Comments from Reviewers

Prairie Daughter: Stories and Poems from Iowa is a wonderfully choreographed and orchestrated narrative of a Midwest Iowa family that is filled with love, passion, values and standards that we find in the back bone of many great families. It is a tribute to Essie Mae Thompson Hill, the mother of this family, who by her inspiration, understanding, passion and dreams left a family with a wonderful legacy and everlasting memories. This is also a tribute to a loving Midwest family, with indelible moments. It is a book filled with great experiences that inspired in its members a way to live their lives with love, values and integrity. In today's America this should be a must read, as it is an inspiration on how all of us should live our lives. This book illustrates that memories are like a great song you never want it to end.

Tracy Ashley Crocker
Registrar General, Order of the Crown of Charlemagne
in the United States of America

\-

Prairie Daughter is a delightful slice of American Pie. Whether we grew up in Iowa or not, one can relate to the stories of a simpler time that live in our collective consciousness. Now living in a time when the world has gotten smaller and moves faster, this book memorializes the type of heartfelt recollections that should not be forgotten and which we would all want to pass on to our grandchildren.

Edward Charles Horton
Marshal, Baronial Oder of the Magna Charta
President General, The Order of the Norman Conquest

An excellent account/autobiography of a life well lived, combining the pulse of mid-America in the early and middle of the past century with anecdotal accounts of actual events – a micro-history of small town/rural communities which creates a pleasurable reading experience. Essie Mae Thompson Hill was a remarkable woman who served as an instructor for pre-flight cadets in the Army and Navy in World War II and was a college professor and mother. Her son, George J. Hill, M.D., skillfully edited this book bringing all the facets of her life together. A good read.

William Beckett Brown III
Geologist, Genealogist, and Family Historian
Governor Emeritus, Society of Colonial Wars in the State of New
Jersey; and Past President, Sons of the Revolution in New Jersey

----

What an engaging way Essie Mae Thompson Hill has for introducing those of us outside her family to her extended family, warts and all, and all without either the lurid tabloid approach of this time in history or, conversely, without a dry pedantic tone. I feel like I have come to know the lady and her world.

Before I began reading the book I would have thought that much of her world would appear quaint to a 21st century reader. I was (and remain) amazed how much of her narrative was similar to my world growing up! Certain historical moments (e.g. WWII) were part of my parents' world, but the day-to-day rhythm of her life was not that far removed from my own childhood.

Jack Idenden
Governor, Society of Mayflower Descendants in New Jersey

PRAIRIE DAUGHTER

PRAIRIE DAUGHTER

Stories and Poems from Iowa

by

Essie Mae Thompson Hill

Edited By

George J. Hill, M.D., M.A., D.Litt.
Captain, Medical Corps, USNR (ret)

HERITAGE BOOKS
2019

HERITAGE BOOKS

AN IMPRINT OF HERITAGE BOOKS, INC.

Books, CDs, and more—Worldwide

For our listing of thousands of titles see our website
at
www.HeritageBooks.com

Published 2019 by
HERITAGE BOOKS, INC.
Publishing Division
5810 Ruatan Street
Berwyn Heights, Md. 20740

Copyright © 2019 George J. Hill, M.D., M.A., D.Litt.

Publication History of the First Editions
© Essie Mae Hill
Prairie Daughter – 1978
Let Thy Handmaidens Speak - 1983
Flapper Fun: Other Poems and Stories – 1988
Essie Mae's Cookbook – (n.d.) c. 1990

Illustrations are from the First Editions of these books, plus others in the personal collection of the editor. Photographs of Lisbon and Mount Vernon, Iowa, by Thomas D. Hill, Jr., taken in 2012. The Frink family photo in the Foreword is from Helen (Frink) Strine.

Cover designed by Debbie Riley

International Standard Book Numbers
Paperbound: 978-0-7884-5876-7

Foreword

The community that Essie Mae Thompson Hill describes in her touching story brings many vivid memories of Lisbon--of streets and homes, of the stores downtown, and notably an aura of serenity and comfort. It seems almost idyllic as I look back on it -- a small community in central Iowa. Most of the people who lived in the town also worked there. While local citizens undoubtedly recognized the importance of the school, the church, the local businesses, my sense is that for many their neighborhood was the center of their life. It was certainly true for my family, the Frinks.

I was the youngest of five, several years younger than my nearest sibling. My family moved from Lisbon when I was six, and my memories of the town are centered on the neighborhood--the McCalls across the street, the Stahls with their greenhouse on the corner, Mrs. Sechrist next door, the Franks down the street. But most especially I remember the Hills, two doors away. There were four in their family--the parents, their older son, George, and most importantly their son, Tommy, exactly six months older than I, my first love!

I must have spent a great deal of time in the Hills' beautiful home because I have as many vivid images of the interior of their home as I do of our own. My sister often would recall that both Tommy and I would eat breakfast quickly, then meet on the walk between the homes for another day of play.

My older brothers were closer in age to George and he, too, played an important role in my recollections--principally those memories are centered on the Treehouse, an architectural wonder treehouse that was the envy of the town. Stories are shared by my brother to this day of Life as it played out in that most impressive addition to the neighborhood. Tommy and I were never allowed to even start the climb, a great sadness for us both.

Tommy and Hona in Lisbon, Iowa - 1940

Tommy and I both cried when we moved in 1941 to a slightly larger, distant Iowa town. He and I kept in touch for a time and whenever his family went through our town, or we through theirs, a stop and a visit were observed. The Hills also moved from Lisbon not long after, but my older sisters and I stayed in contact with Essie Mae until her death.

When I learned some years ago of Tom's untimely death, I sent George a message of condolence, and he and I have been corresponding since. Invariably those inter-family letters have been filled with Lisbon recollections, validating how meaningful were the memories of the life we had known then, especially the friendship bonds which have proved to be so enduring.

It seems trite to dwell on the contrasts between life then and now. That more gentle time Essie Mae shared was nearly 80 years distant, but it is fondly recalled as a significant period in my life as it was in her own. I salute her for writing her story and sharing it with others, and I salute George as well for seeing the value of bringing his mother's lovely writing into the modern age. She was a remarkably talented lady.

Helen Lucille Frink "Hona" Strine
B.A., Cornell College, Phi Beta Kappa
Caldwell, Idaho
hfstrine@mindspring.com

Contents

(*) Poem

Flapper Fun: Other Poems and Stories

_____

(*) Poem

Let Thy Handmaidens Speak

From *Essie Mae's Cookbook*

_____

(*) Poem

_____

(*) Poem

Editor's Preface

My mother was modest, almost to a fault, so it took some time to persuade her to write her recollections. Three of us in her family worked on that problem. Her brother Manly Thompson and her cousin Lester Runkle helped me, by encouraging her to tell stories of her life, as if she were speaking to the family. She began to do this in about 1972, soon after my father retired as a bank officer, and they moved from Aberdeen, South Dakota, to Sun City, Arizona. After 69 cold winters in Iowa and South Dakota, Mother finally could enjoy the year-round sunny skies and warm winters of Arizona. By 1978, she had completed her first book, *Prairie Daughter*. It tells about life as she was growing up in the first decades of the last century, and it includes many stories of her family.

It does not, however, say much about my father's experiences in World War II. Dad asked her not to include these stories, because he was planning to write his own wartime memoir. He had been a newspaper man soon after he graduated from college, and he knew how to write well. He planned to use photos that he took and letters that he wrote to Mother as he traveled across Europe in the last months of the war. He was the American Red Cross Field Director for all three battalions of the 303rd Regimental Combat Team of the 97th Infantry "Trident" Division. He arrived with his troops in Le Havre, France, in April 1945. The 97th Division soon crossed the Rhine River into Germany, and it first engaged in combat in the Battle of the Ruhr. The Division then fought its way across southern Germany to Bavaria. The 303rd Regimental Combat team was the spearhead of Patton's Third Army. One battalion of the 303rd was in Marienbad, Czechoslovakia, on May 8, 1945, VE-Day, and on that day, Dad wrote that he visited all three battalions of the 303rd. After VE-Day, they were instructed to pull back into Germany, to wait in Nuremberg for further orders. Father intended to call his book *A Red Cross Man in Europe*. However, he died suddenly in 1979, soon after *Prairie Daughter* was finished. She hoped that someday, I would assemble the material for Dad's story of *A Red Cross Man in Europe*. It is now next on my to-do list.

Mother worked hard to market *Prairie Daughter*, carefully autographing it for sales to her friends and others. Only a few of the original books remain of the 1000 copies that were originally printed, although used copies are often offered for sale on e-Bay. In the meantime, Mother began to take courses in poetry that were given in Sun City by Arizona State University. She had a busy schedule, giving lectures to local audiences on subjects ranging from poetry readings to geology and Bible history – often in costume. We encouraged her to continue to write stories about her life in Iowa, and thus came the sequel, *Flapper Fun*. In the meantime, she compiled two other books, *Let Thy Handmaidens Speak* – poems about women in the Bible – and *Essie Mae's Cookbook*, which is a book of favorite recipes. It is compiled from submissions by members of her family and their friends, many of them in their own handwriting. Essie Mae's poetry is largely upbeat, inspirational, or humorous. However, in poems such as "Heartstrings" she was wistful, and in her later years, she was sometimes sad, especially after her husband died, and her sons were not able to visit her as much as they had previously.

I have lightly edited these four books, silently correcting some spelling errors and errors in dates, and I used some typefaces and fonts that were not available to her on a standard typewriter. I have deleted some of the stories in the first edition of *Flapper Fun* because they appeared previously in *Prairie Daughter*. I have changed her use of parentheses ( ) to brackets [ ], when they are used to insert corrections or to amplify details within quoted material. Some of my additions and editorial changes are shown within brackets or in footnotes, and others which appear in a different font. I take responsibility for any errors in spelling or punctuation in the present book.

Many things have happened in Essie Mae's family in the past forty years, and I do not wish to continue her story up to the present time. However, I am able to provide additional information that is now available about the life and death of 2nd Lieutenant Marc Pitts, USAAC. He appears in "The 'Floozy' Story" (pp. 104-7).[1] Marc was killed when the B-17 "Skywolf" (423rd Bomber Squadron, 306th Bomber Group), in which he was the bombardier was shot down over Europe in World War II. Findagrave shows that he was born in New York in 1922, the son of Frederic G. and Alice (Fox) Pitts, and he died on 13 June 1943 over Germany. A cross marking his grave is in the Netherlands American Cemetery, in Margraten, Eijsden-Margraten Municipality, Limburg, Netherlands – Plot H, Row 11, Grave 13. Comments about Marc and his family and the 306th Bomber Group are recorded on Findagrave as recently as 29 December 2015. Additional information about his life and the circumstances of his death can be seen on the "Fields of Honor" database, showing pictures of him, his grave, and his medals: Air Medal and Purple Heart.

I will add information about what has happened since 1976 to some of the members of Essie Mae's immediate family by inserting information in brackets about births, deaths, and marriages into her outline of The Thompson Family Record (p. 120-1). The names of family members who are mentioned in this book can be identified by using the Family Record and in the sections of Who's Who in the Thompson and Hill families in the *Cookbook*.

----

[1] For more about 2 LT Marc Frederic Pitts (O-727656) and his family, see:
https://www.fieldsofhonor-database.com/index.php/en/american-war-cemetery-margraten-p/64710-pitts-marc-f; and https://www.findagrave.com/memorial/56302769/marc-f-pitts (accessed 9/19/18)

Prairie Daughter

by
Essie Mae
Thompson Hill

For Essie Mae Thompson Hill, whose voice will always be sweet to her former pupil and lifelong friend. Essie Mae had a chuckle in her throat, a joyous bubbling spring, even explaining the Pleistocene Age.

– Marjorie Holmes,
author of *Two From Galilee*

Essie Mae Thompson
1919

Dedication to *Prairie Daughter* (1st edition)

For my grandchildren

Vicki

Sarah

Lana

Tom, Jr.

David

Jim

My son, George J. Hill, my cousin, Robert Lester Runkle, and my brother, Manly Grant Thompson, encouraged me to write these recollections. They had faith in my ability to make a record of our background and heritage for the family and future generations.

To the extent that this writing does that successfully, the credit belongs to them. For all the shortcomings, I take the responsibility.

Essie Mae Thompson Hill

Essie Mae Thompson
1920

Listen, my children, and you shall hear

      Of the long ago days that I hold so dear —

Of the people, and places, the fun that we had,

      Some of it good, and some of it bad.

It's been said a man can't really savor

      A meal that is ample and good,

Unless he has also known a time

      When he went hungry for food.

So when I see the wonderful things we have now

      Which were absolutely unknown years ago,

I think you'll appreciate what you take for granted

      If I share with you what I know.

                    E. M .H.
                    8/20/76

"Memory is a house of many rooms where one may enter at will."

1

Introduction

Perhaps some time "way back in the dim future" some of the grandchildren will want to know more about how we lived and what we did in the olden days, as they used to call them. They may wish to revive memories of those "Tell me a story, Grandma" times when they were little, and to learn more about places, people, and happenings long gone. As long as they are remembered, they are a "part and parcel" of the present.

These reminiscences are story-time tales, true stories, and stories that could be true, but which can no longer be proven. They tell of our family, friends, and acquaintances, where we lived, how we lived, where we came from, and where we may be going.

Scientists at Cornell College are trying to save some of the "vanishing prairie" before it is too late. But there's "more than one was to skin a cat" and these memories are this Prairie Daughter's way of helping to preserve that environment.

One of the many ways in which The Ages of Man are defined is, that Old Age is that time of life when a person looks back toward the past more than he looks forward toward the future. Although I am now in my seventy-fourth year, according to that definition I am not old, but middle aged, because I can look backward toward the old times or look forward to the future when I have new experiences, with almost equal pleasure. Perhaps an old "saying" in our family, which was a quotation from an unknown hometown orator, best describes my position: "Way back in the dim future."

Looking back, I want to record my thoughts about the old days and my recollections of those times. Looking ahead, if I live long enough to finish all the things that I am planning to do, have already started, and would like to do, I'll be here to celebrate the bicentennial. So I am looking both ways.

I am both startled and thoughtful to have lived through a period of time which antedates the flight of the Wright brothers at Kitty Hawk by six months. Forty years later, when I was teaching in the Navy Flight Preparatory School at Cornell College, the standard airspeed which the cadets used in their Navigation problems was 80 MPH. Now there are many planes which are longer than the distance of the Wright brothers' total flight, and supersonic jet planes travel several times faster than the speed of sound. These are well known facts but this has all taken place during my lifetime.

When I was a child, Aunt Pallie Cory, Mama's sister, lived near Marion, Iowa, about twenty miles from Lisbon. In order to visit her, Papa hired a two-seated surrey or hack and a team of horses from the livery barn. It was the big event of the summer, and travel time took many hours. In 1970, the last lap of a trip which had taken us around the world was from Rome to Aberdeen, South Dakota. Crossing the Atlantic Ocean and half of the American continent took not much longer than our visit to Aunt Pallie. However, I think my Father got the same kind of satisfaction from being the pilot and navigator of his two-horsepower vehicle that his grandson, Lt. Col. Thomas D. Hill, does in navigating a 40,000-horsepower aircraft, which travels thousands of miles in the same length of time.

2

The History of Lisbon

Does the history of Lisbon begin with the settlement of the town, or with the first white man who saw the good land? Or does it begin millions of years before that when, geologists tell us, there were only the warm shallow waters of a great ocean here, and finally later, much later, a succession of glaciers which covered the area and then melted away. As they retreated they left their load of rock and debris, which in time would become the fertile soil of the state, give variety to the landscape, and occasionally furnish a distinctive landmark, such as the huge glacial boulder south of Lisbon, known as Standing Rock. The Indians called Iowa "The Good Land" and Lisbonites share that feeling about their state. The first people to live in this area were the Mound Builders. In the Palisade-Kepler State Park, which is only a few miles from Lisbon, "there are thirteen well-preserved Indian mounds which are reminders that this area was a favored haunt of the Indians before white settlers arrived."[*]

As a result of the exploration by Father Marquette and Louis Joliet, Iowa was claimed by the French. From 1763 to 1800 it belonged to Spain, then it went back again to France. Three years later, as a part of the Louisiana Purchase, it officially became part of the United States.

If "guilt by association" is sometimes assumed to be true, then perhaps we native Iowans can get some satisfaction in having "pride by association." Among the famous people whose birthplace is Iowa are Herbert Hoover and Henry Wallace, Billy Sunday, evangelist, Buffalo Bill, showman, and Grant Wood, artist. Bess Streeter Aldrich, McKinlay Kantor, Paul Engle, and James Norman Hall are famous in American literature, and Meredith Wilson shares life in a small Iowa town with the world in "The Music Man." Another well-known Iowa personality was Senator Bourke B. Hickenlooper whose home was in Cedar Rapids. To give our small boys a "Hickenlooper" was a family expression which meant a swat on the seat of their pants. Mrs. Hickenlooper told us that she gave their boys that kind of punishment one time when they deliberately disobeyed her. I think "misery likes company" and a "Hickenlooper" was a chastisement which was softened by a famous name.

Although Iowa is far from the sea, one of the most distinguished Navy men in recent times was Admiral William Daniel Leahy who was born in Hampton, Iowa, in 1875. In 1944, when he came to Mount Vernon to give the Cornell College Commencement address, he was President Franklin D. Roosevelt's Chief of Staff. In 1944 he was made a five-star Fleet Admiral.

Linn County, in which Lisbon is located, got its name from William Linn, a territorial delegate from Missouri who helped sponsor Iowa Statehood. Iowa became a state in 1846, a year before the first settlers came from Pennsylvania to start a new community. The proximity of Lisbon and Mount Vernon has always influenced the life and characteristics of both towns. One of the early bits of Iowa history which meant a great deal to both communities, and helped to "put them on the map," was the building of the Military Road which ran from Iowa City to Dubuque, crossing the Cedar River at Ivanhoe.

---

[*] *A Centennial History of Mount Vernon, Iowa.*

"That old Military Road had its origin when W. W. Chapman, Territorial Delegate to Washington, D.C., secured in 1840 the passage of a bill providing $20,000 for its construction.* Along the road, running through the present site of Mount Vernon, villages and towns were founded, of which only a few now remain. In the early days, Anamosa and Fairview were prominent hostels [Fairview was the birthplace of my mother]. Travelers along the road gazed with delight at the unending prairies, agreeing with Asa Whitney, a northern Iowa pioneer, who declared in 1846, 'This is the finest country on the globe, capable of sustaining three times the population of any other place. Nowhere is the atmosphere so pure, the surface so gently undulating, or the soils so rich, with not one acre of bad land.'

"Soon four-horse stage coaches of the Western Stage Company traveled the road, and in the forties they carried members of the legislature to the Capitol building in Iowa City. Homesteaders on foot and horseback and in white-topped immigrant wagons traveled on their way to stake out homesteads. [One of these wagon families abandoned a little four-year old girl in Fairview whom my grandparents reared as their own child.] Occasionally a troop of U.S. Dragoons formed a colorful cavalcade in contrast to some lonely circuit-rider with saddle-bags making his way prayerfully to his scattered appointments. The road was surveyed and a furrow plowed by Lyman Dillon with five yoke of oxen." My great uncle, William Manly, had a blacksmith shop in Fairview at the time, and was kept busy outfitting the oxen with iron shoes.

The inscription on the block of marble contributed by Iowa for the Washington Monument reads: "Iowa. Her affections like the rivers of her borders, flow to an inseparable Union." Iowa was the first free state in the Louisiana Purchase.

There has always been some rivalry between Mount Vernon and Lisbon, and like "name calling between two small boys" their nicknames for each other were Pinhook and Dutchtown. The reason for the latter is obvious, because the origin of the first settlers was not classed as "German," but "Pennsylvania Dutch." The odd name of "Pinhook" is said to have come from the wooden hooks used in stores to hang up goods. There must have been a lot of them!

I feel that both Lisbon and Mount Vernon are my home towns.

My baby-home was in Paris (Iowa), my girl-home was in Lisbon (Iowa), and my newly-married home was in Mount Vernon (Iowa) in the brick building which was built about 1859 as a church for the New School Presbyterians. It was never used that way, however, and eventually it was made into an apartment house, owned by S. V. Williams, Methodist preacher, college professor, writer, landlord, and a do-it-yourself maintenance and repair man.

Although our third floor apartment was very attractive, it seemed somewhat less desirable after we heard a muffled "Boom" in the basement, the result of a gas explosion. To keep the furnace door shut after some small gas explosions, Mr. W. had wired it shut! Fortunately, the furnace door was the only thing that was damaged.

In 1847 a group of German people came from Lancaster County, Pennsylvania, by canal boat to the Ohio River, by flat boat down the Ohio, steamboat on the Mississippi River to Burlington, Iowa, and then by wagon to the place we now call Lisbon, Iowa. There were already a few scattered settlers in the area, including Charles Hoskins and his wife from New York, who laid claim to land a mile east of the

---

* *A Centennial History of Mount Vernon, Iowa.*

present town in an area now known as Spring Creek. This was on the road which I took to my first teaching job at the rural school, Valley Chapel. There is still a little cemetery there and at one time there was also a school. Charles Hoskins called the place Yankee Grove, and his land included what is now the eastern half of Lisbon. William Abbe from Elyria, Ohio, built a cabin on the banks of the creek west of Mount Vernon about the same time.

Where, why, and how the name Lisbon came into being as the name for the new settlement is an unsolved mystery, although one theory is that it might have been suggested by a David Dorwart, who came from Lisbon, Ohio, in 1848.

The leader of the group from Pennsylvania was Christian Hershey, who turned away from the financial temptations of the family chocolate business, in favor of religion and specifically, the United Brethren Church. The Centennial edition of the *Mt. Vernon Hawkeye & Lisbon Herald*, August 2, 1975, and the Lisbon Centennial booklet, give pictures and many interesting details of these early settlers, and the names of their descendants who still live in the community. May Hoover Thompson, my sister-in-law, is a descendant of Mr. and Mrs. Charles Hershey, Mr. and Mrs. Jonathan Hoover, and Michael Blessing all members of the original 1847 colony.

The United Brethren Church which was built by Mr. Hershey at his own expense was the first church of that denomination west of the Mississippi River. It has been used as a private residence for many years, and still stands on S. Washington Street, the first house south of the Lisbon Bank. I remember it as the home of Clyde Hoover, and the big rounded mound in the lawn south of the house was a cyclone cellar.

There have certainly been plenty of places in Lisbon where the people could exercise their right to worship God as they choose. In the early part of this century, there were eight different church buildings of different religious denominations. Indicative of the changing times, greater cooperation among churches nowadays, and perhaps less zeal, but better transportation, is the fact that in 1976 there are only two: the Methodist Church and the Federated Church, which represents a combination of the United Brethren and the Evangelical Churches. The little white Roman Catholic Church which is on the opposite corner east of the Methodist Church is now the Lisbon Masonic Hall, and the Reformed Church, the Lutheran, the Seventh Day Adventist and the other churches are all gone. Several of these denominations now have church buildings in Mount Vernon.

The first Methodist sermon was preached in 1840 by Nelson Rathburn in a log cabin east of the creek on South Street, which is the street on which our old home was located. In 1940 an elaborate pageant was put on in the Methodist church to celebrate the first one hundred years of Methodism in Lisbon. An excellent history of the Lisbon Methodist church has been researched and written by Helen Reiger Emerson, whose family members are fifth generation Lisbon people.

The first building was a small brick structure which cost $5300 to build in 1867. There was a heating stove on each side of the room, and the men sat on one side of the center aisle, the women on the other. There was an Amen corner and special pews for the choir along the sides of the room at right angles to the pulpit, so the preacher was assured of plenty of support in his exhortations.

In 1898 this structure was replaced by the present church, which cost about $14,000 to build. The Ladies Aid Society pledged approximately $3000 for extras, such as the beautiful stained glass window, showing Jesus "standing at the door" ($1000) and a Steinway grand piano ($450). This piano was rebuilt in 1974 by the Stuart Franks Family in memory of the tragic death of their daughter Sarah. In 1915 the two-manual pipe organ was installed. The cost was $3000, of which the women of the church paid $2000 and the Carnegie Foundation paid the rest. A few years ago, it was completely rebuilt at a cost of more than the original cost, but it is beautiful, and makes music that is far superior to the modern electric organs in most modern churches.

Examples of women's work:

     1931 Dinner 40¢, 25¢ for children

     1936, '37, '38, '39 Sauerkraut Day dinner 50¢

     1940 Alumni banquet, 158 plates 50¢

Views of Lisbon, Iowa
Chicago and Northwestern RR., Lisbon depot, cow, small animal,
deer, fenced plot, and forest land

By Minnie (née Mohn) Kharas, born in Lisbon
Stenciled and painted on enameled metal tray, 6.5 x 4.5 inches
Signed on reverse side: E M K '49

6

Sauerkraut Day in Lisbon

Small World – Big Day

This is purported to be a true story. George D. Sailor, former postmaster and mayor of Lisbon, when he was standing on a pier in London waiting to board an ocean ship, was asked by a stranger the date of the Lisbon Sauerkraut Day that year. The man was from Clinton, Iowa, . . . but the Day was internationally known!

Without a doubt, people from coast to coast timed their visits back to the old home town in order to meet and greet each other on the big day. In 1931 there were 15,000 people in town, with no accidents, no arrests, no auto thefts, and no alcoholic beverages sold.

The first Sauerkraut Day was held in 1909 as a kind of Homecoming and advertising gimmick. It became so popular that over the next more than a quarter of a century it was often spoken of as "Eastern Iowa's Holiday." No wonder people came! Not only was there continuous free entertainment to go along with the pleasure of seeing old friends, but also free, absolutely free, lunch and coffee, which was served from 11:45 in the morning to 1:00 P.M., and again in the evening from 6:00 o'clock to 7:00 o'clock. The lunch consisted of a serving of sauerkraut, a wiener or two, a couple of crackers, and coffee.

On the third Sauerkraut Day, rain dampened the spirits a little, but the records show that the entertainment went on as scheduled, and it included a successful hot air balloon ascension. This made a very vivid impression on my mind, only nine years old. A year later there were new boulevard lights downtown and a big banner stretched across Main Street which told the public that Lisbon was a "Town Without a Debt."

During the war years of 1917 and 1918 when patriotism and prejudice were at their height, the celebration was omitted, because it was considered inappropriate to feature such a typically German dish as sauerkraut. Not even calling it "Victory Cabbage" could erase the stigma!

Mr. and Mrs. John Hoover, in Dutch costumes, always presided over the food stand, and they had a large part in the continuing success of the day. The wooden shoes which John wore came into Gerald's possession while we lived in Lisbon. I used them for wall planters in my kitchen which had Dutch tulips in the design of the wall paper. Later I used them many times in Christmas programs at school, when we depicted the costumes of other countries. Now they are a part of the treasured family mementoes which George has around the fireplace in his home in Huntington, West Virginia.

There was always such a crush of people around the food stand that many people, including my Mother and Mattie, when she lived in Lisbon, served a sauerkraut dinner at home for guests of the day. When we were little and the Runkles lived in the roomy house on S. Washington, Mattie really had "Open House" on Sauerkraut Day – Lester remembered that his mother used to get a little disgusted with some of the uninvited guests who came to sponge a good, free meal, but she was always very hospitable and no one would ever have guessed her real feelings.

I remember especially one of Mama's dinners on a Sauerkraut Day in the last 1930's. There were about a dozen of us there and it happened to be Gerald's birthday also. One more thing to be celebrated and enjoyed on that special day! Except that my brother-in-law's car was stolen, or he thought it was, and that added an explosive element of excitement which carried over for a long time. You had to know him to know <u>how</u> explosive that was!

The last time the celebration was held was in 1939 when Gerald was general chairman. Needless to say, it was very successful, but times were changing. It became more than the town wanted to do to furnish the six or seven barrels of kraut, almost a half-ton of wieners, crackers, rolls, coffee, cream, etc., which were given away free to the public. Furthermore, no one could replace the Hoovers in preparing it all.

One of the popular features of the day was the exhibits, which were displayed in the scrubbed and scoured garage on the south side of Main Street. People were encouraged to bring in their best things to compete for the tastiest, or the prettiest items in many categories. Produce from field, farm, and garden, trees and vines, needle work of all kinds, flowers, and culinary products.

The prize for the best filled cookies was always offered by Bish (Eldon) Stahl of the Stahl Grocery Co. because he loved Mother's special filled cookies, and he knew she would win the prize, and he would win the cookies.

In 1937 he offered a two-pound can of Butternut coffee as the prize. In 1977 that would be worth about six dollars, but the value shrinks, however, when the first prize that same year for a two-crust apple pie was fifty cents. Other interesting items were:

        Largest head of cabbage: 50¢
        Hickory cake: $1.00
        Best 10 pounds homemade soap: $1.00
        Largest Hubbard squash: 75¢
        Best peck Jonathan apples: five gallons of gas
        Second best peck Jonathan apples: 75¢

Yes, it was fun to live in Lisbon.

A Quick View of Lisbon Along Memory Lane

"Your town will be what you want it to be
It isn't your town, it's you."
– R. W. Glover

The Opera House: our three-story sky-scraper, heated by stoves, which has been the theatre for movies and stage productions, a basketball court, dance hall, school annex used for Commencement and Alumni banquets, lodge meeting room, and finally a wax factory.

The livery barn: odiferous with horsey smells of harness, sweat, urine, and straw.

Macy Lee's Drug Store: where among other things you could buy Lydia Pinkham's Female Vegetable Compound and Sen-sen, a very effective cover-up for an illicit cigarette breath. Fine, except when you smelled Sen-sen you knew what it was covering up!

Bill Leigh (pronounced "Lie") and his ageless parrot, his blacksmith shop, and his huge pile of scrap iron.

Sauerkraut Day, when one year as part of the entertainment a man slid down a wire stretched from the top of the standpipe (water tower), hanging from a strap held between his teeth.

Redpath Vawter Chautauqua and the Hila Morgan Tent Show and another kind of tent show – the old-fashioned Revival Meetings!

The tornado. The family forgot about me asleep upstairs, when they rushed to the basement. Luckily it turned right at our corner, and the only damage to our property was that the Isherwood apple tree forever leaned at an angle that made it easy for climbing. It also left a very penitent family! The town suffered considerable damage.

The hot-air balloon take-off from the pasture north of the U. B. Church.

The F. L. Runkle & Company General Store, with Frank delivering groceries twice a day, pushing a two-wheeled cart.

The Sam Kurtz Lumberyard located south of Main Street.

Henry Kurtz Men's Clothing Store.

The A. K. Runkle Shoe Store, with a sliding ladder to reach the top shelves. Amos Zalesky, club-footed and father of twelve children, in a little room at the back of the store repairing and remaking shoes, tap, tap, tapping, as he used his shoelast.

Pinch McClelland, his ice cream parlor – the fun hang-out on Main Street.

The murder of Mr. and Mrs. Clyde Hoover, by their own son-in-law, in the house that was the original United Brethren Church.

A threatened lynching. [Ed.: Essie Mae said that it was stopped by her father, who single-handedly shamed the crowd and allowed the accused man to escape from town]

George Sturgis Hardware Shop.

The terror and pandemonium of run-away horses. Everyone dashing for cover in doorways, and some brave person running out into the street to catch the run-aways. My fear of big animals goes back (I think) to the time a huge team of run-away draft horses came tearing through our yard and garden where I was making mud-pies, and came very close to trampling me in the wild pandemonium.

Gypsy wagons and Threshing machines – part of the street traffic.

Chris Gish's Meat Market. Sawdust on the floor, the abattoir, east of town. Soup bones and liver given away, free.

Senator W. C. Stuckslager and the R. P. Andreas Family – our notables.

Weekly open-air Band Concerts on Main Street.

Decoration Day with a parade to the cemetery, headed by the band and the veterans of the Civil War, followed by the women of the GAR, and the school children marching in pairs "two by two" clutching wilting bouquets of flowers with which to decorate the graves of the soldiers. A patriotic speech (E. A. Johnson telling the audience that "they that take the sword shall perish by the sword" – a challenge to retaliate, not a warning).

Carrie Schottle's Millinery Shop. New hats, and also ostrich feathers, ribbons, flowers, and lace to make old hats look like new.

Al Floyd's Newspaper office-shack. Lighted by about fifteen oil lamps, one of them with a reflector behind it, focused on the door knob, its only function. Manly worked there for a time. It was a great loss when Al's wife burned all the files of his old papers after his death.

The Interurban – 10¢ to Mount Vernon, 50¢ to Cedar Rapids with stops at the Palisades or Bertram, if anyone wished. The "seedling mile" – the one and only mile of paved road between Lisbon and Cedar Rapids on the Lincoln Highway – about five miles west of Mount Vernon.

The Great Lakes Navy Band, playing in the town square in WW I – school dismissed to see and hear, with John Philip Sousa himself conducting.

No sewers. The well-to-do had water tanks in their attics, and septic tanks in their backyards. This included Mattie and Frank Runkle's home on S. Washington. We were strictly trained not to flush the toilets "unnecessarily."

Kewpie dolls. (How my mother hated them) and ukuleles in the 1920's. Pipe organs in three of the five Lisbon churches. Sometimes operated by a hand-pump behind the scenes.

No paved streets. Mud, Mud, MUD! and dust, which was kept under moderate control by oiling or sprinkling with water.

Stahl's General Store, where I worked for a dollar a day the summer after I graduated from high school. The hours on Saturday were from 8:00 A.M. to 10:30 P.M. or later, but it was very good experience for me. Fill a kerosene can or cut a plug of tobacco. "Bish" was a wonderful and loyal friend when we lived as neighbors to him on E. Market Street. Oh! the flowers, asparagus, smoked sausage, and fruit that he gave us!

Johnson's Furniture and Undertaking Business. Coffins in the back room. When my father died my mother wanted an oak casket, so Howard Johnson made a special trip to Dubuque to get just what she had in mind. Could this be a hang-up from her early remembrances of her own father making coffins in his carpentry shop in Fairview? They were not cheap pine boxes covered with cloth to make them look luxurious. Wood that was frankly wood.

Happy Holidays

One of my earliest memories is being carried by my father to a Christmas eve program in the Methodist Church in Lisbon. This must have been when I was three years old, the winter before Harris was born. When we got to the church we settled in the back seat, and how glad I was to be unwrapped! Mama had tied a white chiffon scarf over my face and around my head for protection against the cold. I couldn't see a thing, and in trying to breathe I had sucked the scarf into my mouth, it froze, and the whole purpose of it was lost. I was really in misery! This doesn't sound like a happy time, but the Christmas eve experiences in the Lisbon church are cherished memories.

Before the pipe organ was installed, the Christmas tree was set up in the choir loft, and it reached to the ceiling, an absolutely heavenly sight to my childish eyes. In later years it was part of the holiday fun to go to Mrs. Stuckslager's Sunday School Class's tree-trimming party at the church. It was an early very version of a "pot luck" dinner and she always bought a big ham. After the meal was over we strung yards and yards of day-old popcorn and cranberries and decorated the tree. The boys climbed the ladders and draped the popcorn strings, while the girls handed them the lights, tinsel, and ornaments which had been brought out of storage in the balcony or in the parsonage next door.

The program was always on Christmas eve, and it was preceded by many hours of practice and rehearsal directed by the Sunday School teachers. The children were seated by classes in the front pews, with the teachers at the end, so they could be chaperones and prompters. The altar, pulpit, platform, and chairs had been removed and, starting with the littlest tots who had to be helped and guided up the steps, the children put on the entertainment. It was strictly a Christmas semi-religious variety show, not a worship service.

In later years, I don't know why I was so scared and nervous when I had to perform before an audience, because from the time I was little I always had to "speak a piece," and I should have become accustomed to solo performances. In 1937, the first Christmas after we moved back to Lisbon as a family, what a lump in my throat I had when George and little two-and-a-half-year-old Tommy spoke their pieces for the first time on that platform in the church. I was very proud of them, for they both had their verses perfectly memorized and said them without hesitation or mistake. Their voices were so soft however that only their mother knew what they were saying, but so many in the audience had known me ever since I had been that age that "Essie Mae's little boys" were a hit. They looked very small and very sweet, as they stood in front of the big Christmas tree, holding hands, and wearing new look-alike corduroy outfits. No one had to give them any help either, in getting on and off the stage, for George was perfectly capable of taking care of himself, and his little brother, too.

At home when I was little we usually put up the tree the day before Christmas, and when James and Manly were still at home they used to go to the woods and bring home a tree which they had cut themselves. There were plenty in the timber, and no one objected. After Papa began working at the school, he'd bring a tree from one of the classrooms after the program was over and school was dismissed for vacation. We had some ornaments, colored glass balls, and tinsel which were saved from year to year, and with the paper chains that we made, not from construction paper, but from the colored pages of an old mail order catalog, and flour and water paste, we had a respectable-looking and satisfactory Christmas tree. No artificial lights, of course, but real candles in special holders which clamped to the branches, or hung with a very heavy weighted ball dangling from the holder to keep it in place. Very hazardous by modern standards of safety, but nothing disastrous occurred.

It was very fortunate that there were just exactly nine of us in the family for whom to buy presents – six in our household, and three in the Runkle's. With a dollar to spend, at ten cents for each gift, I still had ten cents left for a classmate, Christmas wrappings, or just to waste on candy. There were lots of nice things that could be bought for a dime; the only problem was which one to choose. A bottle of perfume, a handkerchief, jewelry (which might turn green and brassy after a few wearings, but who cared), a couple of pencils, or a bolt of lace, lots of things.

After Manly went to Washington, D.C., Christmas at home was upgraded a great deal. One year he sent me a little sewing machine, that clamped to the table and made a chain-stitch seam. Although I was only about nine or ten years old, I already was allowed to use Mama's sewing machine so I didn't use my toy very much, but I loved it, and I loved the thought of such an expensive gift. Another year he sent me a little stove that we could cook on, using denatured alcohol as fuel. It came complete with tiny pots and pans, and it was great for doll tea parties. When it finally looked like Jerry and I would never have any little girls to enjoy them, I gave them to nieces Martha and Sally Thompson. Manly always sent a big box of chocolate candy and Mama guarded it so that it lasted until Easter. It was a real ceremony when the box was opened and we were allowed to choose one piece. Then the box was put back again into hiding in her safe-keeping.

Another great gift was a Kodak box camera. I don't know how old I was, but Lester got one too, and in a treasured picture of me I was still wearing a Red Riding hood, so I wasn't very old. At that time, the camera cost a dollar, with the view finder 25¢ extra. Brother James, I think it was, had a good camera which took postcard sized pictures and he had all the equipment for developing and printing them. We were a lucky family! It was all still useable when Harris was old enough to use it in his own picture hobby.

We always had Christmas dinner at Mattie's, and Harris and I tried to get there as early as we could, because Santa Claus always brought Lester wonderful gifts. When he was very small he got a fancy hobby horse, a dappled gray, with a real mane and tail. It was the talk of the town, the envy of all the children. To show how special it was, in a letter from my classmate, Helen Reiger Emerson, after Runk's death, mentioned that hobby horse as one of her own memories about what a special child he was and how generous he was with his possessions. He let all the kids ride it and enjoy it. The Runkle grandchildren have it now. He also got a Flexible Flier sled, an electric train, and a steam engine. He was utterly unselfish, and we all played with them as if they were community property.

When I was in high school, Mattie allowed me to bring a friend to Christmas dinner, and Minnie Mohn was my favorite. It seemed strange to me that she would desert her own family to be with us, but she added to our jolly time.

12

We had very little money when I was a child, but we had so much fun we surely never thought of ourselves as being sorely deprived. Perhaps that stood me in good stead later when my own family needed things at Christmas. One Christmas morning to make more fun for the boys when we lived in Lisbon, I arranged a treasure hunt for them. It took a long time to find what Santa had brought them, and they could savor each little gift as it was discovered. It made a little bit go a long way! Again, in Lisbon, none of us who were there will ever forget the Christmas when one very dear member of the family downed her pre-dinner cheer a little too fast, and she has never been able to tolerate anything like that since.

There were twenty of us for dinner that year, including Helene Runkle's parents, Frank and Ruby Runkle, Frank's second wife, Rachie, Julius, and Jim High, my mother, Lester, Helene, and their two children, Bobby and Dottie. We had two trees, one in front of each pair of French doors in the front of the house, and there was a veritable mountain of gifts which were waiting to be opened after dinner, including a roll of toilet tissue (<u>disguised in fancy wrapping paper</u>) for every grownup. That brought lots of laughs. I was sitting beside Ruby Runkle while the gifts were being distributed. "Oh, isn't this fun," I exclaimed in great enthusiasm. She had been sitting there unsmiling, and she replied in a very prim, dour way, "Well! I guess you <u>could</u> get used to it!" She never did "get used to it" however, and she always disapproved of me.

Our children always hung up their stockings, and I told them as long as they believed that Santa, who was the Sprit of Christmas, would come and fill them, he would do just that. They could count on it. During World War II, our first Christmas was spent in Mount Vernon. Gerald was away in the Red Cross, and I was so busy with my teaching, shoveling coal to keep the old house warm, battling the elements, and taking care of the family, that I told the boys that they were old enough to skip this stocking-hanging routine.

"Now Mother," they said, "You know you always said that as long as we believed in Santa Claus and hung up our stockings he would come." That settled it, and I rushed down town and got the necessary materials to keep the family tradition going. I have always been grateful that it worked out that way because the custom went on even after the boys were in college and later, and now they carry it on in their own homes.

How could Christmas be anything <u>but</u> a wonderful time, when December 25 was our wedding day in 1930, Tom's and Keiko's in 1959, and Vicki's christening day in 1960. On our 25th anniversary, Tom brought his girl friend home from Colorado University. On our 40th in 1970 we had all twelve of our family together in Aberdeen for several days. On our 45th anniversary, we had a wonderful celebration with dear friends in Payson.

Tom and Keiko's wedding in Minot in 1959 and all the Christmases we spent with them, baby Vicki, and then little Tommy, hold memories that could fill a book by themselves. Christmas with George and his family at the Gaylord Street house in Denver, and again in 1971, when I was released from the hospital to spend the day with them in the High Street house, were happy times, although at the latter time, Jerry and I were separated by 1500 miles. He was with Tom and his family in Oxon Hill, Maryland. Keiko and I were the catalysts in that situation, both of us ill, but the family was wonderful through it all, and we have a tape recording of the activities that day in Oxon Hill. There is also a recording of a family "program" made in Denver before I left there. The highlight of that time was hearing George sing old songs and accompany himself on his baritone ukulele. The double anniversary celebration in Aberdeen in 1970, our 40th anniversary and the Tom Hill's 11th, was probably the highlight of our family relationships. Twelve of us together under one roof! Tom and his family safely home from their year in SE Asia and Japan, and George and his whole family braving 30 degree below zero weather to come from Denver to make the family circle complete. The permanent record of our happy time is a "program" taped Christmas afternoon, in which everyone had a part, starting with singing carols, accompanied by Keiko on the organ, Jerry reading the Christmas story according to St. Luke, Tommy's solo, "The Little Drummer Boy," and George reading the passage about what it means to come home from a first edition of *John Brown's Body* by Stephen Vincent Benet. He had given the book to me as a Christmas gift in 1955.

Should anyone think that repeating something forty-five times would become monotonous, we can testify that "'Tain't necessarily so." The forty-fifth time that we celebrated the time of our marriage was absolutely different from any of the others, and a delight in every way. In 1930 the bridegroom was emotionally overcome, but in 1975, it was the bride who was dissolved in tears. I don't try to explain the former, but I know the latter was emotionally overwhelmed by the tremendous outpouring of love which was evidenced to us by our family that day. We were in our unfinished cottage in Payson North, but we were not alone. The wonderful gifts and messages from loved ones made it the best Christmas ever, and our family seemed very close.

<u>Christmas Is Special for the Hills</u>

Christmas Day brought three celebrations for the G. L. Hill family in Aberdeen.

It was Mr. and Mrs. Hill's 40th wedding anniversary and the 11th anniversary of their son and daughter-in-law, Maj. and Mrs. Thomas D. Hill.

The day also brought a family reunion. A son and his family, Dr. George J. Hill and four children of Denver, Colo., were present along with the Thomas Hills and their two children.

Maj. Hill has completed a year in Southeast Asia with the U.S. Air Force while his family resided in Tokyo, Japan, and will be assigned to the Armed Forces Staff College in Norfolk, Va.

The G. L. Hills visited their daughter-in-law and grandchildren in Tokyo while on a summer tour last year.

--from *The Aberdeen American News*
(23 December 1970)

This may be something of a record in the family. For the forty-six years we have been married I have always devised the Christmas greetings we have sent to friends and relatives. They have included pictures of the family, and our home, the year's news, sometimes written as a letter, sometimes recorded in verse. On our tenth anniversary (1940) our Christmas card was a linoleum cut showing little pictures of the significant happening in each of those years. We have been told that our friend and former neighbor, Mrs. Harry Dilley, had kept the complete collection.

Easter

Three things were very important at Eastertime when I was a child, none of which, I am sorry to say, had much to do with the Biblical meaning of the season. First was a new outfit to wear, a dress and a hat. They might be "recycled," as we'd call them now, a dress remade from one of Mattie's or Rachie's, carefully ripped apart and redesigned, and the hat, an old one but with new ribbon bows and flowers. They were new for me, and I was happy, proud, and satisfied. Easter eggs were a fun tradition in those days, even as they are today among the grandchildren. The rabbit "brought" them until the time Lester and I came home from school early and caught Mama and Mattie dyeing them. They tried to hide the evidence in the oven of the cookstove when they heard us coming, but it was too late. After that we had the fun of coloring them ourselves, always using empty shells from our own eggs that Mother had been saving for weeks.

The third thing that was associated with Easter was selling horseradish to earn money for our offering at Sunday School. How we hated doing it! Our goal was to earn a least a dollar, at five cents a glass that was no small job in a neighborhood where everyone had horseradish. Think what streaming eyes – tears – Mother had in grating it. Yes, grating it, not grinding it. It must have been awful for her but we never thought of that! Only the embarrassment we suffered in asking people to buy it. I was no salesman then, nor am I today, so it was an ordeal to get that money for the church collection on Easter.

One of the nicest things that my brother James ever did for us younger children was to take us on an early spring Easter vacation picnic along the creek south of the school house. He was in college then, at the University of Wisconsin, home on vacation. I was thirteen years younger than he was, so I was about nine or ten years old, Lester a year younger, and Harris only six. We reveled in this attention from a grownup and it has remained a happy Easter memory.

Mayday

We were lucky because we could always count on having "flags" to put in our homemade May baskets. That is what we called the miniature blue iris which grew on the south side of the house in Lisbon. For days we had been busy with wall paper, crepe paper, flour paste, and any little cardboard boxes we could salvage. Last minute preparations also included a fun hike to Reiger's timber to gather violets, anemones, spring beauties, ferns, jack-in-the-pulpits, and May flowers. We might even find a few Morel mushrooms. What a treat! If anyone found them, it was Lester!

Flowers were the feature of the May basket, and it was only in later years that they had to be filled with nuts and candy; a sign of more affluent times, perhaps, but also the shrinking timber areas, and the reluctance of parents to let their youngsters go out on unsupervised exploring expeditions.

This letter written to me by my father when I was eight years old indicates how much Mayday fun meant in our family, as well as the thought and affection he carried in his heart for all of us when he was away from us.

15

Ottumwa, Iowa, May 3rd, 1911

Dear Essie Mae,

    If Papa would write you chaps Every time he thought about you what a Long Letter you would have. I suppose you put out a Lot of May baskets. I Did not see one, only a few on sale in the Stores. I guess the Kids here don't know what May baskets are. If Mama and Harris goes to Marion this week and stays until the Late train they will be good and tired. [Harris hadn't started to school yet, so Mother could take him when she went to visit her father, and I probably stayed at Mattie's house so I could go to school with Lester.]

    You must have tried Extra hard in order to get such a good Grade card. Papa may sneak in home some Night and you will not Know it until morning

With love, Papa

Children's Day

Among the very special days of the year were Children's Day, my birthday in June, and the Fourth of July soon after. Before the days of the Vacation Bible School the summer feature at church was Children's Day when the worship service was given over to a program by the children of the Sunday School. For me that meant learning another piece to speak, and getting a new sash for my perennial white embroidered dress, and hair ribbons to match, usually of pink satin. My hair was dark, long, and heavy, and as I think back on it now, it must have been quite attractive, but I hated it. Mama always insisted that it be parted in the center (only boys were allowed to part their hair on the side!). Only on very special occasions was I allowed to let it hang loose or in curls. My hair was not naturally curly as Rachie's was, so my curls had to be induced by wrapping my hair around "curly rags," then bound with string, and slept on over night. Ordinarily my hair was braided in two braids, which were then looped criss-cross or rolled under and tied with ribbons. I was the last of my girl friends to get my hair cut, because Mama and Papa were so very much against it, although Irene Castle had made the style very popular. In 1923 when I went to DeWitt to teach I finally had it cut, but I concealed it with a hairpiece which I pinned on the pack of my head.

    James and I shared the same birthday, and the year I was thirteen he was exactly twice as old as I and a bridegroom of two weeks. Mattie had a beautiful dinner honoring the newlyweds on June 29, 1916, complete with a gorgeous, chocolate layer cake, with white frosting, and decorated with tiny red roses from the climbing rose vine on the Runkle's front porch. I was very shy, and when it was decided that I should cut the first piece of the cake, while everyone watched me, I was practically in a state of shock. I had never done anything like that before, and the relationship between the angle at the center of a circle and the arc at the circumference was not part of my knowledge. When I finished cutting the first piece, it was enormous! The family who had been watching me started laughing and teasing me about it. Take warning. Never laugh at a thirteen-year-old girl, at least not a shy, self-conscious one, as I was. I went into uncontrollable hysterics, crying, and I couldn't stop. It was awful, and everyone felt very badly. So much so, in fact, that no one has ever mentioned it to me since then, until Lester Runkle and I talked about it last year when we were digging back into our memories.

16

It is good to have had some bad experiences to use as a measuring stick, and at various times since then I have said to myself, "Well, it's not so bad as when I cut my birthday cake."

Fourth of July

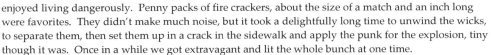

There were no restrictions on the purchase of fireworks, except lack of money. Perhaps lack of communication made people unaware about the casualties, but "ignorance was bliss" and we enjoyed living dangerously. Penny packs of fire crackers, about the size of a match and an inch long were favorites. They didn't make much noise, but it took a delightfully long time to unwind the wicks, to separate them, then set them up in a crack in the sidewalk and apply the punk for the explosion, tiny though it was. Once in a while we got extravagant and lit the whole bunch at one time.

The next size was about the diameter of a lead pencil, and one of those could not only be banged, but made into a fizzler by cracking it half way, spreading it into an inverted V and then lighting it. We had only a few big ones – too expensive, and too dangerous, and we really were very careful. The snake was a small cone out of which came a curling stream of gray ash when it was lighted. It might be several inches long, and fun to play with in between fire crackers. A cap pistol was a good investment because it could be used many times, even another year, if one was lucky. Pinwheels which had been previously nailed to the catalpa trees started the evening show in earnest although we started whirling sparklers as soon as it began to turn dusk. We had paper balloons only a few times, but they were a fire hazard and I think the folks were wise not to have used them much. They were made of Japanese lantern paper and the hot air from a wad of cotton soaked in wood alcohol and ignited, provided the lift. When the fire burned out the balloon came down, of course, usually only a short distance away. There was an open pasture in front of our house which made a fine safe place toward which to aim the skyrockets and Roman candles which were the feature of the evening show. Papa and the older boys built the frame for the skyrockets during the day, and, as I remember it, the display was very successful. The neighbors all joined us to watch and share in the celebration, and the next morning we had fun gathering up the burned-out castings, trying to find any that might still have "potential."

Hallowe'en

Lisbon used to be very tolerant of pranks and mischief on Hallowe'en. This was long before Trick or Treats, and the town put up with a lot of high jinks. There was no municipal sewer system, so few homes or public buildings, including the school house, had indoor plumbing. As a result, there were lots of little backyard "houses" to be set upright again on the day after the spooks and witches had been out. Soap had to be washed off windows, furniture returned to the rightful owners, missing buggies identified, and in some cases "foreign items" brought down off the church spires. I have heard from Irwin Mauch, an old time Lisbonite, who now lives in Tucson, that Manly and his friend George Young, actually got up into the belfry of the school house and rang the school bell long and loud. Very ghostly and mysterious, it seemed. Anything that was out in the open was fair game for the older boys, but I can honestly disclaim participation in anything wilder than scaring folks with a jack o'lantern, a homemade tic-tac and some window soaping down town.

I am glad that I've had the fun of providing some costumes for the grandchildren's Hallowe'en fun, which I think may become part of <u>their</u> memories. The gypsy outfit for Vicki, and David's spotted leopard suit, with long tail, black velvet lined head-cover and paws. Those were the good old days before sadistic grownups started putting razor blades in the treats they give to the youngsters!

<u>Thanksgiving</u>

Thanksgiving was always celebrated with a dinner at our house shared with the Runkles. Traditionally the entertainment was a family "sing" with Frank Runkle pumping away at the reed organ, and Manly leading out in the harmony. Manly had a good voice, and like Harris, and later our Tom, he could sing either the baritone or the tenor; Mother sang alto, and the rest of us carried the melody. Frank stammered so badly that he could hardly talk, but he must have had perfect pitch because he could play anything in any key by ear. He could play a chord accompaniment to music on the radio, and really had extraordinary musical ability. He would have been great in a modern Rock group. He was a wizard with his drumsticks, and he must have been thinking rhythms all the time, because he was constantly drumming with his fingers – a very annoying habit to those around him, but he had many fine qualities, was generous, easily pleased, good natured, and laughed easily. Thanksgiving was a good family time.

Summer Vacation

"What can I do" or "There's nothing to do" were common complaints among youngsters in early modern times, before organized playground activities with salaried directors solved the problem of summer-time leisure. When I was growing up there was no swimming pool, going away to camp, or community recreation program, but I never remember being bored, or lacking something to do.

Even before I started to school, Mama insisted that I learn to sew with a thimble (Lanie has my thimble now), and I had to make a quilt block before I was free to play. Only four square pieces of cloth were put together with crude stitches but, after all, I was barely five years old, and eventually those blocks were actually made into a quilt.

My brother, James, took me to the Cornell Library when I was about eight or nine years old and introduced me to the stern old librarian there, so I could get books from the children's department. James was a student at Cornell at that time. The same librarian was still behind the check-out desk, dedicated to maintaining the place in the best interests of serious students, when I took little George to the library with me when he was about fifteen months old. I was emphatically reminded that SILENCE was required, and even his baby voice was too loud. I was furious, and I picked him up in a huff and stamped out of the building!

I did read many of the books there after James arranged the privilege, and although the wooden sidewalk that once reached from Lisbon to Mount Vernon was gone by that time, I always walked both ways, sometimes with Lester keeping me company. It made a pleasant afternoon excursion.

A different kind of fun was making mud pies. I was literally a killer at that, when I saw one of Mama's young chickens pecking at my beautiful creation, a chocolate mud pie, dusted with some old white flour, and garnished with fresh cherries. I was so angry that I picked up a stick and clobbered that hapless chicken. He ended up with a broken neck and we had an unplanned fried chicken dinner.

Dolls! Dolls! Dolls! I loved dolls, and I could make a whole family out of the hollyhocks which grew along the front of the woodshed. Mother had perennial double poppies in lovely colors, with blossoms about three inches in diameter. She was always glad to have us use them for making dolls, because she considered them merely weeds in her garden and, left to dry, they would reseed themselves and become more of a problem the next year. The head of the doll was the fat, round seed pod of the poppy, and when it was pushed onto the stem of a hollyhock blossom, the result was a lady with a fluffy, ballerina skirt. We cut out long strings of paper dolls, both girls and boys, holding hands, and colored them with crayons and made them dance.

Of course, I had regular boughten dolls, too. A rag doll which wore baby clothes, a china-head doll, and a special one with long dark hair. I liked the little tiny ones best, because my favorite doll-play was making clothes for them, and a piece of cloth only a couple of inches square was big enough to make a dress. Sometimes the cat was dressed in a doll dress and taken for a ride in the doll buggy.

After Manly gave me a little stove, we had real tea parties. Although she was much too old to play with them, Rachie had a nice set of doll dishes in a special wooden cupboard, but she never let me use them. I had some painted or enameled tin dishes, and a set of "silver" with blue china handles.

Mother taught me to crochet, knit and sew before I was in my teens, and I am thankful for that. She tried her best to make a lady out of me, but I was a terrible tomboy, and could climb trees as high as

19

the boys and run just as fast. Lester, Harris, and I all had Indian suits and, although "Cops and Robbers" and "Cowboys and Indians" were not recognized as games then, but we had many "clod fights" with the neighbor kids. We played Train, with the coaster wagon, using the houses along our street as the towns along the C&NW RR. Roller skates, yes, and the necessary key to tighten them on our shoes. If we couldn't locate it when we wanted it, then Mother would say, "Look where it is, and you'll find it."

The Flower Children of Long Ago

Mary Stuckslager was one of the girls in the Daisy Chain at Vassar, but the flower chains for the girls in our part of town were made of white clover. Chains, garlands, crowns, and gathering the materials for them and braiding them in the shade of the broad leaves of the catalpa trees in our front yard was a pleasant way to spend a hot summer afternoon.

Dandelions simply <u>were</u> – no one thought of doing anything about them, except as they fell beheaded by the blades of the lawn mower. No digging, no spraying, or making any extra effort to get rid of them. Some people picked and ate the leaves as greens, like spinach, but our family never did, because it was easier and less time-consuming to get vegetables from the garden. However, we youngsters did pick the long-stemmed blossoms, and held them under each other's chins to "see whether you like butter." The stems could be split with the tongue, and it was a challenge to see how long a curl one could make as the hollow stem separated into two or more parts. The milky juice had a tangy taste and was not unpleasant if you didn't get too much of it.

Perhaps "Daisies won't tell," but pull off the petals one by one as you say, "He loves me, he loves me not," and the daisy <u>will</u> tell.

Kaleidoscope of Memory

As I turn the kaleidoscope of memory I see a panel which pictures the clothes we used to wear. There were the long black cotton or lisle stockings for everyday and glove silk for dress-up. I had one pair, which Mrs. Stuckslager gave me as a prize at a Sunday School Class costume party. We could fake the effect by putting on a pair of black rayon hose over cotton. Along with these there were high button shoes with very pointed toes and spool heels. Two long outmoded pieces of toilet equipment were button hooks and hair receivers, which were small, porcelain, covered bowls into which we stuffed combings from our long hair. A deluxe set was hand painted.

Lingerie included teddies, step-ins, and bloomers made of black sateen in early grade school days. Older girls wore stiffly starched rows of ruffles to help Nature give a Gibson profile to the flat-chested ones. The "falsies" of yesterday. Fortunately, when I became an "older girl" it was the age of the flapper and I was built for those styles.

Although a see-through georgette crepe blouse worn over a corset cover made beautiful with pink baby ribbon strung through eyelet embroidery was high style for young ladies, it was both tolerated and practical for both young and old to have a supply of underwear with long legs and long sleeves. Mother was always apprehensive in the spring about me catching cold by taking off the long underwear too soon. She was also sure that the bare knees and short skirts of the '20's would bring on rheumatism later. She may have been right, although my neck and shoulders were the parts affected in my later years!

Aprons! Before there were electric irons, and wash and wear fabrics, one way to conserve time and energy was to wear an apron. For dress-up it might be of white linen with a four-inch band of crocheted or knitted lace across the bottom, reaching nearly to the hem of the dress which was at least ankle length. They were called fudge aprons. For ordinary wear it was made of blue or gray calico, with big pockets. A Hoover apron was the very popular wrap-around dress of World War II.

A pale complexion was as much of a status symbol as a tan is now. When a lady had to go out into the sun, as women on the farms and small towns had to do when they helped the men with their work, they tried not to "give it away" so they protected their faces as much as possible. Mother always kept a sunbonnet hanging on a nail by the back door, and she never went outdoors bareheaded. For dress-up occasions a lovely embroidered or ruffled parasol was a glamorous and necessary accessory. When Marie came to our house on her honeymoon with Manly she brought me a white one with my monogram on it in addition to an elaborate flower design. I was only twelve years old, and I was thrilled to be treated as a young lady, not a child.

Another picture in the kaleidoscope of my memory shows the beauty treatment. A "switch" was what we now call a wiglet, and for most of us, curls or waves lasted no longer than the first rain or shampoo. In the meantime, a frilly lace-trimmed boudoir cap kept the kid curlers hidden for the girl who wanted to look pretty in bed. Fingernails were buffed to shine, and rosewater and glycerin moisturized the skin.

How the meanings of words change! <u>Freeze dry</u> referred to what happened to wet clothes which were hung outdoors in winter. <u>Shams</u> were covers for bed pillows which were hung on a special frame attached to the head of the bed. It was folded back at night and let down during the day to cover the pillows. A <u>spill</u> was a small piece of rolled up paper with one end folded over, used to transfer a fire to stoves and lamps from an already lighted blaze. To clean the lamp chimneys and make a few spills was a daily chore. A precious box of matches lasted longer that way.

When we used to read "Tales from the Arabian Nights" little did we dream that we would one day have a "genie" of our own which opens the door of our garage at the touch of a finger. No connection between this, of course, and the Aladdin Lamp which burned gasoline and gave a brilliant white light from a fragile gauze wick. The fairy stories of one age become take-for-granted happenings!

The pictures of the first quarter of the twentieth century must surely include fans. Before the days of air conditioning they were a necessity, but they could be a very beautiful accessory as well. I can remember seeing Mother's pink ostrich feather wedding fan in a box in the attic, and I had a similar one when I graduated from high school. Fans made of palm leaves or paper were standard equipment in the church pews in summer, serving a dual purpose of cooling and a place for an advertisement of some store downtown. Fans were also made of carved sandalwood, painted silk, bone, celluloid and later plastic, and have become favorite collector items. Sally Rand and Japan are famous for their fans, and they are a lovely relic of the romantic past.

Among the things which used to be standard household equipment and for which I am glad we have no use nowadays are curtain stretchers and quilting frames, carpet beaters and washboards, ball bluing and stove polish. Gone, but not forgotten, however, are the copper hot water reservoir at the end of the kitchen range, and the copper washboiler that Mother used. I am glad to have Mother Hill's recipe for making homemade soap and cottage cheese, my Mother's recipe for sugar cookies, and Aunt Mattie's for watermelon pickles, all in their own handwriting.

Finally, there are some unrelated pictures in my memory, unrelated, but parts of the whole. The horse-drawn ice wagon, dripping water as it was pulled along the unpaved dusty streets, stopping at the houses which had a sign in the front window indicating how many pounds of ice were needed. The ice was carried by tongs, held against the rubber apron worn by the ice-man. Neighborhood youngsters clustered around, hopeful of a little piece of ice to pop into their mouths.

The arc lights which were the fore-runners of electric street lights. Their chief characteristic was the eerie bluish color of the light, and a constant humming sound. They were very attractive to bugs, especially the big June bugs, dead ones by the hundreds in the street when morning came. When replacements of new sticks of carbon (charcoal) were made we eagerly recycled the old pieces for writing on the sidewalks. Taking care of these lights was a maintenance job for someone in Lisbon, but who knows who? This type of street light was surely the half-way point between the old lamplighter, and modern lights which automatically turn on as darkness falls.

The bobsled ride, a very special kind of winter fun which usually began and ended at the Methodist parsonage. The floor of the bobsled was covered with straw, there were fur robes to snuggle under, and songs and giggling as we rode around the country for a couple of hours, and then back again to enjoy a bowl of Mrs. Ballz's wonderful oyster stew! The song "Jingle Bells" is a special favorite of mine, because I can remember riding in a cutter with a fast pacer horse and jingling bells at the invitation of my classmate, Helen Reiger, who lived on a farm south of town, and still does. She is the half-way person in a five-generation family line of Lisbonites.

Pinch McClelland's restaurant with the now-treasured by antique hunters' ice-cream chairs and tables in the back room where we could savor a ten cent sundae or splurge with a 25¢ banana split. Under the counter in the front he kept a punch board which paid off with a box of candy under the lucky number. My boy friend was a very good customer.

It may be good to record these things but it is not good to dwell on them overlong. In most cases, their modern counterparts are far superior.

Unforgettable are Mrs. Stuckslager's Sunday School Class parties. The big white house, the biggest house in town, the only home with a live-in maid. Soft carpets, oriental rugs, the grand piano bearing autographed photographs of Madame Schumann-Heink and Dr. Frederick Stock. When we entered high school, we were eligible to become members of the Sunday School class which Mrs. Stuckslager taught in the Methodist Church. How we looked forward to that, and how fortunate we were. She was a beautiful lady, not only in spirit and character and generosity, but in person, too, with her luxuriant dark hair, her patrician face and figure, and her gowns from New York and Europe. She was an expert Bible teacher, lessons which she made more interesting by pictures and descriptions of the cathedrals of Europe and the Passion Play in Oberammergau. All that, plus a party in her home once a month. Sometimes she was not only the gracious hostess but provided the entertainment, too. She shared with us the recordings of Alma Gluck and Caaruso played on the huge Victrola, and we loved to listen to the eerie rhythm of Kipling's "Boots" – Boots, Boots, Boots, slogging over Africa.

At other times we worked up our own entertainment. We had a costume party, which I remember especially because I won the prize of a Godey Lady Book for my Little Bo Peep outfit. Sometimes she let us dress up in the things in the trunks on the third floor, native costumes brought back from Europe. A sheet hung in the dining room doorway made a good screen for shadow pictures, while the audience sat on the steps opposite. The parties traditionally ended with homemade ice cream cranked out by Lucian Gish, the family handy-man, and mile-high angel food cake, using the same beautiful china and silver for us naïve young teenagers that she used for her world-renowned friends and guests. She was a wonderful friend and especially to us Thompson "kids."

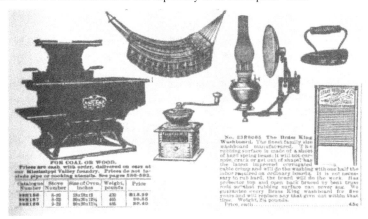

Live or Die, or the Bottle and the Pill
"An Apple a Day Keeps the Doctor Away" and Other Ways to Keep Healthy

Lisbon had four doctors when I was growing up, but the only time we needed professional care, that I remember, was when Harris broke his collarbone at school, and Mother slipped on ice and broke her wrist. We were well doctored at home. The arsenal of ammunition to fight disease and disability included the *Doctor Book.* This was a standard reference book that almost every family relied upon, and which was very fascinating to the children when they were allowed to look at it. We especially liked the Physiology section where there was a full page colored picture of an a-sexual human body. Following this picture there were transparent pages imprinted with the skeleton, the circulatory system, the internal organs, and the nerves. The complete series gave a real x-ray knowledge of the sum total of the human body and all its component parts.

The medicines kept on hand at home, or obtained at Macy Lee's Drug Store, when they were needed, included Lydia Pinkham's Vegetable Compound, a Female Remedy. According to the label it was tonic "which corrects all derangements peculiar to the sex, regulates the system, stops the pains, tones up the nervous organization, brightens the eye, clears the complexion, rounds out the figure, and restores health."

For stomach ache, Mother kept Chamberlain's Medicine, a liquid which she mixed with sugar and water but still tasted bad, Blackberry Balsam, and catnip tea. Dr. Carter's Little Liver Pills, "Every Picture Tells a Story," were a cure-all. For colds and coughs she rubbed our chests with Mentholatum or made a compress of turpentine and lard, or camphorated oil, and a flannel rag. Hoarhound candy and Smith Brothers Cough Drops kept our throat soothed. We used Castor oil and Nature's Remedy when "irregularity" was the problem. We had the usual "children's" diseases, such as measles and chicken pox; quinine was the remedy for fever. These capsules were filled by the druggist himself, and sometimes there was residue of the powder left on the outside of the container. Ugh! After the quarantine sign was taken down from the door, sulphur burned in the house killed the germs. Nothing could live in that odor! A bedpan was a shared medical convenience, available to both the Runkles' and Thompsons' households, and a syringe completed the needed medical equipment.

Many of the patent medicines and tonics have now been identified as being 80 Proof alcohol, so it is no wonder that people felt no pain after taking them. In our home they were used very sparingly, however.

There was no aspirin, sinus medicine, antibiotics, tranquillizers, sterile cotton, Band-aids, Kleenex or Kotex. Iodine was used as a disinfectant, and Denver Mud or baking soda took the sting out of insect bites and skin rashes. Liniment was used for rheumatism, which included all the joint and muscle pains we now group under the name arthritis, without differentiation as to osteo or rheumatoid types. Dad had a post-nasal drip and when he cleared his throat in the morning you could hear him a block away!

Probably the only house call which a doctor ever made to our home was when Doctor Burd made a "duty visit" when Harris had scarlet fever in 1922. Our house was quarantined but Dad came and went through the back door. I stayed with the Runkles, and Harris, who was (luckily) not very sick, recalls that he taught himself to type on an old Oliver typewriter. Far different was the fate of poor

John (Dummy) Sholttle who had scarlet fever when he was a small child, and it left him completely deaf. Since he could hear nothing, he never learned to talk, he was deaf-mute all his life, and in his last years he became blind also.

A doctor kept a supply of medicines and pills in his office, and supplied his patients with remedies for what ailed them, without the necessity of giving a prescription to be filled at the drug store. Jim High had a tonsillectomy in Doctor York's home office, and when I was in college I had a congenital pilonidal cyst removed from my lower back in Dr. Ebersole's office in Mount Vernon. It had a hair in it about eight inches long, and it had become infected. His wife, Jean, assisted as his nurse. She offered me a little glass of wine afterwards! Hospital administrators take note!

Years later, I was in his waiting room when our boys were small, while he attended to a college student. When she left, he said, "She was here a couple of months ago to get something that would destroy some warts on her hands. I was out of my regular remedy so I gave her a substitute and told her to come back in a week or so. I asked her today why she hadn't come. She told me that the stuff I gave her was great, and her warts all disappeared." Then he added, "I wish I could remember what I gave her." The money from the Ebersole's estate built the fine Medical Center which is now located on the Cornell Campus.

Our son George was the first of twenty grandchildren in the Hill family to come into the world without the assistance of their Grandma Jessie Hill, and the first to be born in a hospital, with the exception of Adelia's son, Edward, who was a Caesarian baby. However, Mother Hill was there, and induced his first breath of life while the doctors were attending to Adelia.

My life spans unbelievable changes in medicine, and I can truly appreciate the present, without downgrading the past. I have special pride in the work that George is doing in the field of medicine.

Even without vitamins and scientific diets we were an extraordinarily healthy family.

Natural Foods

I have lived too long to get enthusiastic about Health Stores of today. "Natural foods!" Almost everything for sale in these stores was standard fare when I was growing up so, as far as I am concerned, where's progress, or what's new? Can it be that those old days weren't so bad after all?

Even as late as the 1930's when Harris visited us in Lisbon, the only milk available was raw milk, delivered in glass bottles by "Dolly" (George) Graver's milk wagon. So we drove to Anamosa fifteen miles away to get pasteurized, homogenized milk for him. Doctor's orders for his ulcers. It was no hardship, however, because while we were there we could get some Anamosa ice cream, the best in the area. Nowadays "Raw Milk" is featured in health stores. Washing those bottles every day was an unwelcome chore, but there would be several inches of good rich cream rising to the top of the milk – rich enough to whip. In winter a long plug of frozen milk would stick up above the top of the bottle.

No insecticides! "The Silent Spring!" We flicked potato bugs into a can of kerosene instead of using a spray. Fruit was either wormy or not, and nothing usually was done abut it. "Natural fertilizer" was put on the garden every spring just before it was plowed. There was no regulation against keeping livestock in town, so it was easy for Dad to get what he needed. But, Oh! How mother used to scrub, scour, and scrape the potatoes from our garden before she baked them.

We had fertile eggs, fresh, mild, amber-colored sorghum molasses, comb honey, and homegrown cornmeal. No preservatives added. We ate margarine because it was cheaper, not because we feared cholesterol, which no one had ever heard of. We ate fresh tomatoes from the garden twice a day in summer, and stewed (canned) tomatoes all winter. The selling price was 50¢ a bushel.

Catnip tea was a soothing elixir. Sweet corn and apples were dried in the sun without preservatives or additives to prevent darkening. Even peanut butter was "natural" made from ground peanuts. Salad dressing was usually homemade, using egg yolks left over from making an angel food cake. Rachie's homemade lard made wonderful pie crusts. Convenience food and mixes were unknown, and in Stahl's General Store, oatmeal, rice, dried Navy beans, sugar, flour, and coffee were all stored in bins in bulk along the front of the counter and measured out on demand. Of course, mice were a problem! The big coffee grinder was standard equipment in the grocery store, and Oh! the smell was so delicious! Green tea in bulk, not teabags, was the evening meal beverage. Grapefruit was a novelty and not popular, but bananas came to the store in a bunch in an individual wooden crate. The whole bunch was then hung from a special hook and there was a machete-like knife for separating them. Oranges and lemons came in wooden crates, which were piled up outside the back of the store and were free for the taking. They were good for making "scooters," dressing tables, bookcases, and airplanes. The law protected the dairymen, so margarine was uncolored, white, but a capsule of coloring was enclosed in the package, and a tedious home job was mixing it to make it look "like the expensive spread." "Have you any trading to do" was the expression that people used when they meant "shopping." This, of course, was based on the fact that people coming in from the country actually did trade their homemade butter for staples from the store.

Some of that homemade butter was reserved for special people, little one-pound mounds of it with a distinctive design imprinted on the tops, some of it went to the general public, and some was so rancid, and bad smelling and tasting that Bish Stahl just disposed of it without telling the lady who had brought it in. He didn't want to lose her business, although he didn't have much to lose.

We had a little flock of chickens at home, a few eggs every day, and Mother used to let one or two broody hens "set" in the spring so we had baby chicks. In fact, March 4, 1913, the day of President Wilson's inauguration, Harris, age five years, posed for a picture holding two newly hatched little chickens which we named Woodrow and Marshall.

Even the jelly Mother made was "natural" without any bottled pectin added. What a variety of fruit we had! Sweet Whitney crab apples that we youngsters ate raw in astronomical quantities. Mother and Mattie made delicious spiced and pickled apples from them. We had huge Wolf River apples, so big and soft that they'd squash and splatter when they dropped to the ground. Isherwoods and Wealthys were put down in the cellar to eat during the winter. There was a blue plum tree and a variety of red plum that was large enough for Mother to peel, and that is what she patiently did before she canned them, using a big butcher knife. We had rhubarb in unlimited supply, cherries, and black raspberries. After Rachie was on the farm she kept us supplied with blue Concord grapes. What a bounty of natural foods!

Mixed nuts with almonds and English walnuts were available in the store at Christmas time, but hickory nuts and black walnuts came from the timber, and were husked, cracked and shelled by hand. The black walnut husks stained the hands, and in the fall at harvesting time, the boys at school vied with each other as to who had the blackest hands. It had to wear off, it wouldn't wash off.

I can't say much for the purity of the water we drank from out well, however. Maybe we had built up an immunity to it, because it never made us ill, and we thought it tasted wonderful. So cold and so good! In fact, we thought that Marie (Manly's wife, who was a city girl) was a little finicky because she insisted on having city water to drink and to use in the baby's formula. I am thankful for the good water supply we have now, and for the materials that are added to keep it healthful and strengthen our teeth. Fluoride is a good additive, in my estimation.

Testing, testing, testing, all the time! "It causes cancer in rats, so ban it!" This is the way it is. This is the way it was.

Recreation
Fun and Games

My grandparents and my parents lived about half way in time between the bundling-board period of their colonial ancestors and the era of the passion-pits of the outdoor movie parking lots of their descendants.

They seem to have lived in a recreational desert. Their goal was to achieve physical survival day by day, and to avoid the heat of the hell fires of the hereafter. In other words, work and church.

> "Rest comes at length, though life be long and dreary."
> –The Methodist Hymnal

How they loved to sing about that eternal rest! The large numbers of hymns of those days which refer to rest "when the laborer's task is o'er" testify to the kind of recreation that they looked forward to.

If they had quilting parties, wedding celebrations, or any of the pioneer fun that we read about, Mother never mentioned them. Singing school was the only form of recreation that she spoke of. Her father gave her a lovely walnut reed organ before she left home, and long after I foolishly persuaded her to part with it, I kept the old singing-school books she had saved. They were the nucleus of a collection of this special kind of music book, which I finally gave to Canon David Horning, who was Minister of Music in the Episcopal Cathedral in Sioux Falls, South Dakota. I must be a descendant of the pioneer women who left a string of treasured keepsakes, discarded along the trail, as they traveled in covered wagons toward a new home, because every time we moved I left behind, gave away, discarded, or in some way got rid of things that would have made good family heirlooms, and cherished possessions.

The singing school director might have been an itinerant school teacher or preacher. He used a tuning fork to give the pitch, and the sessions were held in the school house in the evening. This was probably where Mother learned to sing alto, because the music in these books was lined out in four part harmony. This training must have improved the music at church. Without a musical instrument, the preacher sounded the pitch, and sang one line of a hymn. Then the congregation sang it, on and on through all the verses. Most of the hymns had many verses and were expressions of worries and warnings, but the people loved to sing them. Son George has in his possession a tiny hymnal, words only, which belonged to Mother and dates back to those early times. Hundreds of the hymns were written by the great Methodist Charles Wesley.

In my own time, was life a drag and boring for children without jungle-gyms, skate boards and Barbie dolls? How did the older folks spend their leisure hours before radio, color TV, and Recreation Centers in retirement communities?

When I was a little girl, life was not dull, and there were plenty of activities and play equipment, albeit homemade and simple. Many of the toys and games that we had then are sought-after antiques of today. The stereo of that time was not a Hi Fi, but a stereo-scope, a device which was held in the hand and was equipped with special lenses through which adjacent pictures of the same scene could be viewed with a remarkable three-dimensional effect. In fact, in later years movies were made on the same principle, and the people in the audiences were given special glasses made of plastic to wear during the showing. The sets of pictures we used to enjoy might be called the movie re-runs of yesterday, because we used to enjoy the funny little stories over and over again. They were not "Adult movies" in the modern sense, but stories about grownups with a subtle tough of naughtiness, as when the pretty cook's floury hands left prints on the dark coat of the master of the house, the unsuspected evidence of a stolen caress in the kitchen. Scenic wonders of the world pictured on these special cards made Niagara Falls and Mt. Fujiyama as beautiful and spectacular to us as children, as the real thing appeared to us as adults many years later.

Home movies? Not quite, but a Magic Lantern show never looked for an audience and no matter how many times we saw the cartoon comics they were never stale, boring, or trite. "Look in your pockets, Henry," became a family expression when little Harris made this sage suggestion when he saw one of our light-fingered playmates making a great show of hunting everywhere for a lost slide after the show ended. When Henry's pockets were examined, that's where the slide proved to be!

The trees around the house were just right for swings. This could be a board suspended from a horizontal limb by a rope holding the sturdy board with notches in the ends, or a bag of sand, or an old tire. We could appreciate Robert Louis Stevenson's poem which begins, "Oh, how I like to go up in a swing, Up in the air so high," just as children do now on the metal and chain contraptions on their playground Jungle Gyms. The catalpas were perfect for climbing, too, and perhaps it was an expression of subconscious atavistic reversion which made us spend so much time up among the branches.

We played house without a playhouse. Most of the fun was in creating the A-frame tent out of strips of rag carpet, blankets, and old comforters hung over the clothes line. Usually, by the time the boys had helped to stretch out the sides and anchor them down, and the dolls and furnishings were arranged in it, my little girl playmate, Jean Opal McClelland, and I could play in it undisturbed. A ball game or a raid on the apple trees was more appealing to the boys than housekeeping. Before the days of the Little League in a baseball park there was One Old Cat on the street. Lisbon loved baseball, but there was no counterpart to the parental pressure on the youngsters which is sometimes found now in organized Little League baseball for the younger boys.

Perhaps the pleasure I have now in making scrapbooks, collections of poetry I want to save, photographs, trip souvenirs, and newspaper clippings for Club histories, goes back to the endless happy hours we had making the scrapbook which we had when we were children. It was a large, thick hardcover book with heavy pages, which had originally been designed to display samples of cloth for tailor-made men's suits. Gibson girls dressed in high fashion with voluptuous S-shaped figures, advertisements for new cars, illustrations from the *Saturday Evening Post*, and pictures of appealing pets were all carefully cut out and mounted in it. We worked on the floor, and Mama helped us mix the flour and water paste, and allowed us to use her shears, if we guaranteed to put them back on the special nail under the clock shelf.

The wooden alphabet blocks, wooden Lincoln logs, even roller skates with wooden wheels, the metal wind-up tops and trains, the cast iron fire engine and mechanical bank may not last forever, but they lasted longer than their modern counterparts that are made of plastic material which can't be broken, nailed, sawed, will not disintegrated in water, sun, or acid, and yet will come apart in the hands of a modern child before Christmas Day is over. We had a multipurpose game board, usually used for checkers, a blackboard for playing school, marbles, jump rope, and an ingenious wooden spelling board, which Harris saved and finally gave to me.

Other indoor pastimes which have a kind of immortality, were dominoes, Tick Tack Toe, and card games, such as Authors and Old Maid. Mother taught us how to make a Cat's Cradle out of string manipulated around the fingers, an art which knows no generation gap. I learned to make beads out of colored pages of a mail order catalog, using the same method I've seen in the Craft Clubs in Sun City. Beads could also be made from rose petals. It took large quantities of them, and the method was to put them through a food grinder several times, shape them, make a hole with a hatpin, and lay them out on a piece of old sheet iron to dry and turn black. They always had a pleasant smell and looked nice when they were strung with "gold" beads, or paper beads. The seeds from Mother's Job's tears also could be strung as beads. It must have been the same primitive urge for self-adornment which we see in the Indians of the Southwest making necklaces out of the seeds of the Juniper tree.

Mobility was provided by a coaster wagon and a scooter made from an orange crate, fastened to the end of a 2"x4" board mounted on roller skates. Tricycles and bicycles were as rare among the youngsters as automobiles were for adults when I was a child. Al Floyd had an antique model bicycle, with an enormous front wheel and a tiny one in the back, which he sometimes rode on Sauerkraut Day. It took some special know-how even to get on to it. Eventually Lester got a bicycle with which to deliver papers. Of course, he was very generous about sharing it, and I learned to ride it.

Reading was not a game but it was an important part of my life. The relatively few books which we owned must have had a mysterious and miraculous way of multiplying themselves, because I can remember so many of them. There were the classics, such as Louisa May Alcott's *Little Men* and *Little Women*, Poe's mysteries, Lamb's *Tales from Shakespeare*, Van Dyke's short stories, Hawthorne's *Tales of a Wayside Inn*, and Kipling's *Just So Stories*. There were other animal books, such as *Beautiful Joe* and *Black Beauty*, and Jack London's *Call of the Wild*. When I read them aloud to my pupils sixty-five years later, I found that they loved them as much as I had. I don't know how I missed reading *Alice in Wonderland*, but it doesn't have the same impact to read it for the first time as an adult. There was a lot of variety, however, starting with *Mother Goose*, and Hans Christian Anderson's *Fairy Tales* to *Hans Brinker*, the Rover Boys series, and the sentimental novels of the early 1900's such as *The Trail of the Lonesome Pine, Lavender and Old Lace*, and Zane Gray's books. *Pilgrim's Progress* and *The Scarlet Letter* were both part of my reading repertoire, although I didn't understand the significance of either one of them. The Volumes, as we called the set of books officially titled *The Young Folks Treasury*, were indeed a treasury of easy-to-read stories, myths and legends, biographies and history which I read and re-read innumerable times, and which greatly enriched my learning and pleasure.

At school we had a spelldown occasionally, and on special occasions, such as Valentine's Day, we might play Musical Chairs or Fruit Basket Upset. The littlest children played the perennial favorites Drop the Handkerchief, Farmer in the Dell, and London Bridge, while the older ones swung around in the more violent Crack the Whip, raced across the dividing space between two lines of players in Black Man's Base, or chased among the trees playing Wood Tag. Hockey was too rough a game for the girls, but the boys played it incessantly, using a tin can as a puck, and hickory sticks. Harris remembers going out to the timber to get them. The hickory bushes had roots which grew at right angles to the sprouts, the wood was tough and straight, and when they were cut to the right length, they made acceptable hockey sticks. Hide and Seek, Run Sheep Run, and Sardine were for the older pupils, mixed groups. On summer evenings after supper, while it was still daylight we used to go back to the school yard and play those games. Around the chimney on the schoolhouse the swallows would be endlessly circling, finding their way to their nests, and sometimes, we could hear the magic sound of music coming from Pfautz's old fashioned morning-glory-horn phonograph, the only one in the neighborhood. We counted out with "Eine, Meenie, Meinie, Moe" without any thought of racial insults, nor dreamed of vandalism as a part of fun and games. We didn't have the best, but it wasn't so bad, either.

What about the grown-ups and their recreation? Before the automatic washing machine, no-iron fabrics, tractors and combines, daylight saving, the forty-hour week, and compulsory retirement, people didn't have enough leisure time to worry about. The bank in Lisbon was closed during the noon hour, but it was open on Saturday, and the store keepers kept their places of business open twelve or fourteen hours a day. On the farm, the work-time was from dawn until dark. It was "early to bed and early to rise" with prayer meeting on Wednesday night for group therapy, and a trip to town on Saturday night to "trade" and gossip at the grocery.

In Lisbon several fraternal organizations, and after World War I, the American Legion, had meeting halls, and they provided social life for their members. During the 1920's the people interested in playing golf laid out a nine hole course in Peter Ink's pasture north of Mount Vernon. There was a potluck supper for the members every Friday night, and by the time we were married in 1930, this was the nucleus of our social activities. Little George in due time became the special pet of the group, and he was able to hold his own in antics and repartee. It was at one of those suppers that Baby Tommy was introduced to our friends at the age of two weeks.

There was only one black person who lived in Mount Vernon. She was Laura Platt, who had been Mrs. J. B. (Doc) Robinson's "mammy" since she was a little girl "back east." Laura always came with the Robinsons to the potluck suppers, and when it was in season she brought her specialty, which was fresh corn on the cob, roasted in the husk. Oh! How we enjoyed it, and we enjoyed having her with us. She was such a distinctive personality that she has become part of the folk-history of the town. She gave a new dignity and appreciation of her race to all of us.

We had good times in the old days.

School Days

School days, School days,
Dear old Golden Rule days,
Readin' and 'ritin' and 'rithmetic,
Taught to the tune of the hick'ry stick.

You were my bashful, barefoot beau,
I was your queen in calico,
You wrote on your slate, "I love you so,"
When we were a couple of kids.

I don't remember about the "love" but I surely do remember the slates. To me it is a significant sign of the changes in my lifetime to have started to school with that kind of writing equipment, and to have ended my teaching experiences, my last year in a classroom, in a place where I taught my fifth grade pupils to use school-furnished typewriters!

Although my schooldays in Lisbon seem quite primitive as I look back on them, nevertheless we had many good teachers who furnished the Cafeteria of Learning with good things and insisted that we partake. We had a rather limited curriculum, with few extra-curricular activities, except basketball, but perhaps the result was that we got more out of what little we had. I am thankful for the poetry which we had to memorize – "Thanatopsis," "The Chambered Nautilus," some of "Evangeline," parts of "The Lady of the Lake" and "The Vision of Sir Launfal." I tried to make my eighth grade pupils in Sioux Falls do this too, but they resisted it, resented it, and hated it. Changing times!

The ancient history we studied in the seventh grade centered on Greece and Rome, and what we learned was a help later in high school Latin classes. When we were in Athens and Rome in 1970 it seemed to me like the old textbook with all the pictures of the statues of gods and goddesses, the Acropolis, and the Forum were simply coming to life. They looked so familiar, and so natural, because the old Ancient History courses had made them so real, so long ago. The geometry class we had under John R. Lang in my sophomore year gave me all that I knew about arcs and angles when I was getting my CAA Instructor Rating in Navigation in 1944, twenty-five years later.

The school day always started with opening exercises – Bible reading and the Lord's Prayer. Then we either had some singing, or the teacher read out loud from a book she thought we ought to become familiar with. "Kidnapped" was one that I remember. In the Second Room (third and fourth grades) there was a bust of Longfellow on the self above the water pail, and a picture of Sir Galahad on the wall. Above the blackboard in the front of the room there was a picture of the Madonna and Child and a large Stuckslager and Auracher Bank calendar. No whispering or communication was allowed after we "took our seats" and very emphatically there was no gum chewing. When I first went to school we used the *McGuffey Reader*, which was made up of stories and poems, each with a "Lesson" to be learned, in thrift, obedience, good morals, and seemly manners and behavior.

Unless the weather was very bad, we were not allowed to come into the building until the "last bell" rang. Long before that time we had been lined up in front of the door by rooms, jockeying for either the first or last place in the line. We marched quietly in single file up the stairs, into the cloakroom, took off our wraps, and settled in our seats with hands clasped on the desks in front of us, ready and waiting for the tardy bell to ring.

About five minutes after the last child had disappeared into his classroom the tardy bell was supposed to ring with a great "Clang." My father, however, was tolerant of a youngster who came puffing up the hill trying to get inside the building before the bell rang, and he would be counted late, a tardy mark on his record and grade card. If Papa thought the child had a reasonable excuse for being late, and was really trying to get there, he would stand on the stairsteps with his watch in one hand, and the bell rope in the other, frowning to emphasize the seriousness of the situation, but he'd delay the fateful moment until the youngster was safe. Rachel Albright told me in 1970 that she was one of those children, and how thankful she was for Papa's "blindness."

At the end of the day the teacher waited to dismiss the children until everyone was sitting "in position" with desks cleared, hands clasped, backs straight. Then she would say, "Turn," pause, "Stand," pause again, then "Pass" and the children, one row at a time, would make their exit down the stairs in single file. Discipline, regimentation, respect for teachers and authority! Never questioned, or at least not often. It was fun however, to pass a note by pre-arrangement to someone across the room, by leaving it in the *Unabridged Dictionary*. *National Geographic* magazines were the *Playboy* magazines of the school room.

Gone but not forgotten are the ink well, dip pen, and pen wiper, the collapsible drinking cup, and slate pencils. Long hair, long underwear, long dresses, and long black cotton stockings are things of the past, and the old Washington Lisbon School is about to be torn down to make room for a new building.

My two older brothers and my sister had memories that were somewhat different from mine, and they recalled things that were happening in high school when I was in the lower grades of which I was not even aware. In a letter from Manly written July 6, 1975, he said, "Mr. Stuckslager (a member of the School Board for many years) intervened in favor of a school strike which I and two other mavericks led, which resulted in the ouster of school Superintendent Smith." Manly was graduated in 1910. The story speaks for itself! James taught English in the Lisbon High School, and although he was young, he had a reputation for sternness, discipline and precision, according to Elizabeth Stuckslager's memory of him. She laughed about it many years later when she told me, but she said she resented for a long time some criticism he made of one of her themes, which she thought was unjustified.

Palmer Method Penmanship was a special course in my sophomore year, and we learned to make ovals, and up-and-downs, holding pens correctly and sitting in the proper position. My class opted for Macbeth and King Lear as our Shakespeare studies (instead of the usual Hamlet) and we had to memorize large portions of them. After two years of Latin, our class of seven, including two future Phi Beta Kappas, elected to study Virgil's *Aeneid*, instead of the usual third year Latin study of Cicero's *Orations*. I took one more year of Latin in my freshman year at Cornell, and got along satisfactorily with the knowledge I had gotten from Florence Keye's classes in Lisbon.

The school experiences I have had reach from the three R's and outdoor plumbing to carpeted classrooms, in-door swimming pools, and televised teaching. Now the emphasis is on originality and creativity rather than conformity and memorization. There are also switch blades in the hands of the pupils in some schools instead of a hickory stick in the hand of a teacher or principal.

But it is good that no longer is the slow learner or the handicapped child retained in disgrace because he fails to get at least a mark of <u>70</u> (a passing grade) in a majority of subjects. "Did'ja pass?" was the universal cry on the last day of school when the grade cards were given out. It was a traumatic, tragic, humiliating time for the unfortunate children who were retained in the same grade, sometimes several times. Eventually they finally dropped out. Now there are special teachers for children with every sort of disability and handicap, grades, as such, are unknown, and in many cases more money is spent on these children than on the ones who are above average in intelligence. However, it delights me to observe the fine training that our grandchildren are getting in all their schools. The Here and Now is far superior to the Past and Gone.

The Lisbon school is fortunate to have a song which is truly its own, both words and music. It was written by Harold Baltz of the Class of 1919.

Lisbon High School Song
Come sing the praise of Lisbon High School
The school we deem the best;
May we through honor and endeavor keep her
Always the best school of the West.
The crimson and the black are o'er us,
Our colors proud and gay,
May we exalt and raise them
When we meet the world of care.
Chorus:
O L. H. S. we love thee truly,
O L. H. S. there's none above thee,
We want to serve thee,
We want to prove thee,
To the world that you are the best of all.
Unto each you give your blessing,
Above each one your colors fly,
Three cheers and three cheers
For these four jolly years,
We're spending now in Lisbon High.

The time has come when we must leave thee,
Promoted from thy halls;
Then as our youthful castles fall and crumble,
These days of gladness we'll recall,
We'll live these scenes all over;
We'll play these games again.
The memory of Lisbon will make us sing again.

In 1939 an auditorium wing was added to the Lisbon schoolhouse and the building was rededicated. I was president of the Lisbon Alumni Association, and I wrote these verses and read them in honor of the occasion. I read them again as part of my speech at the Alumni banquet in 1970, which was the Golden Anniversary of my graduation class.

Lisbon High School – Fiftieth Anniversary

By Essie Mae Thompson Hill

As we come back to the old school today,
And stand in its loved halls once more,
Our hearts are crowded with mem'ries
Of the hours we have spent here before.

The teachers, the classes, our schoolmates –
Flash 'cross our minds in review,
And we welcome this opportunity
To revisit the scenes which we knew.

They say it has been fifty years
Since that bell first rang out its glad call,
But no matter how far we have scattered
It still rings in the hearts of us all.

If these old walls could speak for themselves
On this happy Homecoming Day,
We would need no other program
Than to hear what they had to say.

But today we see changes indeed,
The result of long, earnest endeavor,
And now we are proud in the knowledge
That our school is better than ever.

But no one can truly appreciate
What an up-to-date school is, I think,
Unless he has tested his muscle
On the old pump when he wanted a drink.

And, did you ever feel more distinguished
Than the times when permitted to pass
The pail with the sponge and the water,
To wash the slates of the rest of the class?

They say that kids now learn to read faster
Than they ever did back in our day,
But think of the fun they are missing
In not having to bleat like a sheep for "short A."

Lisbon has had many fine teachers,
And to them I'm sure all of us say,
"For your work, your ideals, and devotion,
We wish to pay tribute today."

While we look on the past with affection,
We're looking ahead without fear,
For we know that the school which we cherish
Will continue to grow better each year.

Copy of the speech by A. M. Floyd at the 50th Anniversary of Lisbon H.S.

HALF CENTURY ANNIVERSARY

Sunday, August 20, 1939   LISBON PUBLIC SCHOOL

The first one hundred years is said to be the hardest. Thus in the first forty-five years there were five distinct school house buildings erected. While in the last fifty years, this new 1939 structure is the only one built within the half-century. I am very glad to be here at this Dedication and half-century Anniversary.

There is much satisfaction in recognizing that FIFTY years ago, of personally being on this school ground. This school ground was a place of many happy and important incidents, as well as not-to-be-forgotten pleasant memories, dating way-back from the first A.B.C. class; when the sweetest dispositioned fair-haired lady teacher ever known (Miss Lizzie Young) stood at the school room door on Friday evenings, at the closing of the week's school, and embraced each dirty-faced urchin, with such a sweet kiss, that it could be tasted in our dreams, for three nights afterwards. In her room there were fifty-nine pupils that were showered with fifty-nine big, juicy smacks.

Well, this is dear old Lisbon Public schools, almost reaching the ninety-sixth year, and still progressing. This NEW 1939 building is the SIXTH foundation built for Lisbon school purposes. First it was the log school house, in the West part of Lisbon, and located west of the Graver Dairy residence. Then the brick, later known as the Neesley residence. Next the one-story frame, on the present school grounds, with a belfry and well-known bell. The FOURTH was the two-story frame, built just east, beside the one-story frame, all painted white.

The WEST part stands across the street (home of Andrew Beaver). The FIFTH was the brick "Washington" two-story building, of October 21, fifty years ago which still stands intact, excepting that the belfry has been dismantled. But the bell remains; for it, thanks to Supt. Rahn.

When the school board acquired this tract of land, nearly eighty years ago, there was a road running north from a brick-yard, that was located in the field south of the school grounds. The marks of this wagon road could be traced thru the west part of this school ground up until this summer.

There were upwards of one hundred mammoth oak trees and very much hazel brush. The pupils were asked to clean up the brush, which they did, without pay. P. J. Fisher, a former teacher and a resident attorney (perhaps a member then of the school board), said he would bring to the ground a wagon load of apples, in appreciation of the voluntary work of brush-cleaning by the students. There were many longings and keen watching for that certain load of apples . . . that never came.

In summing up the four school buildings, it has been found that the log school house was used eleven years; the red brick six years; the second-story white frame, twenty-five years; and up to now, the present "Washington" brick has thus far been used for a half-century, fifty years, and is seemingly good for another fifty years.

In 1889, the school district voted a bond issue of ten thousand dollars. Jonas S. Gauby was the contractor and he and the mechanics were principally Lisbon residents. Rev. D. S. Fouse, president of the school board, father of S. G. Fouse, was faithfully looking after the details of construction, and seeing to it that there was no undue waste of any kind, and at the same time, insisting that all work should be substantial, from the foundation to the roof. When the building was completed, it was found to be within the ten thousand dollars bond issue, really figuring, it was said only to be $9,998.79. The tax-payers hardly noticed any increase in their usual tax. One farmer, in the district, not many years after, inquired when the new school building was to increase the tax. He was informed that the ENTIRE bond issue had already been paid.

It was a great day, October 21, 1889, when the dedication exercises took place. The program was held in the United Brethren (Federated) Church, consisting of vocal music, and addresses, Prof. Freer, of Cornell College and Prof. Devine, Superintendent of the Mount Vernon Schools, were the principal speakers. Then the brass band led the procession, of school officials, Grand Army soldiers, local societies, students and citizens, marching from the church east to Washington Street (at the creamery); thence south to School street, and then west to the school grounds. The band was playing, flags were flying and everybody enthusiastic. In front of the new building there was a short program, including the presentation of a large flag, by John A. Buck Post, G.A.R. The flag was raised to the staff over the building, and then the door was unlocked and the rooms opened for inspection. The next day the Fall term commenced. The addresses were STRONG with devoted loyalty and much expressed American Patriotism. The people were very proud of the 1889 year "Washington" brick building.

Of the eleven members of the Lisbon Cornell Band, that led the Grand Parade from the United Brethren Church to the Lisbon School grounds on Monday, October 21, 1889 – fifty years ago, two have passed away; William H. Kurtz, cornet player, formerly Lisbon clothing merchant; and Levi J. Cook (or Koch), solo alto player (formerly of Lisbon and later of Cedar Rapids). Those who survive of the band, are the following: Frank Hoover, of California; Fred Zalesky, of Fort Dodge, Iowa; Frank L. Runkle and Wm. H. Hoover of Mount Vernon; Wm. F. Stahl and James Keifer Barnicle of Cedar Rapids. Three are now residents of Lisbon: Cris M. Gish, Orlin O. Walmer and myself, A. M. Floyd.

Well, in the old primitive days of the school, as we progressed from class to class, the school was ruled and operated very much by the rod or hickory stick. In the course of years, while certain boys received their whippings almost daily, yet to me, I escaped with only three, in the entire epoch. One whipping was given by a man teacher, of the Simon Legree type, who was devoid of diplomacy, justice or conservative investigation.

Large, hazel-brush or hickory sticks, long in length, were the "implements of war-fare," that were kept on top of the thirty-foot blackboard, in generous numbers, ready for INSTANT CONTACT. He used these sticks frequently, with or without cause or provocation. He also used tobacco almost constantly, while he was teaching and the school was in session. And a large, friendly, wood-box in the center of the room, was his pride and consolation, when it became necessary to eject an overflow of a mouthful of sappy juice.

The other two flayings were inflicted and thrust upon me, not for any infraction of school rules, but because, as the fiery-red-headed-six-foot-tall schoolma'm said, it was simply on "general principles." Since considering the matter, perhaps she was right. Anyhow neither one of the three inflictions were injurious, or even painful. The lady teacher in after years married a preacher of age and experience only, no other special attributes, and then I had much sympathy for her, like she had previously for me, on "general principles." Bless her memory, for she was, however, a very thorough instructor. Agnes Wilson was her name.

While there were a number of excellent Superintendents of the Lisbon High School, especially U. D. Runkle and P. W. Peterson, who were each called back to be at the head of the school, and served long and well; yet there was another outstanding man to be mentioned. That gentleman was William E. Cort, now a resident of California. He was the head of the Lisbon Schools from the autumn of the year 1884 until the close of the school year in the spring, when he presented the renowned class of 1885, consisting of ten seniors, SIX of whom still survive this life. Prof. Cort was always courteous, clear-minded, careful in making a decision, practiced diplomacy, adhered to justice in all.

The Thompson Family History

The name Thompson means "son of Thom," which was a pet form of Thomas. It was the word in ancient English times for a twin. Thompsons probably originally came from Norway in some Viking invasion because the name is common there, as well as in Sweden, England, and Scotland.

My father's ancestors are believed to have come to New England in the late seventeenth century. They were living in Charleston, Massachusetts, north of Boston, when the Revolutionary War broke out. No records have come down to us which gives any indication about why they chose to remain loyal to the king instead of joining the men who were fighting for independence. But that is what they did, and at the time of the early siege of Boston they escaped in small boats, with hundreds of other Loyalists, and went to Halifax, Nova Scotia.[*]

I always thought it was quite romantic that my grandfather, James Thompson, came west with his bride, Jane Grant, and built a log cabin on the prairie in Linn County, north of Marion, Iowa where their eight children were born. My great-grandparents had twelve children, of whom James was the third child and the first son. Grandfather died in 1889, at the age of fifty-nine, but he had a brother, Charles, twenty-two years younger than he was, who lived to be over ninety years old, and it is from him and his daughter Priscilla that we have learned about the Thompsons in Nova Scotia and America.

Uncle Charles was born in Medford, Massachusetts, after the family had moved back to the United States. He was a remarkable man. When he died he was one of only three surviving firemen who had battled the great Boston fire of 1872. He was a great story teller and conversationalist, and he made many trips to the Midwest to visit with his relatives there, and to try to make them realize what a wonderful place New England was. The newspaper account of the 59th wedding anniversary of Uncle Charles and Aunt Cassie said, "In September, 1933, when he was 82 years of age, Mr. Thompson left Boston by train to visit the World's Fair. He made the trip alone and stayed several days in the Windy City." As a matter of fact, he stayed with my brother James and wife May, in Oak Park, a suburb of Chicago. James was his escort to the Fair. After he thought that aged Uncle Charles had had enough of the excitement and wonders of the Century of Progress, he put him on the train to go back home. But he underestimated the independent old fire-fighter! Uncle Charles just walked through the train, got off on the other side, and went back to the fair grounds on his own. He did everything he wanted to do, saw everything that he wanted to see, all on his own, and left his great-nephew none the wiser.

---

[*] Ed. note: Essie Mae's belief about the Thompson migration to Nova Scotia as Loyalists from Boston is incorrect. We now know that our ancestor, Archibald Thompson, a weaver, appeared in Bridgewater, Mass., in about 1724, in the Scots-Irish migration to America. His son, Archibald (II) first came to Nova Scotia as a young soldier in the French and Indian War, and he returned there with his wife after he was married in 1761. They settled on the Bay of Fundy, not in Halifax. However, after several generations in Nova Scotia, our branch of the Thompson family migrated back to the United States from Halifax. See George J. Hill, *Fundy to Chesapeake: The Thompson, Rundall and Allied Families* (Berwyn Heights, Md.: Heritage Books, 2016).

"I'll believe it when I see it" seems to govern the Thompsons' attitudes about the stories that relatives from different parts of the country tell each other. Fortunately, in modern times most of us have traveled enough to realize that Uncle Charles's stories really were true, however much they seemed like "whoppers" when he was telling them. Nevertheless, we loved hearing them and looked forward to his visits like a man from another world. Evidently that same skepticism was true a hundred years ago, when our Grandfather wrote to his family telling them about the fertile soil and abundant corn crops in Iowa. In Nova Scotia after the corn was harvested the husks were tied together and the ears were hung on the fence posts to dry. So they knew that James's story was just a "tall tale" because there couldn't have been enough fence posts on which to dry all the corn he said he raised!

Priscilla Thompson, Uncle Charles's youngest daughter, has carried on her father's interest in maintaining family ties. She has made many visits to the relatives in the mid-west, and she has done a great deal of research on traditions and records. She has lived in Cohasset, Massachusetts, for many years, but it has been though her familiarity with Brockton, where her parents and grandparents lived and were buried, that we know about the family tree with its branches and twigs.

William H. and Sarah Rundall Thompson

Rundall brothers and sisters

Rachel Manly

Sarah and Mattie Rundall

Essie Mae (Davies) Smith

Cousins – 1904
Lester Runkle with
Essie Mae Thompson

James, Edith, Manly
Father, Harris, Essie Mae and Mother

My Father – William Henry Thompson

Papa was a complex man. He was a good conversationalist and story teller, but he was often morose and silent. His early pictures show him to be very handsome with black hair, deep blue eyes, and a wonderful smile. When he married my mother, he wore a formal coat, and a tall silk "Abe Lincoln" hat. As long as I can remember, it was stored away in the attic at home. Manly claimed it after Papa's death, and he finally gave it to a Little Theatre group in Milwaukee. It was also used in the Cornell 75th Anniversary pageant as part of Abraham Lincoln's costume. In his later years, however, Papa's clothes and hygiene were an embarrassment to all of us. The changes which age and circumstances bring!

My parents Sadie and Will were married September 3, 1889, in Central City, Iowa. They went to Des Moines on their honeymoon. Mother said they sat up on the train all night to get there and went to bed as soon as they got to the hotel.

Among the letters which Mother saved was one written by my Father which told of his plans:

Headed, Paris, Iowa

August 24, 1889

"My dear Sadie,

I am thinking of you all the time and I can't go to bed for a while so I will scratch off a few lines to you. I want to see you so bad to night. I am all alone but my thoughts are with the dearest girl I ever met and how I Love her you will know how much I Love you when I have the right to take care of you. I wish sometimes I could quit thinking about you. I was in such a deep thought yesterday morning that I worked about 60 pounds of butter and put it away and never put any salt in it and had to work it all over again. I hadn't ought to tell you but I don't care. My Dear, Do you Know when the State fair begins. It's 23 and 24 of Sept. Can you be ready by that time. We will see some of the busy world I know you will like the change. There is an ice cream supper at the Alex McDonald's to night. All have gone but poor me Ha What do I care for their ice cream. Your ever true loving Will."

Mother kept a letter from Papa, written January 13, 1889, which tells about Grandpa James Thompson's terminal illness:

"Dear Sadie, Do not think I have forgotten you for the past few weeks for I have not. But have no time now except for my Dear Father. He is very sick. The Dr. thinks he will not live. We are doing all we can for him. Have had two doctors and have gone to Marion today for Dr. Hubbard. He will be here this afternoon . . . Oh Sadie, I am so broke up I can't do anything. I have been going home every night and the worry and the work together is killing me. But I would not care if only we could help Pa.

Excuse so short a letter and all mistakes for I don't know what I am doing half my time. Good by. Your ever loving Will."

He was a very loving father and husband, although I suspect he was not always faithful. But he could be so scowling, stern, and severe with us that we were scared to death of his displeasure. If we disagreed with him, we never argued, and if we were doing something of which he disapproved, a frown was all it took to make us quit immediately.

He thought he was as good as anyone, and better than most, or at least his family was. He supported the church, but never attended services. He always asked the blessing at the beginning of a meal, but in such a mumbling fashion that the only part of it which we distinctly understood was the Amen at the end.

The distaste, distrust, and fear that he had for the Democrats was almost pathological. I think it was based on the tariff problem, although I am sure that he had been a rock-ribbed, hide-bound Republican all his life. At one time he evidently had a good business in the creamery up on the prairie where I was born, and later in Lisbon. In the trunk in the attic where Mama kept his letters and papers there were some old bills of lading that showed he was shipping sweet butter to New York City, as well as selling it locally. However, during the term of some Democratic president or Congress (perhaps Cleveland) the tariff on dairy products from abroad was taken off and he could not meet the competition from the imported material. So his creamery business was a failure, and in order to make a living he sold cream separators in western Iowa, South Dakota, and Nebraska. Mother kept all his letters and they are a wonderful record of those times, and how hard he worked for us "chaps," as he called us children at home.

Harris was born during this time, and Mother always resented the fact that Papa was not at home "when she needed him." Harris was about two weeks old before Papa ever saw him, but that was a very short time, compared with what it was like during modern war times, when babies might be several years old before their daddies saw them. There have been hard times in modern years, as well as in the old days, and mothers have always needed to have courage and stamina.

Papa's work gave him the opportunity to do considerable traveling throughout the Midwest, with special trips to New York City, and to a convention in Niagara Falls. This was in contrast to Mother, who always stayed at home and looked after the children and the household, but he missed her. In a letter to her, written on June 9, 1912, he said, "I am glad to hear you have your new dress and hat. Now you should come to Ottumwa some Sat. and spend Sunday with the old man. Such a trip would do you good. You beat me in a new suit. I haven't gotten mine yet. Don't get time. . . . Now little chaps, help your Ma with the work and don't make any more trouble or worry or expense than possible. Pop will get his suit in good time. With Love, Papa"

Of all the places that he saw and visited, he thought South Dakota was the best. He really fell in love with that state, and he wanted with all his heart and mind to move there to live. He tried in vain to persuade Mother to go. The only times that I ever heard them really argue was after Harris and I had gone upstairs to bed, and were presumably asleep. I was frightened and very unhappy as I lay listening to their angry voices. Mama kept saying, "I'll never sign the deed!" and Papa shouting back at her all the reasons why they should sell the house and move to that Land of Opportunity. Finally he had to give up.

Mama's reason for not wanting to leave Lisbon was that she was afraid that we children would never get an education, if we went out to that God-forsaken territory. She believed in Education, as her parents before her had done! That was more important to her than anything else, including the relationship with her husband. "What's best for the children" was the goal of both of them, but they had different ideas about how to attain that goal. Who can say whether she was right or wrong? Speculations about that are merely guesses, but the fact that we all did get an education satisfied her, and seemed to justify her stubbornness. As far as Papa was concerned, the result was that he spent the rest of his life frustrated, downgraded, and existing on a level far below his potential. That is my opinion, although not all the family agree. His outlook, personality, and habits changed. He had to take a job as custodian of the Lisbon School, and later of the Lisbon Bank also, and he always hated it.

The recollection of what Mother's refusal to move at that time did to my father was what finally made me agree to go to Aberdeen from Sioux Falls when Jerry was determined to leave the security of his position as vice president of the Union Savings Bank to start a new bank in a strange locality, a complete gamble with the future. Even after calling on our friend, Bishop Conrad Gesner, for advice, and hearing his warm recommendation that it would be a good move for us, I still was reluctant to go. However, at last I changed my mind. I told our friend, Marianne Naused, "I remember what happened to my father when Mother refused to leave security and gamble on the future in a new place, and I wouldn't do that to Jerry." Jerry's venture was a success, and what my father's might have been, who knows?

Although Papa did not have much education he had a keen mind, wonderful tongue-in-cheek sense of humor, and a gift of communication. On August 25, 1907, he wrote from Norfolk, Nebraska,

"Dear Mama and Chaps, I have a good excuse today if I did not write. Yesterday I rode 70 miles up on the reservation in South Dakota and did not see but one house. Did not get into Gregory until 11 last night, had supper, got up at 5:30 this morning and came to Norfolk. Did not have any breakfast until one P.M. today. It is now five P.M., have been busy getting out my report and writing. Will sleep some tonight.

"The chaps had ought to be up on the reservation for one summer. Keep them busy catching fleas. They are in the beds in all the towns. Can they bite, did you ask. Worse than bedbugs! I will write more next week. This is just to let you know that I am feeling well again. You must not worry about me getting hurt. I am trying to lead such a life that I may be spared to see you all. Accidents will happen in any kind of work, but in traveling I take no extra risk. Baby Harris must be a nice baby. It don't seem right for Pop to be away. Girlie [that was the family name for me] writes such nice letters. [I was four years old] What's the matter with Lester boy. He don't write Uncle Willie. When I started to write I tried to think I was not tired but such a jaunt as yesterday is something awful. I am going to sleep one hour until supper. Can you imagine such a strip of country, for seventy-five miles with one house. [He drove a horse and buggy] This one Co. is all prairie. More than 100,000 acres. In one herd of cattle there are 15,000 head, 200 cowboys are now rounding them up for shipment. With love, Papa"

In another letter written in the summer of 1907 to Rachie, he said he had driven to Norfolk, Nebraska, from the southern Black Hills in South Dakota. He comments on the "lightness of the air," saying,

43

"I suppose one could get used to it. So many interesting things to see one tires out in a few blocks in walking. Of course, you don't have to walk as there are horses to ride, all kinds of nice cabs of every description. At one part of town some boys have a large tent where they keep 20 of these little burros or donkies all saddled up ready if you care to go up the mountain climbing. Manly would enjoy a ride on one of these donks. [Manly was fifteen years old] Tell Manly that he can buy one of these donkeys here for $15.00 broke to ride. They put one saddle girth around the body of the donk and one back under the tail so as to keep the saddle from slipping over the head when going down hill. Your pop didn't have time to take in all the sights while there. We will all come up here some time when we get rich."

He was in Ponca, Nebraska, on March 1, 1907, two weeks before Harris was born. He wrote,

"Dear Chaps at home, I came to Sioux City yesterday, and I found your letter at the hotel. Essie May's and Lester's letters were just all right. They can just beat you all in writing. [Lester was about a year and a half in age, and I was not yet four.] Today I have been in Nebraska for the first time in 44 years. [He was forty-four years old, so that was his way of saying that he was there for the first time.] I saw and talked with the man that first came to Neb from Iowa. I suppose the next few days I will meet with ½ doz that will tell the same story. These old whiskered farmers are chuck full of <u>con</u> talk. We at home have the wrong opinion of the west. In fact there is no going out west. Here I am 350 miles west of Linn County and it all looks the same to me. Of course in some localities it is not so well improved but all seem to be doing well. This town of Ponca 1200 people, is a very nice town if it were not for the drink element but you don't see any drunk people. . . . I feel very much at home here in Neb. If I could just run down a Jack Rabbit I would quit work. Our commission house here in Sioux City gave away 350 jack rabbits yesterday. The warm weather caused the decline in the market. Some colored people came with sacks to carry home the Jacks. Fine eating, Manly. How would a Sunday dinner go flavored with dead rabit [sic]? Essie May [notice the spelling] Girlie you can write better than Rachie. You tell Rachie Papa said so. Tell Lester Uncle Willie said for him to go to school and learn to write so he can keep store for his Pop. I can read his letters but no body else can. Love to all, Papa"

On November 2, in 1907, he wrote from Sioux City,

"Dear Mama and Babies, Your letters all came to hand, one yesterday and one today. It seems good to hear from home. Our chaps will be of the age some day when they will realize how much good letters do one when they are among strangers. Money can't buy all the things that are useful in this world. We lack ready cash a great many times in order to satisfy what money can buy. Pop hopes he will always have the health and strength to keep the chink coming in, as James says . . . such a fine day here and tonight the streets are crowded with well dressed people as I sit here in my room. One can hear all kind of noise. How little one knows what is going on in the world outside ones own house unless you have opportunity to see . . . I ate breakfast about 9:30. Had stewed prunes and grape nuts first and then salt mackerel with potatoes and fried eggs and bacon and corn cakes with good cream and sugar . I don't believe I will eat much dinner. Today would be fine if you were all here. We would take a buggy ride around the city. Girlie would like that. Manly, you ought to be here to sell papers. Such a business as it is in large cities. Will close with love to all, Pop."

He thought of us "chaps" often and tried to share his experiences with us at home.

There is nothing that my father would not have done for me. Among the special good times we had together was building a barn on the back of our lot in the summer of 1924. I wore overalls and a big hat, and finally went up on the roof to help him lay the shingles in straight rows, lined up with a cord and blue carpenter's chalk. Quite different from the quickie method that our carpenter used in putting the roof on our Payson, Arizona, cottage, using rolls of pre-notched composition material. Another good time we enjoyed together was in target practice with a couple of guns which he brought home from the bank, especially for that purpose. He put up the target on a tree back of the school house and he made me feel that I did very well. It was dangerous, probably illegal, but no one else knew about it, and we had a good time together.

Mother disapproved of my Catholic boy friend, because she felt the same way that Dad did about the Democrats. So I privately asked Dad, "Is it all right with you if I go with him?"

"Yes," he answered, "I think he's a nice boy, but don't let him get his hands under your skirt." I was so shocked that I could hardly answer, "Oh, he wouldn't do that!" That was more advice than Mother ever gave me. My sister Rachie married (unhappily) when she was twenty years old, but I was twenty-seven before I got married, so Mother had a long time to worry about me.

Papa and Jerry liked each other from the first time I took him home to meet my folks. He was, in fact the first fellow that I ever took to home that they both liked. A few weeks before we were married, Manly said to Dad, "Is Essie Mae really going to marry that fellow (Gerald)?

Dad replied, "Well, she better! He's been calling me 'Dad' for three months." Jerry knew how to win over my folks. My father adored "little George" as he always called him. I am sorry that I didn't tell him that I was expecting another baby the last time I visited him in the hospital in Iowa City in September, 1934. Dad was very, very ill, but I know it would have pleased him to know.

He finally gave in to my persuasion and came to hear me sing at a Cornell Baccalaureate service, and I was very proud and pleased. Characteristically, he left immediately after my solo was over. At our family reunion in Cedar Rapids in 1974, Manly told us about his early memories of our creamery near Paris, Iowa (Linn County) where I was born. He said we had an ice house, and consequently we were the only family able to have ice cream in the summertime. A great treat and a wonderful attraction to all the kids in the neighborhood.

Another characteristic of my father was punctuality. His life was geared to time. At mealtime Mother would start taking up the food even though no one was in sight, but by the time she finished, everyone would be seated in the right place at the table, ready for Papa to ask the blessing so we could start eating. I don't remember ever coming to the table after the meal had started, and dinner was at twelve o'clock and supper at six. Papa used to say that in all his years of traveling, he never missed a train. He was packed, waiting at the station ready to go when the train came in. Even during the last year of his life when he was no longer working, Mama got three meals a day <u>on time</u>.

Minnie Mohn Kharas laughs about Papa's response to her invitation to her wedding. She was married in the Reformed Church in Lisbon which she had attended as a child. Services were no longer held there, and there were no furnishings in it. We brought in portable chairs and went to our house to get ferns and flowers to decorate it. Papa was sitting in the shade in the back yard when we got there. Min said, "Mr. Thompson, I would like to have you come to my wedding tomorrow." He grinned and replied, "Well, Minnie, I'd like to, but the *Saturday Evening Post* will be coming, and I've got to finish a continued story in it." Probably Clarence Buddington Kelland! At any rate she remembers the Indian blanket he gave her for a wedding gift, still wrapped in the same paper from the store.

There were two untouchables in the kitchen that belonged to Papa. They were in the east window near the side door where the cistern was. One was his razor strop which he never used for anything but sharpening his razor, but which Mother found convenient to use occasionally for quick, painful corporal punishment. The other was his Jew's harp – we always thought it was a "juice harp." He used to play "Turkey in the Straw" and other lively tunes, including "Weevily Wheat." I have been told that on the first day I went to school I volunteered to sing it:

> I won't have none of your weevily wheat,
> I won't have none of your barley
> For I must have the best of wheat,
> To bake a cake for Charley.

I had three older siblings in school at that time, so the story got home, and became a family joke. Harris learned to play Papa's Jew's harp and still cherishes it.

It was always exciting when Manly came home from Washington, D.C. He and Papa had very lively discussions, lots of bantering, an exchange of jokes, and political arguments. Manly, as an adult, could get away with disagreeing with our father, but we younger ones never had the nerve to do it. They also had an annual wrestling match. It was fascinating and a little frightening to watch them tussling on the kitchen floor. Manly told me that he finally quit doing it, when it became too easy for him to win. He didn't want to make Papa think he "wasn't as good as he always was."

Dad used to go to Stuckslager's timber in mid-summer to get big pails' full of blackberries, which Mama fixed for eating fresh, and canned, and made pies and jam from them. We had raspberries at home, but this was a nice change. I can remember him making apple cider, which was delightful, and butchering a hog, which was horrifying. Sometimes on a Sunday afternoon he'd make some parched corn in the big iron skillet. I'm sure he'd be scornful of the parched corn which is now sold for cocktail party appetizers.

Sunday afternoon also meant a nap for papa, lying on the couch in the dining room with a newspaper over his face. He snored so loudly the walls of the room almost rattled, and we kids nearly had hysterics with smothered laughter. Whatever the Sunday afternoon activity was, the morning began with preparations for Sunday School. Papa's part was to cut our fingernails, using his pocket knife, and to give us our money for the collection – a penny! Those Sunday mornings were the only times in the week when Mama and Papa could be alone together, and it must have been a precious time for them.

He valued honesty and integrity, and detested hypocrisy and deceit. "These modern inconveniences," "Split leather," and "The guarantee's run out" were his ways of commenting on things which he considered slip-shod, poor in quality, or a misrepresentation of fact.

In some ways he was ahead of his time. He had the greatest scorn for soft white baker's bread, which we, as kids, thought was far superior to Mother's homemade bread. "It'll be the death of the human race," he used to say, and that was long before dietitians worried about all the vitamins, minerals, and good stuff that were lost in the flour refining process.

I have always felt that my parents had a lot of affection for each other, although there were times when Mama gave him the "silent treatment" and the atmosphere was pretty well charged with hostility. In all honesty, I must say that he probably deserved it. But Mama always helped him put on his coat when he went to the bank in the evening, and he always kissed her goodbye. However, Harris says she told him with sadness in her voice, one summer evening as they sat on the south porch, "Your father and I haven't slept together in ten years." Knowing Mama's vague way of talking about personal subjects or sex, I am not sure what she meant, but I do know she always laughed at his stories no matter how many times she had heard them, and she always tried to please him in every way, except to move to South Dakota.

At the time Mattie died, Dad bought a lot in the Norwich cemetery near Martelle, large enough for six graves. About six weeks after Mattie's death and burial, he himself died and was buried there, Mama's brother, Uncle Will Rundall, was also buried there. Now all six spaces are filled – the two Rundall girls, their brother, and their spouses.

When Mama arranged for the markers on the graves, she also had a blue spruce tree planted near Papa's grave. This tree has grown so large that it almost covers all the markers and is the most beautiful thing in the cemetery.

This is the Norwich Cemetery north of Martelle, Iowa. My mother's parents, Silas and Rachel Rundall, and grandparents are buried there. She told us that it was originally part of the original Rundall farm. We claim this as a family tradition, although a large granite grave marker in the cemetery gives the credit to another family.

My father had the infinite patience that it takes to keep tools sharp. This included his pocket knife. He used his whetstone as the Greeks do their worry beads. In leisure times he didn't fidget or give the impression that he had any nervous tension because he could always reach down into his pocket and come up with his knife and whetstone. He used to like to play mumbley-peg sometimes on a summer afternoon. This is an old-fashioned game of skill in which each one of a group tries to outdo the others in tossing his knife so it will stick by the blade, into the ground or a wooden sidewalk, the challenges becoming increasingly difficult. Overhand, underhand, left handed, and from all sorts of positions. When Papa did it, it was something special, and good summer amusement.

I pay tribute to him for his good mind, for his love and devotion to the family, and especially for the many things he did for me. I qualify my words with sadness because of the gap between what he could have done and been, and what he did do. Perhaps that is true of all of us.

Father, Mother, Edith, Mattie, Frank, Manly
Harris, Lester, Essie Mae

Will Thompson

William H. Thompson

Mother – Sarah D. Rundall Thompson

Who needed a psychologist's couch when we had mother? She was the safety valve and the best listener that ever was. Joseph Fort Newton, a famous preacher and columnist in the 1920's wrote,

"A friend is one with whom we can think aloud, blurting out anything that is in our minds, without restraint or fear, knowing that if it is true, it will be treasured; and if it is foolish, it will not only be forgiven, but forgotten and gone; sifting the wheat and the chaff together; keeping and cherishing that which is good, and, with the breath of kindness blow the rest away."

To me, Mother was that kind of person – a friend, and a confidante, as well as a parent. Not only did she listen to my problems and complaints, but she listened to me read my themes, my application letters, my programs, and she gave me confidence when I sang or did anything in public. She was a good speller, better than I in arithmetic, and she was always ready to help me learn my Latin and Spanish vocabularies, by pronouncing the words for me. As I rushed around in the morning getting ready to catch the interurban to go to an early class at Cornell, she could stir the oatmeal with one hand while she held the book with the other.

Inheritance or environment, what we are born with or what we learn, which makes the personality of a person? That is debatable, of course, but for the inheritance records, my mother's grandmother (my great-grandmother) was Sarah D. Walter of Chester County, Pennsylvania. When she was 19 years old she married William Manly, born in Cecil County, Maryland. She bore eight children, and died when she was thirty-six years old. My mother was named for her grandmother, Sarah D., but she was always called Sadie. She was born on April 2, 1865, exactly one week before the end of the Civil War, and she was twelve days old when President Lincoln was assassinated on April 14, 1865.

Mother's mother was Rachel Manly, the third child of William and Sarah D. Manly, born in Fairview, Iowa, on July 4, 1832. She sometimes used the "thee" and "thou" of Quaker speech, my mother recalled, although the family at that time was Methodist. She was married to Silas Rundall on her birthday in 1856, died in 1881, and is buried in the Norwich cemetery, north of Martelle, Iowa.

Among Mother's keepsakes was a copy of my grandfather Rundall's obituary. This says that "Silas William Rundall, the second of a family of eleven children, was born in New York City, March 1, 1832.[*] At the age of ten years he moved with his family to Ohio. Here he was converted early in youth and joined the Methodist Church, in which organization he remained a faithful and willing worker in the service of the Master.

"At the age of seventeen he was apprenticed in the carpenter trade, in which he soon became a skilled and competent workman. Seeing opportunity farther west, he moved to Iowa at the age of twenty and settled in Fairview, Jones County.

"Four years later, July 4, 1856, he married Miss Rachel Manly . . . Their married life was blessed by four children, all of whom survive. This happy family circle was broken on August 26, 1881, by the death of the mother. Later he was married to Mrs. Mary McElhinney, who survives to miss the loving care of a kind husband.

---

[*] It was later learned that Silas William Rundall was born in Peekskill, Putnam Co., N.Y., not New York City (see George J. Hill, *Fundy to Chesapeake: The Thompson, Rundall and Allied Families*, 125.)

"Mr. Rundall's whole life was characterized by an unswerving loyalty to the highest principles of life. He was a pioneer in church and school life. Soon after his first marriage he organized and personally supervised a Select School for young people in Fairview, which existed for many years. In church circles he was Sunday School Superintendent for twelve years and class leader for twenty-four years. Mr. Rundall always enjoyed the closest possible communion with Christ. This made his life one of unselfish usefulness, the memory of which is treasured by his family and friends.

"The closing scenes of his life were passed at the home of his daughter, Mrs. W. H. Thompson, of Lisbon. Here he was tenderly cared for by his sons and daughters, something that filled his last hours with untold satisfaction. 'He was ready to go,' he said. 'He had done his work, and welcomed the end, which would permit him to leave "This outgrown shell by life's unresting sea." ' " He died in 1912.

In the summer of 1905 the ten Rundall brothers and sisters had a reunion in Marion, Iowa, and their pictures were taken together. George Hill has one of these pictures, with all their names. As far as I know there are no records telling about Grandpa Rundall's ancestors, or why, how, or when the whole family came to eastern Iowa.* My brother Manly recalled our grandfather as being quite a different personality than described in his eulogy. He said, "My recollection of him is that he was a loud mouthed bigot, absolutely sure in his own mind that whatever his conclusions were it was God's will. Mama did not dispute with him on the occasions of his visits, but on the other hand, it was obvious that she was not in harmony with many of his views!"

Another of Mother's keepsakes was a letter from her father dated Jan. 6, 1896, and written in Central City, Iowa. It is addressed to my father and says,

> "W. H. Thompson
> Lisbon, Iowa
> Will,
>
>> I am sick up at Josh's [John Mann, Grandfather's brother-in-law].
>> See Mattie and have her come as soon as she can. Let her have what money she needs. Answer by telegram when she can come.
>
> S. W. Rundall"

Rather dictatorial! He must have been the only person in the world who could and did order my father around, and I think this letter shows the basic character of both of them.

I remember I was very unhappy when on one of his visits he made me ride "side saddle" on his foot when he played "horse," his knees crossed, and bounced me up and down. Little Harris, being a boy, was allowed to straddle his foot. This was my first experience with sex discrimination. I wasn't accustomed to it, and didn't like it, or him.

Grandpa Rundall died in our home when I was eight years old, and I can remember the undertaker arriving and doing mysterious things, buckets being carried in and out of the downstairs bedroom, and then the casket being brought in. Finally we were allowed to come into the front room

---

* Essie Mae didn't remember that Silas was buried beside his parents in the Norwich cemetery, Martelle, Iowa, and that he and his siblings came to Iowa with them. See *Fundy to Chesapeake.*

and peek into the coffin where Grandpa lay. It was the custom at that time to keep the casket in the home until the funeral. That was true even as late as 1934 when my father's funeral service was held in that same room. Part of the custom, too, was that someone had to "sit up with the corpse," usually a friend or neighbor, who volunteered this duty.

Mother's three great loves were Family, Education, and the Methodist Church. The circumstances of her early life must have molded and influenced her personality in her later years. She had a hard time as a teenager. When she was fifteen years old, she was told that her mother had cancer and a life expectancy of about a year. Her mother spent that year training my mother to take charge of the house and to look after the three younger children, Will, Mattie, and their cousin, Jim. There was great deal of love between my grandparents, but after my grandmother's death, it was not long before my grandfather remarried (according to my mother's recollection). The children were stunned. He had not told them of his plans. He simply brought home a "new mother." To their dying days the children detested her, and always referred to her as "the old lady."

Mama's two brothers left home as soon as possible, and she did too, as soon as she could get a teaching position. Between the older foster sister, Aunt Pallie, and Mother, they took care of little sister, Mattie. From the time my parents came to Lisbon, when I was a baby, Mattie lived in our home, and my father considered her part of his family responsibility.

After she married Frank Runkle she was childless for so long that she wanted to adopt my older sister Rachel. Although she would have had a much more affluent life than he could provide for her, Papa wouldn't consider giving up his little girl. It was a wise decision, because after several miscarriages, Mattie finally had her own little baby Lester, and the two families had such strong family ties that we were almost one unit with two headquarters. Lester and I were a year and a half apart in age, but grew up as brother and sister, with all the benefits of two very loving but different types of homes. When we were small we were often dressed alike, and my family nickname was "Girlie" because Lester couldn't say "Essie Mae."

My Rundall grandparents held education in the very highest esteem. While others in their families were concentrating their energies on getting land and making money in the mid-nineteenth century, Grandpa Rundall neglected his carpentry and cabinet making to build a schoolhouse in Fairview and get an educational program started. The lady that he recruited from Cornell College to teach in his school was Rachel Manly, who was purported to be both pretty and smart. She became his wife in 1856, the mother of his children and my grandmother.

The only photographs of them which we have today show them looking old, dour, and grim, but they were actually quite noted for their compatibility and affection, according to stories which are told by relatives.

Mother's cousin, Cora Siver, told Helene Runkle that for several years after their marriage my grandparents were very disappointed in not having any children. Then one day, according to Cora's story, a family came through Fairview in a covered wagon, going "west." They had with them a little girl about four years old who was unwanted, and whom they intended to abandon. My grandparents took her, loved her, and reared her as their own, although they never legally adopted her. "What will people say," in other words "gossip" was always an important criterion for my mother's actions, and I wonder whether that is a psychological imprinting which dates back to the gossip in the town at that time that this little girl was unwelcome because she "had some black blood." Not true.

In addition to this little girl and their own four children, Silas and Rachel Rundall also took into their home and reared a nephew whose mother died when he was born. Jim Rundall was the name he used, and my mother, who was ten years old when he came to live with them, always considered him as her special little brother. He became one of the early United States secret service men, and lived in the San Francisco area. Mother and he had a happy reunion when Manly took her to visit him when she was in Ogden, Utah, in 1928.

Mother was not a talker, but she had several meaningful expressions which have become family folk-lore. She was satisfied and quietly proud when I got good grades in school, but very apprehensive when I reported a compliment on my appearance. "Pretty is as pretty does," she would say. When we misplaced our belongings, we could expect no sympathy from her when we couldn't find them. "Look where it is and you'll find it," and she was absolutely right! A fundamental rule in our house was "Children should be seen, not heard," so we were expected to listen to grownups without talking. "That's the word with the bark on it" meant that there was to be no back talk or argument about an order that she gave us.

Other family saying included "a flpperty flopperty" which described a hearty meal, "chiv'lings" or odds and ends, and axioms such as "The least said, the soonest mended" (the silent treatment in a quarrel) and "What can't be cured must be endured." "Take a Dutchman as he means, not as he says" offered understanding and tolerance to a person who got his tongue tangled, and "If you can't say something good about a person, don't say anything" was a basic rule of Mother's life. "Let your head save your heels" was her sage advice to me, many times.

On Mother's blacklist were unwed mothers (sex without marriage), Catholics, and a neighbor who did not replace a small tree which he accidentally cut down when he was mowing along the street with a power mower. Papa had planted the tree on our curb, and Mother never forgave the neighbor for cutting it down. When I reminded her of what the Lord's Prayer says about forgiveness, she literally turned her deaf ear to me. She was also quite prejudiced against the young man who took her son-in-law's place in the Stuckslager and Auracher Bank in Lisbon, after we moved away. I am sure she hadn't realized the extent to which she had been getting personal loving attention from Gerald, and she never liked or trusted the way his successor handled her affairs.

When she got her loom, Papa was absolutely furious. She probably had anticipated this, because she hadn't told him anything about it before it came. To him it was just one more blow to his pride. His wife weaving rugs for money! It was only after Gerald intervened and calmed him down that he allowed it to be set up. "What do you know about weaving?" he exclaimed. "I can read, can't I?" she replied. Mother never had a lesson or any instruction, but she studied the instructions, learned to string the warp, and to weave attractive patterns. She made quantities of rugs and carpet strips, place mats, tote bags, and covers. People admired her work, and she always had more than she had time to do. She enjoyed weaving, especially when her customers allowed her to work out her own patterns and designs. She also liked the little extra financial independence that it gave her, for gifts to the children, and contributions to the church. In fact, she left a small legacy to the Lisbon Methodist Church, which I was told was used to buy new offering plates. She used to say that she could tell a person's character by the type and condition of the materials which were brought to her to weave.

Her flowers were a great joy to her. She had a real "green thumb." I think if she stuck a broomstick into the ground it would have blossomed like a rose. She always saved the seed for the next year, and she was interested in the changes in color from one year to the next. Her flowerbeds were not artistically laid out, nor did she have any interest or talent in arranging cut flowers. She just loved growing them, and she had a wonderful mixture of forget-me-nots, Job's tears, zinnias, pinks, Sweet William, and bachelor's buttons. There were moss roses, four o'clocks, and day lilies. Pink and yellow roses, and a thick mass of ferns along the north side of the house. Hollyhocks along the woodshed, bittersweet on the clothesline posts, and big shaggy double poppies everywhere along the sides of the vegetable garden. The taller flowers also included touch-me-nots, cosmos, snap dragons, and phlox. She set out the bulbs of dahlias, gladiolas, and cock's comb, and kept the sweet peas and nasturtiums picked so they would continue blooming. All these and many more, all loved, admired, and tenderly cared for.

In her scheme of gardening, the poppies, horseradish, a certain kind of white radish that came up as a "volunteer" each year, and dill, were all weeds, or at least nuisances. She couldn't get rid of them entirely, but she did all she could to discourage them. Now a bunch of dill sells for 59¢ in the grocery.

How tastes change! Mother liked asparagus, but none of the rest of us did. There was some that grew wild along the sidewalk leading to the school house which she used to gather and cook with peas. This disguised the asparagus to a certain extent, and peas were such a favorite vegetable that we were conned into eating it. She should have eaten all the asparagus herself, because she liked it so well.

My father thought the season would be a failure if he hadn't been able to get his potatoes planted on Good Friday, so that we could have new potatoes and fresh peas for Fourth of July dinner. Of course, no one had lettuce except in the spring when we eagerly watched the pale green leaves come through the black soil, thinned them out, and finally decided they were large enough to eat with a sugar, vinegar, and cream or water dressing. We could make a whole meal out of Mother's homemade bread and fresh radishes and lettuce from the garden.

Oh, how she hated weeds! When Rachie scolded her for using her waning strength to pull the weeds that she saw growing along the sidewalks on the farm after she went to live there, she would just wait until Rachie went to town leaving her alone. Then she'd put on her sun bonnet and go out after the dandelions and sticky grass, just quietly continuing the battle against them.

She was not an outstanding cook and she never tried to be. She left that accomplishment to Mattie. However, she did have two specialties for which she should be remembered. Her sugar cookies, plain or filled, were so good that little grandson, Billy Thompson, said "I ate Grandma's cookies until my arm was tired." Everyone dropped out of competition with her in the Sauerkraut Day baking contest for filled cookies because she always won. I have her recipe, but I can't make them as good as hers. Is it because I don't have an old-fashioned kitchen range in which to bake them?

She also often made what she called bread cake, which was really like a light, sweet coffee cake, made with bread sponge. It had raisins in it and cinnamon and sugar on top. She baked bread routinely, and remembering the smell and sight of those fresh loaves still makes my mouth water.

Cinnamon rolls, buns, and "fried bread," also came from the big crock of dough. She would never teach me anything about cooking or let me work in the kitchen. She always said, "You'll be having much better equipment than this and to learn now would just be a waste of time." So she'd shunt me back to my books or sewing.

She had a beautiful serene expression, spoke softly, and would rather listen than express her own opinions. She wore her ash blonde hair parted in the middle and drawn back behind her ears. On special occasions she would roll the sides on kid curlers (wires wrapped in soft leather) over night, or use a curling iron heated on the kerosene lamp, so she'd have soft waves in her hair.

Mother was one of the healthiest persons I have ever known, although she was not particularly strong or robust. She loved all kinds of vegetables, ate very little meat, and even after Papa died, and she had only herself to cook for, she always fixed three good meals every day. I am sure she was never in a hospital in her life, except to visit someone else who was there. We children were all born at home.

She had the firmest belief that her Heavenly Father was taking personal care of her, and therefore she had nothing to worry about. One time one of our Methodist preachers in Lisbon told her that she was not a Christian because she could not name the exact time she "was converted." What he said did not bother her at all, because she knew that he didn't know what he was talking about. She felt in her heart that she had always been a child of God, consequently she didn't need to be converted to something that she already was.

She always listened quietly and appreciatively to my stories about the evolution of life on earth, but it made no difference at all in her belief about the Creation. Tolerance was one of her outstanding characteristics. She believed in teaching us children right from wrong, good from bad, but when we were adults, she thought that we were responsible for what we did, and she did not fret, worry, or nag us about our actions then. She did not attempt to regulate our lives, never criticized, or expressed her disapproval or disappointment.

At the time of our niece Kathleen Thompson's wedding in Oak Park, Illinois, Harris's and Helen's home was the headquarters for the Iowa relatives. At the end of the meal that night, Harris poured each of us except Mother a small after dinner drink of Cointreau. I was sitting beside her, and without saying anything she quietly put the tip of her teaspoon into my glass, tasted it, and then thoughtfully said, "Mmmm. Orange, isn't it?" She didn't approve of all that we did, but she was uncritical and tolerant.

My friend, Ruth Pinkerton, voice teacher at Cornell, admired Mother very much, and once told me, "You can't expect your children to be as nice as you are, because they don't have as nice a mother." Interpret that, if you can!

Her favorite reading was the Bible and related materials, such as the church publications, the Classmate, and the Sunday School Quarterly, a lesson guide. She never made a fetish of Bible reading, however, by thinking that there was any special virtue in reading it from cover to cover every year, as some people do. She enjoyed "The Guiding Light," a radio program based on the lives of Old Testament characters.

When we went to Sac City in 1946, we became acquainted with Mother's first cousin, Lincoln Manly. His father was an older brother of my Grandma Rachel Manly Rundall. Lincoln was about five years older than my mother, but they were born in the same little village, and had the same family background, so his remarks recorded by the *Sac Sun* when he was almost 88 years old shed some light on what life was like in early pioneer times in Iowa and what Mother's life was like at that time. This was the environment of her childhood which helped to shape her personality.

Lincoln said, "I was born in Jones County, at Fairview, Iowa, which was four miles south of Anamosa, on November 4, 1860. Fairview was halfway between Dubuque and Iowa City on the Military Road. All freight was hauled by oxen. They told me that my birthday was the beginning of Lincoln's first term as President, and I was named for him. My father was a life-long Republican. He was a blacksmith. Pa had a frame that swung the oxen off their feet, and then he nailed the shoes on them.

"I failed to get much schooling, because I always had so much farm work to do. But my younger brothers all graduated from Cornell College. There was lots of talk in our county when the state proposed a state prison in Anamosa, because there was so much stone west of there. [Grant Wood's painting "Stone City" immortalized the place where the stone used in the building of the state prison and many other buildings in Iowa was quarried. It is only a few miles from Anamosa and Fairview.]

"I never heard my father whistle or sing, but mother was a fair singer. All of us children could sing. . . . I sang tenor, and the other boys sang as they saw fit, but we surely had a jolly good time. No whiskey or tobacco in our house. My mother died at forty-eight years of age, of cancer. Pa died at 83 years. My mother was turned out of the Quaker church because she would not say she was sorry because she married out of the church."

Among the similarities between his story and my mother's are that both of them were born in Fairview, Iowa, had stern, grim, religious fathers, and gentle Quaker-reared mothers who died of cancer in their forties. They were both good singers and enjoyed singing in church all their lives.

A "stranger than fiction" story concerns one of Lincoln's younger brothers, Wilson Edward Manly, known as "Ed" in the family. He went to west China as a missionary in 1893, and when he retired in 1937, he was replaced by the Reverend Olin Stockwell, whose father was a brother of Grandma Hill. So, half way around the world, Gerald's cousin and my cousin became colleagues, co-workers, and devoted friends.

Marian, daughter of Wilson Edward Manly, was a medical missionary in the same place. She and Olin were both arrested and jailed by the Communists. Marian was released after a few days, but Olin was kept in prison for two years. This is Olin Stockwell's letter in response to my inquiries about the Manlys and his imprisonment:

"You write concerning family history, particularly the W. E. Manly family. We first knew the Manlys through their two daughters, Marian and Grace, at Ohio Wesleyan, and later as our missionary colleagues in west China, when we went out there in 1935. Marian, who graduated at Ohio Wesleyan in 1918, was not only a fine doctor, but an artist and writer as well. She was the one who collaborated with Han Su-Yin in her first book, *Destination Chungking*, and set her on her distinguish writing career. She is now spending her last days in a nursing home in Oregon. Grace was a wonderful leader in educational and evangelistic work, and died in West China in 1944 from bubonic plague, which she contracted while working in the villages of west China. There was a brother, Gordon, who was an engineer, working in dam construction in India and other places. He and his wife, now retired are living at 509 E.

Gorham St., Madison, Wisc. 53703. I am sure that he could fill in other details that you may want. Your George knew his first wife when she had cancer of a special kind.

"I do not know when the Manlys went to China, but I think that your records, '1893,' are right. This makes him among the earliest missionaries into west China. 'Uncle Ward' as we new him, was a man of abounding energy, great enthusiasm, and hopes and dreams that extended far beyond his grasp. Florence was a woman of wisdom and spiritual depth, and great love and appreciation of the Chinese people. We lived with them for the first year we were in west China – at Chengdu – and then they lived with us for a second year while they were winding up their affairs and preparing to return to the States for retirement. I took over from Uncle Ward in evangelistic work there in west China in 1935.

"I was arrested (by the Communists) in November 1950 and released at the end of November 1952. The two books that were published, *With God in Red China*, and *Meditations from a Prison Cell*, are both out of print. I never published the poetry, and as I read it now, know that it is not worthy of publication. I leave it buried in my files." [By Olin Stockwell]

My mother lived to be almost eighty-five years of age, a rare, wonderful person.

Will Thompson and Sadie Rundall
Wedding picture, September 1889

Miss Sarah Rundall

Lady Sadie Thompson

Sunbonnet Sadie

57

James, Essie Mae
and Harris

Essie Mae Thompson - teacher
Dean Clark
Willie Pisarik
Clair Achenbaugh
Glen Stoneking
Preston McCall
Leroy Davin
Rachel Albright
Faye Gardner
Clarisse Johnston
Helen Garl
Nita Floyd

The Second Grade
Lisbon School
1918

*Essie Mae with John Paul
and Mr. Simonton at
Washington D.C.
1922*

*Essie Mae
helping roof father's barn
1924*

*Essie Mae
The old fashioned
Yellowstone "Songbird"
in "The Cowboy's Dream"*

There Was a Little Girl

There was a little girl, she had a little curl
Right in the middle of her forehead;
And when she was good, she was very, very good
And when she was bad, she was horrid.
                                        – Henry Wadsworth Longfellow

What's in a name? When that name is Essie Mae, what is in it, is a beautiful lady, a great deal of love, and a friendship which lasted from 1902 when the beautiful lady came into our home until she died in 1975 at the age of 92 years and eleven months.

It is no secret in our family that I was a planned-for, hoped-for, and greatly loved and cherished baby. My parents had been married almost fourteen years, Papa was forty years old, Mama was thirty-eight, and they had three children – James, thirteen, Manly, about eleven, and Rachel Edith, nearly nine. Nicely spaced about two years apart, equivalent to the length of time Mama nursed each of them, plus one "period," plus nine months. She told me that. My coming was different.

During the school year before I was born, my folks were living "up on the prairie" in north Linn County near the now defunct town of Paris, Iowa. My father operated a creamery, but our home was on part of the land that had been my grandfather Thompson's farm when he came from Nova Scotia. It was near the rural school which provided the elementary education for the youngsters of the area. The teacher of that school roomed and boarded at our house, and her name was Essie Mae Davies. Elmont was the name of the school, and I think the name also referred to the district.

After she left Elmont to go back to college, married, and made her home in Atlantic, Iowa, we seldom saw her, but the loyal, loving friendship remained. It is best told in the letters which I have saved and treasured.

On December 10, 1974, she wrote to me: "My heart is saddened by the death of James. I can see him now in memory [this was 72 years later]. He was the last of you children to go to bed when I lived with your family in Elmont. I can see Manly too, when he leaned on the kitchen table watching your mother making that 'one egg cake' that we all liked so well.

"You may remember that I was born in Elmont, but not in the house where your parents lived. The one I was born in was used as a corncrib then. Those were happy days in Elmont. When we were old enough to attend high school we were sent to Central City. After graduation I went with the teacher to Mt. Vernon and enrolled in Cornell College. She went because she had a beau there and wanted to be near him. By then I knew I wanted to be a teacher, so I left Cornell and enrolled in Cedar Falls Normal School [now The University of Northern Iowa]. It was when I was home for Christmas one year that the directors of the Elmont school came to Paris and asked me if I would teach at Elmont. The teacher they had, had no discipline, and could not control the pupils. In those days many who were going to college left to get jobs so they could continue in college. I was one of them. My father loaned me the money though.

"When I was teaching there at Elmont that year, there were two Arab youths hired by the farmers. They had come to this country to escape their native country and learn English. They wanted to go to the Elmont school and did come. It was my custom to read a message from the Bible on opening school. One of them stood up one day and said their fathers were armed Arabs to fight the Jews.

"Write me more about James and his family. I have the last words your mother wrote to me after your father's death. A post card. It says, 'I think of you often and will love you always.' That's the way I feel about all the family."

The day I was born was also my brother James's birthday – his thirteenth. He was out in the field plowing corn, and when he came in for dinner he was told he had a baby sister. His thoughts and comments are not recorded. By that time Essie Mae Davies had finished the school year and departed, but my folks gave their new baby, born June 29, 1903, her name. I am not too fond of it, but I am proud to share it with a wonderful person.

After Essie Mae Davies graduated from Cedar Falls Teachers College in 1904, she went to Logan, Iowa, to teach and there met a lawyer, Tom Smith, whom she married. They lived in Atlantic, Iowa, had one daughter, Kathrine and one granddaughter, Suzanne. Essie Mae never forgot our family, and her affection for us was extraordinary. In another letter to me when she was 92 years old, January 15, 1975, she said,

"My thoughts go back to the time he [James] was a little boy about eleven years old, I think, and I taught him at Elmont. He was always a quiet lad, not talking much, but interested in what was going on. It was after supper that we gathered around the table in the dining room and discussed the events of the day. I will never forget how kind your parents were to me, and accepted me as one of the family. I know I was with your family when McKinley was shot."

My brother Manly described a visit to her in November 1966. He was on his way to Denver to visit his son John, and stopped in Atlantic to see Essie Mae. He wrote:

"I stopped at Atlantic and visited with Essie Mae Davies Smith. The visit was so pleasant [evidently to both] that she told me to visit her again enroute home, so she could learn about your children and mine. [Telling about George Hill and John after he had visited them in Denver.] Well, there was nothing else for me to do – after all, Mama and Papa would expect me to 'mind the teacher.' Besides that, I was delighted to visit her again. She seems to me one of the very few extraordinary persons I have met in my whole lifetime—one of perhaps a half dozen. Mind you, I was 9 and 10 years old when she was with us, and she could not have been more than 20 years old. Yet I remember her so well, and it is obvious she remembers all of us, especially Mama and Papa, with great affection.

"She was in her eighties, yet she still retains that vitality she had as a young woman. I know you will take my word for this, but I will illustrate by a couple of minor incidents. She had gotten from the library and was reading a book published two or three years ago, *The Feminine Mystique.* Maybe you read it – I tried to but couldn't finish it – quite out of sympathy with the viewpoint the author was expressing. The book made quite a splash at the time it first came out. Maybe I didn't state the penultimate sentence correctly. I thought the author over-emphasized the main theme of the career woman, and improperly down-graded the role of women in their age-old careers of wife, mother, and homemaker. Well, anyway, here Essie Mae Smith is reading the book casually with no fanfare, just as an incident of keeping up to current events.

"Another straw in the wind. On my second visit, I phoned her from the hotel down town, and asked if I could call on her. She said certainly, come right up, which I did. When I got there, I noticed that she had on a nice dress, but had not completed fixing her hair. So she soon excused herself and when she came back into the room her hair was fixed up real pretty.

"We visited about an hour and a half each time, and there was never a dull moment. She told me about her life and background, and almost demanded I tell her all about our family, including our children and grandchildren. When I say our family, I mean you and our other brothers and sisters.

"You can tell perhaps by what I have written, what an impact she had on me. I told the children, both yours and mine, about the visit and urged them to do themselves a favor if it is ever possible, and pay her a visit. Regardless of what they may be able to pass on to her, I know they will come away with more than they brought."

More about Me

Too Good to Quit, Not Good Enough to Go On

Mother had a good alto voice and I like to think I inherited some of her talent and ear for music. In the Lisbon school operettas, the lead went automatically to Ella Johnson, but I usually had a solo part. My first solo in church, when I was about fourteen, was "Flee as a Bird to the Mountain, Ye Who Art Weary of Sin," accompanied by Harold Baltz, and coached and encouraged by his mother.

When I was teaching in De Witt I started taking voice lessons and when I went back to Cornell for summer school I continued taking voice lessons with Prof. John Conrad. In order to get my money's worth, I memorized everything he gave me, without having to be told, so when school started in the fall he thought I was ready to sing solos in the student recitals. I didn't have enough training in piano to go as far in music as he wanted me to (go to New York and study, and all that), but he was an excellent teacher, and I've put every moment I had as his pupil to good use. He was a bachelor, at least twenty years older than I was, very suave, and sophisticated. I had known him from "afar" for a long time, when he used to come to Lisbon to sing, or was a guest of the Stuckslagers, so when he occasionally asked me to go as his guest, his date, to a party or dinner after I was on the faculty, I felt like Cinderella.

I have shared that voice training with pupils, some of whom have become quite successful. I couldn't take them far, but they give me credit for getting them started right. Peggy Frink majored in Voice at the University of Iowa, then went to New York City where she was soloist at the First Presbyterian Church for many years, and was understudy to the lead in the musical "Top Banana," starring Bert Lahr. Peggy said, "She was disgustingly healthy."

I don't know why, but twice I was asked by the Cornell College administration and the people who were making the arrangements for Commencement, to be the soloist at the Baccalaureate exercises. When Horace Alden Miller, organist and composer, presented a radio program of his own music he asked me to do the songs, thereby arousing some ire among the conservatory faculty, because he ignored the voice teachers. When Wilma Briggs was national chairman of music for the American Legion Auxiliary, she gave patriotic speeches over the radio many times, and I sang the songs at the proper intervals.

However, I think probably the times that my singing really went to people's hearts were when I sang at funerals. The hymns did not overtax my musical ability, my voice was pitched low, so it was easy on the ears, I had good diction and sincerity, so I felt I could really bring comfort through song. I guess that's what I am best remembered for around Mount Vernon and Lisbon. "Too good to quit – not good enough to go on!" The story of my life.

Valley Chapel

Five thirty and I had to get up! It was dark and cold outside, but thanks to Dad, the house was warm and the old black horse would be standing in the alley hitched to the buggy ready to take me to the country school four miles east of Lisbon, and one more horrendous day in my first year of teaching. Mother was getting the oatmeal and coffee ready for breakfast, and while I got into my long legged, long sleeved underwear, combed my long hair, and laced up my high shoes, she packed my lunch. The last thing to do was to put on my three-buckled galoshes, and get out to the buggy where Dad was waiting to tuck a fur robe over my lap and knees. By that time, it was about seven o'clock and beginning to get light.

One morning when Dad went out to the woodshed which served as a barn, he found that old Nig had "committed suicide." During the night the horse had evidently gotten fractious, and in rearing around and kicking he had broken his neck. I was really relieved. I was scared to death of him. He was an old race horse and hard to control, and I am sure he sensed my nervousness and fear. Although I had to depend on "shank's mare" the rest of the year, I really liked it better than driving the horse. I was only eighteen at the time, and a walk of eight miles a day was no problem at all. I started while it was still dark and by the time the sun rose above the horizon I had an unobstructed view of the beautiful colors on the clouds over the whole sky. When I went home I could enjoy the sunsets as I went westward back toward town.

"Valley Chapel" sounds like an idyllic place. What a misnomer! When I went there to teach no one seemed to know what had happened to the chapel, if there had ever been one. The main building there was a typical one-room rural school, painted white, with a tiny "mud room" at the front, where the pupils hung their wraps and left their lunch buckets. The school yard was a corner of a corn field. Corn fields on every side, and in the fall when I first went there, not a house was visible from the school. I felt completely isolated. A mile to the south were the double tracks of the C&NW railroad, and a half mile south of them was the unpaved Lincoln Highway. The country roads leading west toward Lisbon, and north and south, were little more than dirt lanes, deep mud which froze into ruts making travel by any means hazardous, and almost impossible at times. On one occasion old Nig stumbled and fell in trying to pick his way through them. If anyone thinks that helping a fallen horse hitched to a buggy struggling to get up is not a frightening experience, he hasn't had to do it himself.

In addition to the schoolhouse there was a dirt-floored shed for the ponies which half a dozen of the boys rode to school. There was also a pump, a woodshed, and two "four-holers." These two buildings needed no designations for "Girls" and "Boys" – the kids knew which was which. Three things which I never did that year were (1) miss a day of school, (2) drink the water, and (3) use the outdoor facilities.

I had to get an early start from home because the fire in the heating stove had to be started in time to have the schoolhouse warm by the time the children got there.

Papa had to teach me how to build a fire in the room heater, and I started it fresh every morning, not banking it, as some teachers did in their schools. While the room was heating, without taking off my wraps, I swept the floor, and during the rainy times, which were often, that was a big chore. I couldn't bear to stay there in the afternoon after the children went home, so by the next morning the mud had dried and stuck to the floor. Another job that had to be done frequently after I got there in the early morning was to wash obscenities off the blackboards.

Break-ins! It seemed impossible to keep the intruders out. Hobos from the railroad sometimes got in and slept there, and I shudder now to think what could easily have happened to me, but that was one thing that did not frighten me, because I never thought about it. More often the older boys in the neighborhood got into the schoolhouse, especially on weekends. They wrote graffiti on the blackboards, knowing full well who was the teacher, and who would be reading it! I should have gone to the president of the District and insisted that something be done to stop it, but I was too ashamed, and considered it just one more thing I had to put up with. I think the ring leaders were the older boys in his own family – school dropouts.

Even now it seems hard to realize that a neighborhood like that could be only five or six miles away from Cornell College. I felt like I was in a foreign country. I had twenty-seven pupils during the spring term, fifteen of them from three families. Among them were Hudacheks, who spoke Bohemian at home, Lenicheks, Albaughs, Fishers, Stonekings, Spoors and others. My round faced, round headed, blonde little first grader had the interesting "international" name of LaFayette Hudachek, which was suggested by Dr. Kate Hogle, of Mount Vernon, who delivered him. (Dr. Kate was also Mattie's doctor when Lester was born, and Mattie always praised her for her gentle hands during a difficult delivery.) I used to see two of the Hudacheck girls occasionally after they grew up and were married, and I have always been glad for the wholehearted affection they showed toward me. Too late I have come to appreciate that family, who had many things in common with the Bohemian family about whom Willa Cather wrote in *My Antonia*. The children, all of them, became fine American citizens, a credit to their heritage and to this country.

In spite of the hard time I had that year, if I had to live my life over, I would be glad to go back there, to give myself another chance with those children and I hope I would do a better job. I was so young and inexperienced, had never been in a rural school, and knew nothing about the problems involved, so my "best" was none too good. But on the whole, I must have done some good. I sent to the State Library Association for books, and also took out books from the Cornell library and from home, and read out loud to them every day, as well as encouraged them to extra reading. To relieve the dreariness of the place, I bought little white ruffled curtains for the windows. I got a huge book of designs and patterns from the Latta Scholl Supply Company in Cedar Falls. Not creative, but fun for the older girls, there were patterns for pictures they could put on the blackboard. The patterns were made of thin paper with perforations in them in the outline shape of the design. The girls would hold the paper against the blackboard and pat it with a chalk-filled eraser. The chalk dust came thru the perforations and when they took away the pattern there was the vague outline of a Santa Claus, a turkey, or a Hallowe'en witch which could be filled in with colored chalk also supplied by the teacher. It was a good reward or something for them to do while classes for the younger pupils went on, and the girls loved to do it.

I made a homemade hectograph duplicator out of a purple gel in a shallow pan, and also supplied a soft ball and bat, and finally a basketball. I had to furnish my own handbell, which I swung vigorously to call the children in from the playground. Runk came out to the school on Friday afternoon several times, taught them new games and gave a spell-binding Chemistry demonstration in which he "magically" changed water (a clear liquid in a glass) to "wine" (red) to "milk" (white). Doc. Knight would have been proud of his Freshman Chemistry student, as well as surprised at the use to which the new knowledge was being put. The Runkles had a Model T Ford, and it was wonderful to have a ride home.

There were three eighth grade girls among my pupils and after they passed their examinations to enter high school (at Mechanicsville) I added Latin and Algebra to the thirty or more daily classes I already had, in order to give them a head start on the work they'd be having in town school in the fall. No class ordinarily lasted more than four or five minutes. If there were only one or two in the class, they came up to my desk and stood beside me to read, talk, or recite. If there were more than that in a class, there was a "recitation bench" in front of my desk where they sat to recite. There were both single and double desks in the room, the smaller ones in the front, and getting larger toward the back. I have seen desks like those in antique stores now, priced at $40 to $60 each, but I am sure that when Valley Chapel was torn down they were probably given away or burned.

For me it was simply a question of being able to grin and bear it, and not much to grin about! I hated the whole thing. The kids were dirty in speech, clothing, habits, and attitudes. I was shocked, appalled, and sometimes frightened. I took some laundry soap and a brush out to school one day and laid them beside the water pail on the shelf in the back of the room, with the threat (or promise) that "If anyone used the kind of language on the playground that I had been hearing, he was going to get his mouth scrubbed out." I never had to do it, but I suspect that only the volume of the uttered words changed – not the content. My salary was $80 a month, which was twice as much as many teachers in South Dakota were paid during the "dirty thirties" if they were lucky enough to get a job. With this I was able to get some pretty clothes for the first time, take my first trip outside the state of Iowa, and get a financial start on my second year of college.

The school year was only eight and a half months long, so by the middle of May, it was all over and the boys were free to go out into the fields and help with the corn planting and other spring work. School was out on Friday, and the next day I got on the train headed for Chicago. It was a "local" that stopped at every station, but I loved every moment of the trip. As we neared Chicago I was confused and amazed to see dozens of tracks on either side of the train. I had had to cross two tracks when I got on the train in Lisbon, but I couldn't see how I could possibly walk across so many tracks to get to the station in Chicago. It was all new to me, getting off the train in the sheds, the Redcaps, the crowds, the hurrying, the strangers. But there was my brother James, waiting for me. He had been able to come right to the train to meet me and he soon retrieved my luggage, and then we rode the El to Oak Park. He surely was a welcome sight that evening. I stayed a week with James and May, then I had another new experience – my first ride on a Pullman. James briefed me about the hammock for clothing, the protocol of tipping the porter, and the dining car procedures. I went to Washington, D.C., and visited Manly and Marie for two weeks.

In addition to the money I earned that year, I also got experience, which counted a great deal in future job-hunting. In fact, when I was hired by the Sioux Falls School system thirty years later, I was given credit points and a few extra dollars because of that year in an Iowa rural school, while five years of teaching on a college level were given no recognition at all. By the time I was trying to activate my teaching certificate after all those years, Practice Teaching had become one of the requirements. The State Department of Education in South Dakota waived this for me, however, after deciding that my Valley Chapel year must have been good enough "practice." It was practice all right, trial and error, and a prime example of grim determination to survive. When I taught in Aberdeen I counseled, supervised, and provided and example for practice teachers all the time, and I had a happy liaison relationship with the faculty at Northern State Teachers College. So that year 1921-22 was like many other hard times; it proved profitable in the end.

In order to get my original "certifit" as Mr. Ed Hudachek called it, I went to Marion, the County seat of Linn County, and took written examinations in eight or ten school subjects, such as Orthography, Geography, and Arithmetic. A passing grade was all that was required to get the county certificate, which I have kept through the years. Undoubtedly the highlight of the year was the Christmas celebration. It was an SRO performance, and a Double Feature, too. A combined Christmas program and a box social. Lamps and kerosene lanterns for lights, all the traditional recitations, songs and group exercises, Santa Claus in person, and then one of the fathers, who was a professional auctioneer, stepped up to provide the real excitement and fun – the selling of the beautiful, mysterious, anonymous lunch boxes.

My friend, Minnie Mohn, and I thought we could fool everyone by decorating our boxes identically – white crepe paper and red satin ribbons, and inside, fried chicken, sandwiches, potato salad, pickles, deviled eggs, chocolate cake, Mother's filled cookies, and fudge. The idea was to award each box to the fellow who was the highest bidder. When he opened it and found the girl's name inside, they shared the goodies together for their supper. The men were not supposed to know whose box they were bidding for until the hammer fell, when they could claim their prize and find out who was to be their partner for the evening. It didn't turn out as we had planned, however. Min's was the first one sold, and the bidding stopped at a reasonable level. When the second one went up for bids everyone knew it was "Teacher's," and when the auctioneer finally said, "Sold" the price had reached $13.50, and my boy friend got it. The total for the evening was about $45.00. I bought some playground equipment with some of the money and turned the rest over to Mr. Hudachek, and that was the end of that, except for memories of a wonderful, exciting evening. Teacher's box at $13.50 broke all records for box socials!

Teaching at Dewitt, Iowa   1923-1924

When I am asked, "What age-group or subject matter did you like best to teach?" I reply, "Whatever I was teaching at the time." (Valley Chapel was the exception). To this day, I have a special loving feeling toward third grade children, because I so much enjoyed my year in DeWitt with youngsters of that age. And this, in spite of the fact that my classroom was located downtown above the fire station, a temporary arrangement because the old school was overcrowded, and the new school was in the process of construction. However, this was no hardship for me after my one-room country school. To hear the fire engine zoom out below us periodically furnished excitement and an always welcome interruption of classwork. The two-by-two orderly marching parade of the little folks, many of them holding hands, on their way to the city park for recess and recreation (R&R of the 1920's) never failed to bring smiles and tender looks along Main Street.

Six of us teachers lived and ate together in the home of a lovely, white-haired lady, Mrs. Irwin. It was a year of good times. My friend, Alice May Large, lived in a beautiful home only a block away, and I was entertained there and at her family's lake cottage many times. That friendship started in college in 1920, and we still exchange Christmas gifts and visits fifty-six years later. DeWitt was a friendly town, and the townspeople, especially those in the Methodist Church, entertained us with lovely dinner parties, from soup to nuts, and from bouillon cups to finger bowls. This was the first time I had ever lived away from home and away from Lisbon. I was the youngest of the teacher-group, with the least college training and the least teaching experience, but I felt that people of all ages liked and accepted me. I had several friends among the high school girls, who invited me to their picnics, I sang duets with a woman about three times as old as I was, I dated the "catch of the town," and I started taking private voice lessons. Nothing came of the dating, but as a result of the voice training I was accepted into the Glee Club as soon as I went back to Cornell, and before long was the alto soloist. For the next four years, I took voice lessons from John L. Conrad, and I am still reaping the benefits of the wonderful training that I got from him.

Other Teaching Anecdotes

One of the best Christmas presents that Santa Claus ever brought the Thompson children was a blackboard. It was also a desk. The blackboard was on one side of the flip-down lid, and on the other side was a large map of the United States. Above the blackboard was a roller on which were the alphabet, capitals and small letters, in Spencerian script, the numbers, and a series of line drawings of animals and familiar objects. All these were models there to be copied. This blackboard was the inspiration and focus of my favorite thing-to-do, which was playing school. Of course, I was always the teacher, and Harris and any other person who happened to be available were the pupils. I would like to claim credit for Harris's excellent record in school, but I am afraid I can't. I think he learned to recognize the letters of the alphabet from the name on Mama's washing machine wringer before he started to school in the first grade at the age of four and a half years. He had an inquiring mind, and Mama was patient and willing to help develop it.

I became really "hooked" on teaching when as a sophomore in high school, the primary teacher asked the superintendent to allow me to take charge of the second grade reading class, while she took the first graders to the basement for special lessons. There were two grades in her room, as there were in all the grade school rooms in Lisbon, and this arrangement was a progressive effort to give more individual attention to these children in the time before nursery schools, kindergartens, and teachers' aids. I don't know why I was picked to be her helper, but I have always been grateful to Lena Smith and Supt. John R. Lang for this special privilege and experience.

When I see TV advertisements now for various kinds of toothpastes, I am reminded of what Colgate used to do to sell their product in the 1920's, and to promote dental health among school children. It was a give-away type of advertising, and all a teacher had to do to get a free tube of toothpaste for each child was to send to the company the number of pupils she had. The teacher got the credit for providing the children with a useful gift, the children benefitted by better teeth, and the company got good publicity. Many of my pupils in DeWitt and at Valley Chapel did not even own a toothbrush, and I took advantage of the Colgate offer in both places.

Another tooth incident: At the South Dakota School for the Visually Handicapped in Aberdeen, everything is furnished by the State to those children whose parents cannot afford to buy things for them, including toothpaste. When I was teaching there, I felt that dental care was an important part of hygiene, and to that end we had daily tooth inspection. I'll never forget the time when I finally decided that "Surrender was the better part of Valor" as far as those daily inspections were concerned. I also learned to be a little more reasonable and understanding, too.

One of my pupils was a tall, handsome sixth grade Indian boy who had beautiful, even, white teeth, but he absolutely refused to brush them. In the over-all picture, it was a minor thing, of course, but I stubbornly resisted making an exception to the rule which all the others conformed to. For his own good and to show my authority, I guess, we had quite a battle over it. Fortunately, it "dawned onto me," as my Swedish roommate used to say, that it was utterly ridiculous to make an issue of it, because white man's ways are not Indian ways. When this boy left the comparatively luxurious school dormitory and went back to his home on the reservation, every drop of water that the family used had to be carried in pails or tubs at least a quarter of a mile, and it was used sparingly for only essential use. It surely would not be wasted by teeth brushing. He would have enough problems reconciling the two standards of living, coping with a drunken father in an overcrowded, violent household without worrying about his teeth. So I gave up, and didn't try to force him any longer.

While I was teaching in DeWitt, Miss Alice Betts, Dean of Women at Cornell, wrote to me asking if I would be interested in coming back to Cornell and being an assistant in the Geology Department at 35¢ an hour, which was the standard wage. I was, I did, and I spent the last two years of my college course as assistant to J. R. Van Pelt, who was the acting head of the department at that time. During those two years I lived with Mattie and Frank Runkle in Mount Vernon. I worked, studied, dated, danced, dined, sang and had an incredibly good time. When, as a senior, I protested a B grade instead of an A, which I felt I deserved because I had gotten A's on all my papers and examinations in Education under Professor George Tyson, he said, "No one who dates as much as you do, could possibly know enough about my course to get an A." He sounded severe and serious, but I was amused by his reasoning, and let it drop. Later when I was on the faculty, I spent many a Sunday evening in his apartment, listening to his radio, which was outstanding at that time. It brought in music from KDKA in faraway Pittsburg. Not alone, of course! There was always a room filled with congenial people.

It was quite by accident that I became a Geology teacher. I intended to major in history and art in college, but both those classes were such a disappointment and disillusionment that I signed up for the beginning course in Geology just to fill out my schedule for the second semester of my freshman year. This course was "Elements of Geology," taught by Dr. W. H. Norton, using the textbook which he had written. It opened up a whole new world to me, changed my philosophy, beliefs, and life. I have never been the same since. When I graduated, I decided to take the job that was offered to me by the college, to be an instructor in the Geology Department for one year, although I had been elected High School Science teacher in LaGrange, Illinois. Professor Van Pelt was granted a year's leave of absence to work on his doctorate at the University of Chicago, and rather than bring in someone from outside, the college wanted me to fill in for him. He never did come back, and I stayed there for five years, until I was married.

Cornell was in severe financial straits because of the failure of the Emmert Foundation, and four of us out of the graduating class of 1926 became low-salaried members of the staff. These included Martin Munson, speech and debate; Judd Dean,

68

athletics; Walter Gray, admissions; and Essie Mae Thompson, geology. It was a very difficult time in the history of Cornell, but for us it was a lucky break, and I don't think the college suffered because of our work. I will be forever grateful to Dr. Harry Kelly and Dr. Norton for their encouragement and help. I felt that they were backing me all the time, and I never had the slightest hesitation in telling them my problems or asking their advice. What wonderful friends they were!

When I told Dr. Burgstahler, the president of the college, in the fall of 1930, that I was planning to get married at Christmas time, he said, "What if I told you that would be the end of your teaching here?" "I would still get married," I answered. "Well, if that's the way you feel about it, you may finish out the year," he replied.

This made Cornell history! Except for Mrs. Norton, a generation before, there had been an unwritten, but firm rule against married women being on the faculty. When I became Mrs. Hill instead of Miss Thompson, that broke the barrier and established a new precedent. This kind of prejudice seems incredible now. However, when I met Gene Harker, one of my former pupils, here in Sun City, he said, "Well you may have been living with Toot Hill for forty years but you're still Miss Thompson to me."

How I Learned What Mother Never Taught Me
To Cook, To Keep House, and To Take Care of a Baby

One of the happiest summers I ever had was in 1923 when I lived with the Frank Shaws in Mount Vernon. He was director of the music conservatory at Cornell, and she (Julia) was on the faculty as violin teacher. They had two children, three-year-old Virginia, and little John, about nine months.

They were very good friends of the Stuckslagers in Lisbon, and led a social life which was very much more sophisticated in style than most of the college faculty. Until I went there that summer I did not know them, nor did they know me. I had finished my second year in college and had signed a contract to teach third grade in DeWitt in the fall, but what to do in the summer was still a problem. Without my knowledge, Mrs. Stuckslager recommended me to Mrs. Shaw, as a live-in mother's helper for the summer, and it proved to be a mutually happy and beneficial arrangement. I was paid only a dollar a day, plus board and room, but I loved being there so much that I would have been glad to work for nothing. I was completely inexperienced at housework, but Mrs. Stuckslager didn't know that, and Mrs. Shaw was so sweet and patient with my shortcomings that I soon learned what I needed to know. I loved her and the whole family devotedly, and I still use some of her special ways of doing things and have taught them to others. I am sure that the confidence they had in me, and the freedom they felt in being able to go away for weekends without having to worry about the children or household made up for my deficiencies.

By the end of the summer I knew that a *torte* was a delicious cake confection, as well as a legal snafu, which was the tort I had learned in Business Law. From Mrs. Shaw I leaned how to prepare a baby's formula, feed, diaper, and love him; how to keep a house clean and shining; and how to follow a recipe and "get it all together" to make a meal. I also had the pleasure for the first time of handling and working with beautiful dishes and silver, oriental rugs, and antique furniture, and at the same time enjoying the warm friendship and appreciation of truly superior people. It gave me new confidence and a better opinion of myself.

Mr. Shaw sat at the grand piano at least eight hours a day, practicing, practicing, practicing. He smoked cigars as he played, with a huge brass ashtray at the left hand of the piano. I adored them both, and toward the end of the summer, I mastered the art of getting Mr. Shaw's favorite breakfast – pop-overs, bacon, and hash browns, all cooked over an old fashioned cookstove. Luckily I had learned to build a fire when I taught at Valley Chapel. The next year the Shaws moved to Oberlin, Ohio, where he was head of the music department at Oberlin College. Mrs. Shaw was quite young when she died and after her death he married Mary Stuckslager Van Metre, from Lisbon, a widow, who was Dean of Women at Oberlin at that time. My "baby," little John Shaw, grew up and married one of the Seiberling (tire) girls.

Signs of the Times
The Semi-Centennial Year – 1926

In 1926 I was graduated from Cornell College. This year was the mid-point between the 100th anniversary of the Independence of the United States, and the Bicentennial celebration in 1976. It was also approximately the mid-point of the decade which has been called the Roaring Twenties. Perhaps that time would be called more appropriately the Purring Twenties in Mount Vernon and Lisbon, because we lived a satisfied, quiet, contented sort of life. Our experiences were far different from those that the characters in F. Scott Fitzgerald's books were having. He was the favorite author of the time, and supposedly writing realistically about the times.

Prohibition was the law of the land, but we had never known the alternative. Iowa had been a dry state long before the 18th amendment was passed. In Lisbon the question of the sale of intoxicating liquor was settled way back in 1877, when the town council extended the city limits so far out into the country that the saloon keepers who had to set up their shops outside those boundaries gave up because they were too far away from their customers. One hundred years later, the town still does not reach to those boundaries, but one can satisfy a thirst on Main Street.

However, in 1926 there were places down along the Cedar River or in Solon where a potent home brew could be obtained, and some people made homemade wine. Speakeasies and bathtub gin were just titillating subjects to read about without actual experience. This was the time of Al Capone, rum runners, and the infamous St. Valentine's Day massacre in Chicago, which was only a few hours away from Lisbon in time and distance, but not near enough to make any imprint on our lives. I do remember watching strange cars go past our house in Lisbon with mounds of something in the back seats, covered with blankets. We were sure they carried loads of illicit liquor being taken across Iowa by backstreet routes – probably true.

The styles of the times included rolled stockings, cloche hats, long strings of beads, and a female profile as unfeminine as cooperating Nature, a tight bra, and a formless dress could make it. The dresses were cut with straight sides to a point below the hips, then the skirt flared full and swirly to knee length. No snaps or buttons were needed because they were loose enough to pull on over one's head. The only difference between the front and the back was a little lower neckline in front. Nevertheless, I was greatly mortified after I had sung in a recital in the chapel at Cornell, to discover that I had been out on the stage with my dress on backward!

The Black Bottom, the Charleston, and the Jitterbug were the popular dances, but the Virginia Reel at the Washington's Birthday Colonial Ball was the only kind of dancing that the students at Cornell were officially allowed to do until 1927 when the "dance barrier" was finally broken by such persistent reformers as Toot Hill. At a prearranged moment, a whistle sounded and the students in the gym started dancing. After the first time, the college rules were changed to allow the students to attend dances in the gymnasium, but only with the written permission of their parents. Toot never got parental permission, but that didn't stop him from doing it! A new chapter in Cornell history had begun.

In 1923 another kind of Cornell history was made when the Delta Chapter, Iowa, of Phi Beta Kappa was installed on the campus, luckily for me. In 1928, the 75th anniversary of the founding of the college was celebrated with an elaborate pageant, written by Jewell Bothwell Tull. Gerald L. Hill (Toot) was publicity director of Cornell that year, using the news-writing skill he had developed in his undergraduate days. He put it to good use during that historic time.

On the political scene, I cast my first presidential ballot in 1924 in the Lisbon Opera House for Calvin Coolidge and he was in the White House in in 1926. General Von Hindenberg was president of Germany and Benito Mussolini was the Fascist dictator of Italy. Germany was admitted into the family of the League of Nations in 1926. People truly thought that the "War to End All Wars" had made peace forever secure. It never crossed our minds that there would ever be another war which would involve all of us, or a depression which would almost wreck the nation. There was nothing on our minds but satisfaction with the signs of progress and prosperity, and we were very content. Yet in only seven years, 1933, Hitler and the Nazi party would win the elections in Germany. How innocent we were!

As a matter of record, the national sports champions at that time included Helen Wills, Bobby Jones, Babe Ruth, Red Grange, and Jack Dempsey. On the local scene, Dr. Harlan Updegraff was President of Cornell, and Frank Shaw was director of the Music Conservatory. The newest building on the campus was the Law Building, dedicated in 1925, given by Rev. Marion Law in honor of Dr. W. H. Norton. It included the Departments of Biology, Physics, and Geology with classrooms, laboratory, storage rooms, and display cases for Dr. Norton's collections and activities, especially designed by J. R. Van Pelt. The year 1926 also marked the twenty-third time that Dr. Frederick Stock and the Chicago Symphony Orchestra had come to the campus for the annual three-day May Music Festival. My brother Manly remembered sitting on the lawn outside the chapel, listening to the concerts. I recall how bedazzled I was when the Stuckslagers' Pierce Arrow picked me up when I was a Sophomore in high school, and I sat in the front row of the balcony, dividing my attention between the soprano soloist, Helen Stanley, and the glamorous gowns and beautiful people around me – the trills of Miss Stanley and décolleté necklines I had been taught that nice girls did not wear!

Prosperity? I was hired for $1350 in 1926 to be an Instructor in the Geology department. That was increased to $1800 in my fifth year – 1929-1930. A sign of the times is that I lived very happily, paid my college debts, and saved money on that salary. The heads of the departments were paid only $3000, but from Dr. Norton's estate, Cornell received about $100,000. Money went a long way in those times!

For the fiftieth reunion of the Cornell College Class of 1926, Elmer Miller prepared a list of outstanding events which took place on the campus during the years 1922-1926. Here are a few of the happenings in the semi-centennial year 1925-1926:

1925

Oct. 23   Lecture, "The Grand Canyon of the Colorado River," by Dr. William M. Davis, Harvard University

Oct. 24   Dedication of Law Building, the Rev. Marion Law present

Nov. 11   Armistice Day Address, Dr. Henry Clay Standcliff: "Germany Blamed"

Nov. 17   Cambridge University Debaters' victory over Cornell. Question: "This House is in favor of the Principle of Prohibition." Cambridge – Negative side. Cornell team: Martin Munson '26, Ralph Tallman '27 and Robert Ellis '27

Nov. 19   John Drinkwater Lecture "An English Dramatist's View of London"

Dec. 10   The student body in a mass meeting voted their approval of the petition to the trustees which was prepared by student committee on the dance problem

Dec. 11   Trustees' Decision of Dancing Issue delayed until June

Dec. 13   Handel's *Messiah*. Soloists: Ruth Pinkerton, John L. Conrad, Herbert Gould

1926

Feb. 3   Prof. W. E. Slaght, Prof. of Psychology and Philosophy, granted Ph.D. by the University of Iowa

Feb. 12   Lecture "Art and Life" by Gutzon Borglum, Sculptor

Feb. 19   50th Annual Aesthesian Banquet, Home of Helen McKune, 314 5th Ave., S.

Feb. 20   Colonial Ball – Grand March leaders: Charles and Margaret Barker, Kenneth Truckenmiller, and Helen Hunt. (Charles, Margaret and Helen were all present for our 50th Anniversary. Truckenmiller, deceased. I sang a solo.)

Feb. 20   Basketball, Northfield, Minn. Cornell 33 – Carleton 28

Feb. 22   Basketball, St. Paul, Minn. Cornell 48 – Hamline 30

Feb. 26   Basketball, Alumni Gym, Mt. Vernon   Cornell 40 – Monmouth 16

March 17-28   Cornell Women's Glee Club Tour in Iowa (Essie Mae Thompson, Soloist) Rockford, Hampton, Mason City, Waverly, Charles City, Iowa Falls, Rudd, Reinbeck, Parkersburg, Waterloo

April 23   Seventh Annual visit of Carl Sandburg

May 15   Fourth concert by Chicago Symphony Orchestra: Frederick Stock, Conductor; and Alfred Wallenstein, Soloist, cello

June 7   Annual Concert, Cornell Conservatory of Music. (I sang "Sapphic Ode" by Brahms, and "Secrecy" by Hugo Wolf)

June 9   Graduation Day. Address: Prof. Nathaniel Butler, University of Chicago and Adviser to the President. "Liberal Education and Training for Life"

June 14   Dean Clyde Wildman granted Ph.D. degree by Boston University

Summers in the 20's

The Black Hills
Colorado
Yellowstone Park

Camping - 1927

. . . in the Black Hills

. . . at Long's Peak, 1928

My Introduction to South Dakota
A Summer in the Black Hills, 1927

After this, the only way was up! If a girl is looking for romance, it seems reasonable to "be where the fellows are" and a ratio of one to ten sounds like a sure thing. From my experience in the Black Hills in 1927, instead of pure bliss, it is pure misery. Six weeks when I was the only girl in a group of ten fellows in a graduate group of Geology students scarred me for life!! The Geology Department of the University of Iowa, for a number of years, had offered a very good summer field course in Geology with headquarters in the tilted sedimentary rocks near Whitewood, South Dakota, in the northern part of the Hills. The camp was located in the city park, and consisted of canvas sleeping tents, and one large multi-purpose tent which served as a kitchen, dining room, classroom, and conference room. Besides the eleven students that summer were Dr. Runner, his wife, and two small children, and a college girl who was the cook and companion for Mrs. Runner. She stayed with Mrs. Runner while the rest of us were out scrambling around, up hill and down, cracking and collecting rocks, mapping, and studying during the day. She was a banker's daughter from some little town near Iowa City. She certainly wasn't like the Stuckslager girls, who were the only other banker's daughters I had ever known, but she was more typical than they were.

In the correspondence which Dr. Runner and I exchanged in connection with enrollment in the course, he assured me that I would have a girl partner, so I was looking forward to a good time in every way. My Dad made me a sturdy wooden chest with leather strap hinges in which to take my gear. (I finally gave it to a friend in Sioux Falls, and she told me recently that she still has it.) I had boy's corduroy jodhpur-type pants, which were tough and serviceable, but very uncomfortable. Also, high boots, heavy wool shirts, and a flannel-lined rubber raincoat. It was heavy, and necessary, but it added greatly to the load I had to carry with me every day. The chest was none too large by the time I put in wool blankets, my tools, reference books, clothes and personal things. I also took about a half dozen horse blanket pins to use in making a pocket out of the blankets into which to snuggle and try to keep warm. Sleeping bags would have been a godsend, but unknown then.

I went as far as Omaha on the C&NW, and had a nice telephone visit with Ralph Kharas while I waited for the one-passenger-car train which went by single track to Rapid City and Whitewood. Three were no eating facilities on the train, and somewhere out in the dust and heat we stopped for our noon meal. A hack carried the half dozen or more passengers into town (I wish I knew which town), to an eating house. We all sat around the oil-cloth covered table, and the food was served family style. I was very shy, and just tended to my own business without talking "to strangers." The others who were eating there were all men, presumably ranchers and salesmen, and a few townspeople. Oh! it was hot on that train in mid-June. And dry and dusty! I thought the day would never end the time seemed so long! I spent some of the afternoon hanging on to the rail of the little porch on the back of the passenger car, watching the endless prairie roll past, the dust coming up behind in a cloud as the train rolled along. I thought of the art lessons in perspective from Prof. Mills, as the rails of the track seemed to meet on the horizon, the ties between them growing shorter and shorter in the distance. I remembered as a child, listening to my parents argue about going to South Dakota. Dad thought it was the Land of Great Opportunity, but Mother absolutely refused to go. From what I saw that day, I was on her side!

It was dark when we got to Rapid City, and from there to Whitewood I was not alone. An Indian girl sat with me. She had just graduated from boarding school and was retuning home to her people on a reservation. At that time, I knew nothing about South Dakota's involvement and their problems with the Indian population, so I had no in-depth appreciation of what she told me. She had great uncertainty about the future, and after all these years I wish I knew more about her, and what became of her.

The "home" that was provided for me was a small canvas tent without a floor, a canvas cot, pillow, a couple of candles, a water pail, and a wash basin. The "Ladies" toilet was a board nailed between two trees with a pit dug beneath it, a can of slaked lime, and a strip of canvas for a screen. The toilet tissue was hung on a nail in one of the trees. I bought a little rubber mat to lay between my cot and the wooden chest that had to serve as my wash stand and dressing table, writing desk, clothes closet and vanity. I hung my clothes on a rope stretched from one side of the tent to the other, and when it was dry, it stretched and the clothes dragged onto the ground, and when it rained the rope shrank, and pulled in the sides of the tent. To get a tub bath it was necessary to go into town to the hotel, which was beside the railroad tracks, and pay a quarter for the convenience! I have an empathy with the pioneers who lived in sod houses, but for security, warmth, and protection from animals and elements, sod houses were luxurious compared with my tent.

After the first talk session when Dr. Runner told us what we'd be doing and what to expect in the daily routines, my partner gave up, quit, repacked her whirly accordion pleated party dresses, and headed for a job in the Deadwood-Lead area! When I realized that I had no partner, and would have to be working alone, I wanted to quit too, but I had too much at stake to do it.   I am sure I was a drag on the group, because if the fellows had been alone, they could have covered more ground, gone faster, and felt freer than they could with me along with them. But they weren't unhappier about the arrangement than I was. They gave me absolutely no quarter, help, coddling, or encouragement. Their way of coping with the situation was either to tease me or ignore me, and I don't know which was worse. I was never strong physically, and since the field work was geared to the majority – the fellows – I was so exhausted trying to keep up with them in hiking and climbing, that I was a wreck physically, mentally, and emotionally all the time. Shy, and easily embarrassed, I suffered over taking care of bodily functions, and I was so frightened that I wished I could drop dead when we had to go through or near a field where cattle were grazing. I was sure I was going to be gored to death by one of the bulls! The fellows warned me that I couldn't look to them for help if they charged us, and I was sure they meant it.

We packed our own lunches from the materials the cook set out, and we carried them in our rock bags. By the time we stopped for lunch the identity of the sandwiches was hardly recognizable, but we were so hungry we could have eaten a real rhinoceros' tail, as the fellows called the baloney meat that went into them. On a quick trip to Lead I had hobnails put on the soles of my boots, and I kept them for many years as a reminder of that summer, and the blisters! But they made walking and climbing a lot easier, and I was thankful to have them the next summer in the Rocky Mountains.

If the days were bad, the nights were worse! First the cold! Cold water for washing, cold rain, and cold, cold, bed. Even newspapers under the blankets were totally inadequate insulation from the cold, and they didn't make a very soft mattress on the canvas cot, either. But if you're tired enough, eventually you fall asleep even though your feet seem to be freezing. People in the military learned that! Then there was the loneliness. No one to talk to, to commiserate with, to share the disillusionment and unhappiness. Scary sounds in the night! My tent was set up well away from the others, to make sure I had privacy, and that's what I had more than enough of. I also had no feeling of protection against snakes, skunks, bugs, packrats and other repulsive animals, because there was no floor in the tent and no way to make it secure. The sides were loose and anything could crawl into it. There were horses, too, which I was sure might capsize it. Actually, there was nothing to be afraid of, but if what FDR said twenty years later is true, then I really had something to fear, for "fear itself" was my chief companion.

I stuck it out, but only for the first term. I was told later that the second term was much more pleasant. The camp moved to the park in Deadwood, where there were permanent cabins – no more living in tents. The work was also easier in the igneous and metamorphic rock, or perhaps everyone had become more accustomed to the rigors of the days. The fellows didn't have to slow down for me, so they were unhampered, and also went on trips to caves, mines, and the beautiful canyons. In the years since then, I have visited all those places, and the Black Hills have become a favorite vacation place. We have had many good times there, and I can completely enjoy the beauty of the Hills, without any hang up about the miserable time I had in 1927 in climbing them. I like to tell people, however, that some of the gouges and scratches on the rocks are not the result of weathering but MY HOB NAILED BOOTS.

Nothing is all bad, however, and seeing President and Mrs. Calvin Coolidge at the Spearfish rodeo on July 5, 1927, was the high point and redeeming factor of the summer. Their presence was one of the most historically significant times in the whole history of South Dakota. He made his famous "I do not choose to run" pronouncement that summer and also dedicated Mt. Rushmore as the location of the famous Shrine of Democracy, which was carved by Gutzon Borglum.

Ordinarily we worked only five days a week that summer, but in order to take the day off to go to the rodeo we worked the previous Saturday, and felt that we had really earned our holiday. It was my first experience at a rodeo and it was quite interesting. I rode to Spearfish with several of the fellows in one of their cars. Why didn't the Runners ask me to go with them? There was no socializing between the students and teacher, so if the Runners were there we weren't aware of it. Five years before this I had seen President Harding dedicate the Lincoln Memorial in Washington, D.C., and now I was to see President Coolidge!

A rodeo always opens with a parade around the arena, and South Dakota put its "all" into this one. A military band, high school bands, and Indians from the reservations, dressed in long feathered head dress and colorful costumes, walked, danced and shook rattles. And finally came the dignitaries in open cars slowly circling the grounds. President Coolidge was wearing a ten-gallon hat and looking very bored, dignified, unsmiling, and sour. But the lovely first lady, Grace Coolidge, was smiling and gracious, and I felt very excited and glad to be there. Their portraits hang in the State Game Lodge at Custer, which was the summer White House, and how young they look to me now! When we were in Lincoln, Nebraska, in 1974 attending the National Gem and Mineral Show I had an opportunity to tell Lincoln Borglum, the son of the man who carved Mt. Rushmore, about the experience that summer. He was the principal speaker at the Awards banquet, and I was happy to get his autograph to add to my collection of "Famous People's" signatures.

When we got back to camp that night, long after dark, one of the fellows and I sat up on a high hill above the camp, and although we just talked about the events of the day, I had a vague inkle that I was not entirely just a nuisance to all my classmates. In fact, when it became known among the group that I was leaving, everyone was quite nice to me. One of the fellows took me to Lead, where I could get a train to Hot Springs. He was a Catholic, and I know it was a sign of "special interest" when he asked me to go to church with him. I had no hat to wear, which was tradition then, and it seemed so silly to me to cover my head with a handkerchief, as he suggested, that I sat through the service bare-headed. I regret it now. It was just an unkind gesture of stubborn prejudice. He was really very nice, but not for me. I also tried to return the interest that one of the other fellows maintained during the following year while he was getting his degree at SUI, but it was hopeless. He went to Wyoming later, and I understand he "made it big" in oil. No regrets there either! Not sizzling, but fizzling romance in the Black Hills.

As far as geologists are concerned, the area is ideal for research, and it has probably been more thoroughly studied by earth scientists than any other place of equal size in the world. It is like an open book of paleontology, historical geology, physiography, mineralogy, distrophism, canyons, caves, and ore deposits – the whole scope. The granite of Harney Peak, which is the highest elevation east of the Rocky Mountains, is 1,700,000,000 years old.

The Badlands National Monument nearby is a classical example of the effects of erosion, and it is also important as a source of many well-preserved fossils. One of the most unusual fossils in the world is on display in the School of Mines Museum in Rapid City. It is the skeleton of an oredont and her unborn twins. The oredont resembled a pig, and lived about 40,000,000 years ago. Dinosaurs also lived in this area long before that, and the pieces of dinosaur bones which I have remind me of a poem which Dr. Norton used to read to his classes in Organic Evolution.

The Dinosaur

Behold the mighty dinosaur
Famous in prehistoric lore.
But only for his power and
strength.
You will observe by these remains
The creature had two sets of brains
One in his head, the usual place,
The other at his spinal base.
Thus he could reason "a priori"
As well as "a posteriori."

So wise was he, so wise and
solemn,
Each thought filled just a spinal
column.
If one brain found the pressure
strong

It passed a few ideas along.
If something slipped his forward
mind
'Twas rescued by the one behind.
And if in error he was caught
He had a saving afterthought.

As he thought twice before he
spoke
He had no judgment to revoke.
Thus he could think without
congestion
Upon both sides of every question.
Oh, gaze upon this model beast,
Defunct ten million years, at least.
– B. L. Taylor

The ceremony of the dedication of Mt. Rushmore was held in August 1927. At that time, Coolidge said: "We have come here to dedicate a cornerstone which was laid by the Almighty. Here in the heart of the continent, on the side of a mountain which probably no man had ever beheld in the time of Washington, in territory which was acquired by Jefferson, and which remained almost unbroken wilderness beyond the days of Lincoln, which was especially beloved by Roosevelt, the people of the future will see history and art combine to portray the spirit of patriotism."

After Coolidge's speech, he ceremoniously presented Borglum with a set of drills, and Borglum went over the lip of the precipice on a very thin-looking cable. He drilled six "master points" while the crowd watched in suspense. The original plan included a Hall of Records, to be 100 ft. x 80 ft., dug into the top of the mountain. It was to be reached by a monumental set of stairs and decorated by a frieze depicting American History, and statues and mementoes. This plan was never carried through, although the excavation was begun.

There was also a plan to carve the history of the United States in three hundred words, written by President Coolidge. This was an almost impossible task, and Borglum was not satisfied with the copy submitted to him, so this too was not carried out. Work on the whole project stopped in 1928 because of the lack of money, but with a national legislative appropriation on a matching basis, the head of Washington was finished in 1930. It was an uphill fight all the way. The depression and lack of money, Borglum's disagreement with people who were trying to help, and unexpected problems with the rocks of the mountains all added to the difficulties. But in 1936, President Franklin Roosevelt dedicated the figure of Jefferson, and later Lincoln's head was dedicated.

I give these details because we were at the Rushmore Memorial in 1938, and Jerry and little George had a very unusual experience – one which would be entirely impossible to duplicate in these later years. It was late in the afternoon when we got there, and the men who were working on the face of Theodore Roosevelt had finished their work for the day. What an opportunity! There were 400 wooden steps which led from the great mound of debris at the foot of the carvings to the top of Lincoln's head. The workmen used them then but, of course, they have long since been removed. While Tommy, whom we thought was too young to go, and I watched from the deck of the studio, George and his father climbed those steps and stood on the top of the Monument, above Lincoln's head. They even brought back to me some pieces of the granite, very light colored, almost white, and very coarse grained.

Manly lived in Ogden, Utah, in 1927 and on my way home from the Hills that summer I detoured to visit him, and the family. Bill was thirteen, John was eight, and Betty only three years old. I was there about two weeks, and in that time, I saw a great deal of new country, and had some wonderful experiences. Bill acted as guide on hikes and climbs in the spectacular Wasatch Mountains overlooking the Great Basin. After trying to keep up with the fellows in the Black Hills, to be with Bill was a delight. I remember how interesting it was to see the effects of the violence of nature, in the form of tremendous boulders which had been rolled along through the canyons by seasonal torrential floodwaters, and to note that the boulders themselves were often made of a conglomerate rock formed of rounded boulders as large as six or eight feet in diameter. Manly took me everywhere! Timpanogos Cave, named after a great Indian Chief, spectacular artesian water fountains, Ogden Canyon, Great Salt Lake, interesting and historical Mormon buildings in Salt Lake City, the State Capitol, and the huge wild bird refuge, where tens of thousands of birds were milling around.

The most complicated excursion was a weekend camping trip to the Wasatch Mountains. Imagine the preparations! The planning, and the provisions that it took! This was 1927 and there were six of us (Bill gave up a Boy Scout expedition to go with us), plus a canvas tent, stove, cots, bedding, and food – all of it packed into a 1925 automobile! Little three-year-old Betty showed her discomfort and disappointment by shedding many, many tears. In fact, she howled most of the time, as I recall, and I really don't blame her. But I will always remember how good the pancakes tasted which Marie made for breakfast, and how beautiful the lake was, with a perfect reflection of the pine trees around it, in the glass-smooth surface of the water. It was raining when we got there, it had rained during the night, and it was cold, cold, cold, but the morning was beautiful.

The Wasatch mountains are sisters of the Sierra Nevada Mountains, forming opposite sides of the Great Basin. At one time they were continuous, first horizontal, then arched upward, until the top collapsed. You can see remnants of that great arch, scattered all over the salt flats, as smaller isolated ridges and low mountains, around which the road west from Salt Lake City winds or crosses over at convenient passes. A happy ending to that summer!

Summer in Colorado – 1928

In 1928 I tried a new locale for my field work in Geology. This time it was in the Rocky Mountains near Boulder, Colorado, and after the unhappy time I had had in the Black Hills the previous summer, this experience was pure joy. A summer school bulletin from Colorado University gave a description of the summer camp, and it seemed exactly the answer to my needs, expectations, and capabilities. As soon as I got to Boulder, ready to start the summer field course, I was impressed with the friendliness of everyone I met. I stayed at a rooming house across the street from the campus for several days, during registration and the orientation meetings. Then our group left the campus in buses and went to the camp, a ride which took a couple of hours. There were twenty-five in the class, and more than half of them were females. Quite a different type of set-up from the Black Hills group.

There were a couple of girls from Texas, and we loved their accent and their enthusiasm for the cool climate and beautiful mountain scenery. There was also an old maid school teacher from Rhode Isnad, tall, thin, and set in her ways and opinions. She stirred my resentment when she said, "Everybody knows that the poorest teaching is done in the college classroom." I resented that greatly at the time, but now I think it is probably true. My roommate was a seventeen-year old girl from Cincinnati, much more worldly wise than I was. I enjoyed her companionship very much, but there were some things I knew more about than she did! Geology, for instance. Our "home" was a log cabin located on the bank of a cold, swift-flowing little mountain stream, and the sound of it tumbling over the rocks was as good as a sleeping pill at night.

We had a big dining house, and on each table there were salt and pepper shakers in the form of little dogs. "Pebble Pups" were what the students were called, and these marked our places. Only the faculty members were called "Rockhounds." The recreation center was called the Gas House, and it featured a huge round pit-fireplace in the center of the room with a canopy over it, and a pipe which extended through the ceiling to draw off the smoke. From the porch on a clear night one cold see the lights of Denver, fifty miles away. We spent three days in the field each week, and in the laboratory the rest of the time, listening to lectures, using the microscopes, studying slides, and identifying our bring-back rocks. I learned a great deal that I put into use in my own teaching.

Instead of long hikes, most of the time we were taken by bus to the day's field-study location. I am sure no one appreciated this more than I did. There's no better place to find a variety of minerals in a short time than in a mine dump, and we were expected to bring in a great deal of material. It was a delightful, low-keyed approach to all the problems and the learning. We sang, joked, and told stories as we rode along. While we were looking for rocks we also learned about flowers from one of our group who taught science in Colorado Springs. The flowers were gorgeous – the bright red Indian Paintbrush, golden poppies, purple columbine – Colorado's state flower, which grows wild up there in the mountains – and the exquisite little blue forget-me-nots which grew above the timberline. The last week of the term we spent in Rocky Mountain National Park at the Columbine Campground, getting into condition to climb Long's Peak. Each day we climbed one of the smaller mountains, and became accustomed to the higher altitude. Fortunately, I was not bothered, but even after living in the mountains for more than a month some of the class members had trouble with nausea and nose bleeding.

Undoubtedly the most famous peak in Colorado is the one named for the early explorer Zebulon Pike. But Long's Peak is not only several hundred feet higher, it is also more of a challenge to get to the top. On Pike's Peak, one can drive a car, or ride the cog railway, if one chooses, but even the horse trail goes only part way to the top of Long's Peak and the rest of the way has to be traversed on foot. There is a sheer cliff on one side which is 2500 feet high, and at the bottom is Chasm lake. To reach the top that way is no job for an amateur "Sunday" hiker. We rode horseback as far as we could (the Boulder Field) in order to make the trip in one day. I was glad to get off the horse and onto my feet, although from then on there was only a vaguely marked trail, sometimes merely a painted stripe across the boulders.

In many places we had to walk dangerously close to a precipice, and once we climbed on hands and knees. When we reached the top of the mountain, which was a flat area about the size of a city block, and had signed the registration book, the "Prof" who had been our leader celebrated for us all by standing on his head on top of the highest boulder. Hundreds of people climb to the top of Long's Peak every summer. However, in all the years since then, I have never talked to anyone else who has made the climb. On the way home, I went by bus to Colorado Springs, and took the tourist trip to the Garden of the Gods, Manitou Springs, and to the top of Pike's Peak, which was somewhat of a disappointment after Long's Peak. When son Tom was trying to decide where to go to college, I recommended Colorado University, and he graduated in Aeronautical Engineering there in 1956. At that time, the family drove up to the camp where I had such a good time, but the area was fenced off. My little log cabin is probably long gone from the mountain, but not from my mind.

Yellowstone Park – 1929

What Ft. Lauderdale was to the Ivy League in the 1950's, Yellowstone Park was to Cornellians in the '20's. With two important exceptions: first, the season was summer vacation time, instead of Easter, and second, the students were part of the work crew. The object was the same, however: fun, shedding conventional behavior, and burning the candle at both ends. The stories about it as "the place to be" were passed around campus whenever there was talk about what to do during summer vacation. Faculty members also enjoyed the summer there, and added their stories to those of the students. Different, but still interesting! Among those were Dr. Harry Kelly, head of the Biology Department, and John Robert Van Pelt of the Geology Department. They were "ninety-day wonders" – temporary rangers, giving lectures and guiding tours for the tourists.

I had had three pay-as-you-go summer sessions in the West, studying Geology, and in 1929 I decided I wanted to follow the crowd to Yellowstone to see and learn about the wonders there and get paid for it, as well as have fund doing it. The competition for jobs was so keen that to be accepted, one had to be not only willing and eager to work, but also to help with the entertainment of the guests. Some kind of musical or entertainment training was a must. Three of us from Cornell went out together from the Twin Cities on the Northern Pacific Railroad to Livingston, Montana. Betty Cole, daughter of the Cornell President, who had a beautiful alto voice was one of our group. She later was head of the Massachusetts State Girl's Correctional Institution at Framingham, and is well known for her work in penology. I was assigned to Old Faithful as a "pillow puncher," so after the beds were made and the cabins cleaned in the mornings, I was free to hike, explore, watch the geysers and hot springs, or whatever was interesting to do, until evening, when I usually took part in the shows for the guests.

Rudy Vallee was the popular singer of the time and his trademark was the megaphone which he used as an amplifier for his voice, but he had no patent on its use. I used a megaphone, too, so I can say my entertaining life reaches from megaphone to microphone! I was the Old Fashioned Girl in the outdoor amphitheater production of the "Cowboy's Dream," singing "Smilin' Through," and looking like I'd just stepped out of the pages of *Gone with the Wind*. I was not the girl of his dreams, however, nor was the Spanish senorita, the Dutch girl, the flapper, or any of the others, who tried to win his heart by song or dance. The one who won his heart was a cowgirl, of course, who came riding into the firelight on her horse, and together they rode away into the friendly darkness!

I also sang in a variety show which was put on in the big indoor auditorium one night a week, and sang the low alto in a quartette with two girls from Minneapolis, and a girl from Broken Bow, Nebraska. We sang in shows, and in the Old Faithful Hotel when special entertainment was needed. This included a regional bankers' convention. In between times I sang "background" songs in the dining room at the Lodge, and ever since then I have had an empathy with the musicians who perform where everyone is eating, talking, and certainly not listening to the music. The Pillow Punchers serenaded the guests when the buses arrived, and we also sang in the evening in the Old Faithful Lodge when the colored lights were turned on the famous geyser when it erupted. Our song was "Hail to Old Faithful, She plays every hour, Hail to her beauty, Hail to her Power."

      Yellowstone had a language all its own. For example: College help – Savages. Cabin girls – Pillow Punchers. Tourists – Dudes. Dishwashers – Pearl Divers. Evening dates – Rotten logging or blanket parties. Porters – Pack Rats. Baggage Loaders – Boot Boys. Summer Rangers – Ninety Day Wonders. If you've never tasted coffee with salt petre in it, you don't know how awful coffee can be. It was supposed to have a quieting effect on youthful exuberance, but the purpose was defeated because no one could stand to drink the vile-tasting stuff. My job was tent girl, which I deliberately chose so that I could have free time after the work was done in the mornings. We worked in pairs, and my partner was a sixteen-year-old girl, Dorothy Johnson, who had just graduated from high school. In spite of the difference in our ages, we formed a friendship that has lasted more than forty-five years. She taught in Tipton when we lived in Lisbon, and after an unhappy marriage she went to Fresno, California, to teach handicapped children. We visited her there and were very impressed with her skill and devotion to her pupils.

      Two groups of personal visitors came to the Park, which delighted me. My father came with Manly and his family. This trip was part of the entertainment which Manly gave Dad when he visited the family in Ogden, Utah, that summer. The other was a surprise visit from President Herbert Burgstahler (of Cornell) and his son Cy. He took Dorothy and me on the complete tour of the Park, and I surely appreciated that, because I had no car and I had no way to see anything except the area at Old Faithful, and there are so many other famous, unique and beautiful places to see.

      In a letter Dad wrote to Mother before he came to Yellowstone Park, he said,

"Dear Mama,   Ogden, Utah, July 10th, 1929

      Your letter came today. The time goes by so fast for me out here. Can't hardly realize what changes have taken place in Liston. Somehow after Will Huey was taken sick I never expected to see him again. If the old lawn mower is too hard for you to handle, hire some boy to do the work. You Must Not Overwork Yourself.

      Manly and I are having some good times. Manly is a very congenial fellow to visit with. Well posted on all current events of the day. If I never have the good Luck to visit in his home again this visit will stand out in my Life as one of the most wonderful experiences I ever had. We surely have been blessed with a fine family. Yesterday Manly had some business up at Brigham. One of the head Foresters of Salt Lake City met us. This man told me that the Department thought a great deal of

Manly from Washington to Ogden and all throughout the West and also that Manly had been very successful with his Law cases. Today Manly is to meet some man from Washington D.C. at Salt Lake City. Last night we drove up Ogden Canyon to fish. Did not catch any, but a very beautiful drive. On Saturday of this week we start for Yellowstone Park. <u>Hope to see Essie Mae.</u> <u>We plan to be gone a week.</u> Billy and John Paul are fine boys. Bettie has grown tall. Everything is jake with us. Feel fine and sleep well. Was glad to hear Helen has a school. Harris pay is about what I expected.

With love, Papa"

One thing leads to another and the aftermath of that summer in Yellowstone will continue to the end of time. After I came home from Yellowstone I used to go to Lisbon on the interurban every weekend to visit Mom and Dad, and the ticket office was in the Iowa Railway and Light office at the east end of Main Street in Mount Vernon. Toot Hill worked there and sold me the tickets. He had been a "Savage" at Lake Camp three years before, and we found we had lots of mutual experiences to laugh about and talk over, in that fall of 1929, while I waited for the car to come. In fact, there was so much to talk about that we began dating. The big date was December 25, 1930, when we were married in the Methodist Church in Mount Vernon. Call it "The Saga of Yellowstone Park." We revisited it together in 1934, when we left baby George with his grandmother in Ogden, Utah. Jerry (Toot) made another trip there in 1948 with George, fifteen years old at that time, and Jim High, on their way home from Two Dot, Montana, where George had spent his first summer on the McFarland-White ranch. My father wrote this letter to us when we were in Ogden, Utah, with Mother and baby George in 1934. We originally planned to take George with us when we went to Yellowstone Park, and Dad indicates here both his love for little George, and his doubt about our ability to look after him properly.

"Dear Folks,   June 22, 1934
Your card written Wed. came in this A.M. [He answered it very promptly.] A good rain Wed. eve and another good one today. More to follow. Lester and Frank picked the cherries yesterday. Dorothy [Runkle] has the speckled hen chicken pox. Mattie has been with them all week. Wind and hail has done lots of damage in counties south and east of Des Moines. A big elevator at Central City blew down.

<u>If you folks go to Yellowstone Park be sure and hold Little George by the hand while going among the mud bowls and water holds. In fact hold onto him all the time.</u>

This letter will be all from me. You will get in Monday. After that date you will be on the <u>go go</u>. Feeling fine.

Love Pop"

Gerald and Essie Mae (Thompson) Hill

Family Reunion - 1930

Thompson Family home - Lisbon

Hill home Lisbon 1936

A Century of Progress – 1933
"We Were There"

The 1933 Chicago International Exposition in Chicago was called "A Century of Progress," and the official book of the Fair says, "Although it chances that Chicago was incorporated as a village in 1833, the Exposition is not solely intended to be a colossal demonstration of exultation on the advancements of Chicago within the limits of a century. This is truly in every sense an Exposition belonging to the world. The one great motif is the rise of mankind during the last hundred years, the most outstanding 100 years of scientific discovery of miraculous improvements in the living conditions of the people of the earth that has ever been seen."

Yes, we were there! On opening day and the day after, with our friends, George and Elizabeth Anselm of Mount Vernon, with headquarters in her father's luxurious apartment overlooking Lake Michigan. Later in the summer we rented an apartment near the Fair Grounds with the Runkles and spent a hilarious week. At that time, we covered the Fair thoroughly from Sally Rand and her fan dance on the Midway through most of the "intellectual exhibits" of Art, Science, and Culture. We had the official Guide Book, and we missed very little.

Gone were the Grecian imitations in the architecture of former Expositions. They were replaced by modern functional styles, constructed of new materials, and dazzling with unique lighting effects. The influence of this fair on life in these United States since then is incalculable, and I am grateful to have lived before it, through it, and after it.

Forty years ago, the big problem was <u>money</u>, not <u>safety</u>, when we went to Chicago. Lester and Helen had no qualms about walking to our apartment late at night from the Fair Grounds, climbing the outside stairway, and finally locating the right place by examining the garbage cans at the back doors. Nowadays college students do sociological research by examining garbage, but in the summer of 1934, it was a question of "where am I," not "who am I." There probably wasn't very much in our garbage can, because we ate very frugally, and we could get almost enough for our lunch from the free samples we were given by exhibitors, such as Heinz.

Previously there had been the Expositions in Paris (the Eiffel Tower), in Queen Victoria's England (the Crystal Palace), in the United States in Buffalo, N.Y., St. Louis, and in Chicago in 1893, which left the Field Museum as a permanent part of the city's treasures. The Century of Progress divides the old from the new, and inspired the efforts of the scientific world toward discovering new wonders in the future, rather than imitating and perpetuating the cultures and achievements of the past.

To us, "A Century of Progress" was the greatest, not excepting Expo 1970 in Tokyo, when our family, Keiko, Vicki, and Tommy were with us.

Interesting Guests

Among our fond memories are some interesting guests we've had since we've been married. The Lisbon house was located just right to let us help our Mount Vernon friends with their entertainment, but we were not restricted to them, or by them. The best example of this was the "after the May Festival Concert" party that Grace and Dick Barker, and Dean (of the College) Jay and Mary McGregor, and the Hills hosted at our house in Lisbon. There were about fifty guests, including the associate conductor the Chicago Symphony Orchestra, and we scheduled it as an open house get-together after the first concert in Mount Vernon on a Thursday evening.

We had fun getting ready for it, making the lime punch pepped up with plenty of bottled goods, and the sandwich loaves, with attractive garnishes. The weather was perfect, the house looked lovely, flowers everywhere, the dining table beautiful, the two pairs of French doors to the porch open wide, the punch bowl ready to be filled. We were ready for our expected guests, but about 4:30 in the afternoon, unexpected guests arrived!

Paul and Marie Hill from Des Moines drove up in front of the house. That would have been fine, because they were always very welcome, unexpected or not, but they brought with them Jerry's missionary aunt, who came "to spend a few days with us." Surprise guests pose problems! She was a lovely, gracious, sweet person, but the type of party which we were having that night was not right for her. She would have disapproved utterly, and it would have been an embarrassment. However, my wonderful understanding mother came to the rescue and invited her to be her guest that night. Oh! What a narrow escape from a family disgrace!

When the Rust College singers came to Lisbon to give a concert in the Methodist Church, we had the boys at our house and Lib Franks across the street entertained the girls. All of them had breakfast at our house. Those negro students were not accustomed to being guests in a white folks' home, or to being waited upon, but it was a pleasure for us to do it. When we got home after the concert the four fellows stood in front of the fireplace and gave us a private concert that was really outstanding.

Charles Hisatomi's visit after he was released from an internment camp in California after World War II. He was enroute to Cleveland for employment, and hearing about what he and his family and parents had gone through made us aware of another phase of the hardships, tragedy, and injustices of that time. Charles (who was a Neisi) had been a pupil of mine in geology, and after he graduated and went back to his home in California, for some unknown reason, he sent us a crate of avocados and other fruit as a gift every year at Thanksgiving time. He was a most loyal friend. George and Tommy had heard about him all their lives, and they learned to enjoy avocados at a time when they were unknown in the local grocery. It was a great delight to give them the opportunity of meeting him, and to have him in our home. We also had Dr. and

Mrs. C. F. "Judge" Littell from Mount Vernon with us that evening at dinner, and as we sat at the table, Charles Hisatomi said in a thoughtful voice, "This room is larger than the whole house that we've been living in in the internment camp."

Cornell now has a fine health center on the campus, built as a memorial to Dr. and Mrs. Francis Ebersole, and financed largely by money from their estate. However, in the 1920's and 1930's when a student got sick he was sent to the Infirmary, a little cottage back of the Chapel, which had a few beds and a nurse on duty. One day, when we were living in Lisbon, Dr. Ebersole, who was an old friend, phoned me to say that there was a mumps epidemic on camps, and could I take care of a couple of girls in our home, while they were ill. I could, I would, they came, and we had a delightful time. They were among our "interesting guests."

The Lisbon house was ideal for dancing, and we had lots of dancing parties. Peggy and Marilyn Frink's teenage friends, the Delts [ΔΦΡ (Delta Phi Rho), Jerry's Cornell fraternity], congregating for Cornell Homecoming reunions, and parties for my Lisbon Sunday School class. Too bad our own boys were too young to take full advantage of the place, although I am sure they remember the birthday and Hallowe'en parties and Christmas dinners we had there.

Probably the most famous guest that we have had in recent years was Marjorie Holmes, my former pupil, and the author of many inspiring books, which have become known throughout the world. Harold and Alice Holmes and the Hills were the only people she took time to visit last year when she came to Phoenix in connection with her newest book, and was on a very busy schedule of interviews and TV and radio appearances. In her book *Love and Laughter*, she says about me, "Essie May Hill . . . had a chuckle in her throat, a joyous bubbling spring, even explaining the Pleistocene Age." She autographed a copy of her book for me, writing, "For Essie May Thompson Hill, whose voice will always be sweet to her former pupil and lifelong friend."

These are a few of the interesting guests who have added much to our lives, and whom we remember fondly.

Come Peace of God, and dwell again on earth,
Come with the calm that hailed Thy Prince's birth,
Come with the healing of Thy gentle touch
Come, Peace of God, that this world needs so much -

Methodist Hymnal
Mary Rowland and Lily Rendle

Sons Thomas & George

Essie Mae and Gerald -
serving with the Civil Air Patrol
1943

Cadet
John Thompson
with Grandmother

Capt. Manly Thompson

Manly, Great-Grandmother
(Sadie Thompson) Marie, John
Virginia and Peggy

Our War Experiences

In the bicentennial year, 1976, the national focus was on our Declaration of Independence from England, and the birthday of our country when "a new nation was brought forth on this continent."

> "For everything there is a season;
> A time for love and a time for hate;
> A time for war and a time for peace."
> – Ecclesiastes

Two hundred years ago was a time for war, when "the embattled farmers stood beside the rude bridge" and fired into the advancing Redcoats "the shot heard 'round the world." One of the many blessings which we in these United States were thankful for in that historic year 1976 was that we were not at war. Strife and disagreements and problems, yes, but not war, as has happened so many times in the history of our country.

The surrender of General Robert E. Lee at Appomattox took place less than forty years before I was born. When I was growing up in Lisbon, Iowa, the Civil War veterans, The Grand Army of the Republic, led the Memorial Day parade to the cemetery, and participated in the services.

Our family's first real wartime experiences began in World War I with brother Manly's enlistment in the army. He was living in Washington, D.C., married, and the father of three-year-old Billy. He was stationed in nearby Ft. Meade. He was exceedingly patriotic and hated being retained there as an instructor rather than being sent overseas into the fighting areas. Our family was very proud to be able to hang a service flag with one star on it in the front window of our house in his honor, and I wore a miniature service flag on the sleeve of my middy blouse, which was the popular dress style for school. Manly's picture was included in the souvenir book which contained all the service men's pictures from Linn County and their records.

Our Home Economics teacher inaugurated a contest to find out who could collect the most wartime recipes which used substitutes for sugar, flour, butter, and other scarce or rationed ingredients. I had an advantage because that is the way Mama cooked all the time. So with her help I amassed enough to win the prize. There were dozens and dozens of them, and I wish I had kept them. The prize was a pretty potted purple hyacinth, but I worked very hard and I was very disappointed. However, Mother set it out in the flower garden under the dining room window on the east side of the house, and it grew there for many years. In the end, it came to be a source of pride and pleasure to me, as I became more appreciative of her love for growing things and her knack with them.

To be a part of it, in any way, shape or form! Among my keepsakes I have a certificate from the UNITED WAR WORK CAMPAIGN which testifies to the fact that "Essie Mae Thompson of Lisbon, Iowa, having completed her payment of One Dollar from her own earnings toward the United War Work Campaign Fund, is therefore enrolled as one of the Victory Girls and is thus helping to provide comfort, and cheer for an American Fighter through the work of the seven organizations represented in the campaign." These included the YMCA, YWCA, Salvation Army, etc. So I was a Victory Girl and wore a service flag on my arm in World War I, and thought I was really helping to defeat the Kaiser!

World War I ended when I was a Junior in high school. Things were really wild that day, inhibitions lifted, and happiness and excitement knew no limits. The false Armistice on November 10, Lester's birthday, made us realize that the end of the war was imminent, and gave us an extra day in which to prepare our posters and arrange for the parade. We marched en masse to Mount Vernon, went to the big bonfire, and ended the evening by going to a public dance in the lodge hall which was above Bauman's clothing store. I never did tell Mother about that, because she would have disapproved so completely and never trusted me again. By that time, she accepted the fact that we did dance a little at our private parties or she closed her mind to it, but a public dance was not the environment for her darling daughter!

Lisbon, like every other town in the country, large or small, was very strongly affected by the war. Everything we thought or did was motivated and influenced by it. Among the incidents of that time which will always remain as a part of Lisbon chronicles is the fact that Otis Besse, a close friend of Manly and the husband of Clarissa Runkle, Lester's cousin, was aboard the USS *Cyclops*, when it disappeared. No trace of it was ever found. It simply vanished. Its disappearance is one of the unsolved mysteries of U.S. Naval history. The ship with a crew of 309 men left Barbados in the West Indies on March 4, 1918, loaded with a cargo of manganese ore. Its destination was Norfolk, Virginia. When it failed to arrive, it was first thought to have been torpedoed, or had struck a mine, but there was no debris anywhere around, and no records of mines, so the speculations were dropped. Many other theories for its disappearance were investigated, but nothing could be found.

After a long investigation, the Navy finally announced, "The disappearance of this ship is one of the most baffling mysteries in the annals of the Navy, all attempts to locate it having proved unsuccessful. Many theories have been advanced, but none satisfactorily accounts for her disappearance." President Wilson said, "Only God and the sea know what happened to that great ship."

There has been considerable attention given lately to the "Bermuda Triangle" where scores of ships and planes seem to have mysteriously disappeared. The course of the *Cyclops* lay within this area. Recent research by Lawrence David Kusche brings new light to the mystery of that ship's disappearance. He has discovered that there was a storm at that time with winds capable of capsizing it. No attention was given to this in the investigation. Also, in 1968, a Navy diver, searching for the missing nuclear submarine *Scorpion* near Norfolk, came upon the remains of a ship with an unusual superstructure like the *Cyclops* had for unloading cargo. Unfortunately, the exact location was lost because a storm came up and the diver had to leave the area, but it holds hope that the fate of the *Cyclops* and Lisbon's Otis Beese will be known. To honor his memory, the American Legion Post in Lisbon is named "The Cyclops."

Before the Armistice was declared, a terrible thing happened in the fall of 1918 which eventually caused more than twice as many deaths as occurred in World War I and World War II combined. I refer to the "Flu" or the Spanish Influenza as it was called. The war was almost over, the Kaiser was beginning to make peace overtures, and in America people were beginning to feel that victory was in sight. The first case of the disease in this country occurred in Ft. Devens, Massachusetts, on September 7, 1918. An enlisted man was hospitalized with a fever and headache. That was not an uncommon happening, but this was different – how very different! A little more than three months later there were 550,000 Americans who had died of this sickness – the Spanish Flu. It was world-wide epidemic, and eventually 22,000,000 people died of the disease.

In Alaska whole villages were wiped out, and in India more than 10,000,000 died. Thousands of men in military camps throughout the United States died before they had a chance to go overseas. Women, like Mother Hill in Clarion, and Mrs. James Baltz, wife of the Methodist Minister, left their homes and worked around the clock with the doctors, risking their own lives to care for those who were sick. Our neighbor, Martha Pfautz Mohn, a young wife and mother, died, leaving a little baby to be reared by her parents, who already had twelve children! As far as I know, I was the only one of our family who got it, and I don't remember much about the experience, except how weak I was when I finally got out of bed about two weeks later. Before this time there had been sporadic epidemics of "the flu," but none of them as serious as the new type which broke out in 1918. The Russians and the Chinese were both blamed for it, but the name "Spanish" was finally given to it because in the early months of 1918, there were so many deaths in the cities of Spain. It has never been determined where it actually started or why it was so deadly. In the ensuing years, scientists have developed "shots" to counteract the violent effects of the flu viruses which still make people fearful. The latest is the "Swine Flu," with a proposal to inoculate everyone in the U.S.A. Time will tell the outcome of that plan.

Between the Armistice which ended the fighting in World War I and Pearl Harbor, which was the beginning of the United States participation in World War II, twenty-three years elapsed, during which I changed from a naïve school girl not yet sixteen, to a housewife and mother nearing the life-begins-at-forty stage of my life.

Our family's personal involvement in WW II really began when husband Jerry accepted an invitation to join a group of young fellows who were organizing a flying club. They bought a small plane, a Piper Cub, and based it in a pasture which

90

had been converted into a tiny airfield about three miles east of Lisbon. In order to get gas and instruction in Aeronautical training they joined the Civil Air Patrol. This was a newly created auxiliary of the Army Air Corps. Members were able to get experience in marching in formation, flight instruction, as well as to wear an official khaki uniform, and to get training which could give a head start in military service.

While I was helping Jerry to prepare for the CAA examinations in Civil Air Regulations, Meteorology, and Navigation, I learned enough to eventually pass the tests myself and, more or less on a dare, went one step father and earned Instructor Ratings in these subjects. We also began attending Civil Air Patrol meetings in Cedar Rapids, and eventually I was asked to be an instructor in Civil Air Regulations there. The *Cedar Rapids Gazette* sent a photographer to the meeting one night and a very flattering picture of me and a couple of the girls who were in the class appeared in the newspaper to show that "Rosie, the Riveter" had counterparts in other phases of the war effort. This publicity led to an invitation to teach in the Air Corps Flight School which was in operation at Coe College, Cedar Rapids, Iowa.

This was in the Fall of 1943, more than a year and a half after Pearl Harbor, and many things had been happening during that time at home and elsewhere throughout the world. Nephew John Thompson had completed his pre-flight training in the Navy Flight School at Iowa City, had gotten his wings as a Marine pilot, married Virginia White, and they had come to our home in Lisbon to spend their honeymoon. We were very proud to have them, and all of us felt that anything we could do for a person in the service of our country was a personal contribution to the winning of the war. As a result of one incident while they were there, Jerry became what John calls "his favorite uncle," and son George became convinced that the Marine Corps was the toughest and best branch of the military services. The crew from "Floozy," the B17 bomber which had made an emergency landing north of Lisbon in the Fall of 1942, were scattered all over the world by this time, and a couple of the fellows were perilously near the end of their lives. We had fed, bedded, and entertained them while they waited for the plane to be repaired, and we had great affection for them.

Jerry was getting ready to go as a Field Director in the Red Cross, after he failed to get into the Navy because of his eyesight. Brother Manly, who had been in WW I, was again in the Army, and his son Bill and our niece, Harriett Thompson, were both in the Navy. Nephew John Thompson had been sent to the South Pacific after he completed his preliminary training in Iowa City and had gotten his wings in Texas. Bill Thompson was in the Mediterranean, and Harriett, a WAVE, was in Washington, D.C. There she met and married a fellow officer Al Ronander, a chaplain. At home, ten-year old George organized the neighborhood youngsters into a "Write a Fighter Club," and he furnished most of the materials and ideas for them. He also was responsible for being the family supervisor of the blackout practice sessions, which were the order of the town every week or so. Marc Pitts, Tommy's special friend, the Bombardier on "Floozy," had come and gone, leaving a permanent imprint on his young acquaintance.

It gave me a good feeling to have the skills and training that were needed at this time. I never hesitated for a minute to agree to do all that was asked and expected of me. During the time that I was teaching at Coe College in Cedar Rapids, I had only four classes a day, but they started at eight in the morning, so I had to leave home before the kids went to school, or Jerry to work, and I didn't usually get home until the latter part of the afternoon. I took my lunch and drove off campus to eat. I was quite alone, without sociability or any group associations. I couldn't get anyone to help with the housework at home, so I canned, cooked, and cleaned as usual after I got back to Lisbon. Two or three nights a week both Jerry and I went back to Cedar Rapids to a CAP meeting, and I can remember climbing into the back seat of the red Ford about 10:30 or 11:00 o'clock, and sleeping in complete exhaustion all the way home.

Eventually, the administrators of the Navy Flight Preparatory School at Cornell College in Mount Vernon heard about this work and learned that I was a certified CAA Instructor in Navigation, Meteorology, and Civil Air Regulations. They asked me to join the staff there. Gerald went to his wartime work in the Red Cross, we sold our Lisbon house, and the boys and I moved to Mount Vernon.

Although the time I had spent teaching at Coe College seemed difficult, as it turned our however, it was like the preliminary bout before the main event, which was, of course, those war years in Mount Vernon. I personally shoveled thirteen and a half tons of coal that first winter to "Keep the Home Fires Burning" in the house which we rented for $25 a month after we sold the Lisbon house. Wow! (There was ceiling on rents which prevented the landlords from taking advantage of the demand for housing.) The kids said the house was held together by the wall paper.

Actually, the old house had been converted into a multiple housing dwelling and I became "live-in" landlord. The kids and I lived on the first floor. I rented the second floor to two married cadets and their wives. They each paid me fifteen dollars a month to live there. The husbands were only allowed to come home on the weekends, but the wives kept each other company and the rent they paid more than paid the rent for the whole house. On the third floor there was an old bachelor who had lived there long before I took over, and he was my "handy-man" – a real jewel. Instead of paying rent, he took care of the snow shoveling in the winter and the garden the rest of the time. I have never been furnished with such beautiful flowers or vegetables as he provided for us. He "went with the house" and eased my life considerably. Very quiet and unobtrusive, but once in a long while we'd hear him go up the stairs singing as he went – the final moments of a "swinging weekend."

After I had finished my day's work with the Cadets in the Flight School on the Cornell Campus, I still had to keep the family fed, clothed, and entertained, as well as make weekly trips to Lisbon to continue my teaching in the Civil Air Patrol. All in all, it was just about all that I could manage. Mother worried, and I used to say, "This is taking ten years off my life." However, the ratio between pain and pride, sadness and satisfaction, has become reversed in my mind and memory as the years have passed, and the recollections of the hard times are giving way to the recollections of the happy times during those years. *"Forsan et olim meminisse iujabit."* (Perhaps some day it will be pleasing to remember even these things.) – Virgil, *The Aeneid.*

Among the good things which came from those years were that the boys learned to be independent, helpful, reliable, and resourceful, and the three of us enjoyed a wonderful congeniality and companionship. It didn't hurt them a bit to have to adjust to a very modest home and way of life, to make new friends, and to figure out ways of making extra money for themselves. For instance, George, eleven and a half years old, was the laundry liaison person for the student cadets. He used to come home with his pockets bulging with money, and a practical problem in arithmetic in figuring out how much of it belonged to him, and how much went to Mrs. Rex Dean who was doing the washing. After he got a job at the Stoltz Dry Cleaning and made so much money, I had to beg off on my promise to duplicate his earning, because I was going broke trying to keep up with him. He secretly saved enough to surprise me with the money to buy a *Webster's Unabridged Dictionary* which had been my hope and dream for a long time. It became one of my most prized and cherished possessions. I loaned it back to him when he went to Yale.

In between the time I had to spend studying my own homework and helping the boys with theirs, we had fun together. I rode belly-buster on their sled down Presbyterian Hill, and enjoyed school and church activities. It was a sharing time. Among other things, we read books together, and one that we especially enjoyed and appreciated was *Mama's Bank Account*, which was later made into the movie *I Remember Mama*. We learned that one "Mama's bank account" was just about as much of a worry and problem as another's!

Other times which are good to remember are seeing each of them perform on the Cornell stage with the college drama students. The plays were directed by Bertha and Al Johnson. George was in the premier performance of *Love Your Neighbor* written by Al, and a representative of Row Peterson Publishing Company was in the audience on opening night. It was finally bought and published by that company and George's picture is included in the published edition with the original cast. Tommy was cast in the part of the little brother in *Family Portrait* which is the story of Jesus's family after He left home for His ministry. George started his Boy Scout experiences during this time, twelve years old, and we remember the induction service in the basement of the Methodist Church. How proud and happy, and tearful, I was when I pinned his Tenderfoot badge on the pocket of his oversize, secondhand, blouse. He went on to become an Eagle Scout and still devotes time to the organization.

Eleven-year-old George and I had an interesting experience early in the summer of 1944. Fleet Admiral William Leahy did the college the honor of coming from Washington, D.C., to give the Commencement address. One of the four 5-star admirals in the Navy, he was the senior military aide to President Franklin Roosevelt. I was teaching in the Navy Flight Preparatory School on campus and, "for something to do" George had been learning Morse Code with the cadets. Commander Totten P. Heffelfinger (a Twin Cities financier), Commanding Officer of the Navy unit, was also in the class. As a member of the faculty I went to the formal reception for the Admiral and took George as my escort. When we went through the reception, Commander Heffelfinger smilingly and graciously introduced George as "my classmate, George Hill." George's comment afterwards was, "Admiral Leahy is just like an old grandpa." When D-Day occurred a few days later, we all realized the "big secret" the Admiral had known all the time that he was on the Cornell campus. George eventually became not only a "classmate" of Commander Heffelfinger, but a fellow alumnus of Yale College.

As the war neared the end, the number of incoming cadets was reduced in proportion to the need. Most of the regular Cornell faculty members who had been temporarily drafted from their regular positions in the Music Conservatory, in the English, Physics, and Geology Departments to teach in the Navy program, returned to their regular positions, and the extra instructors, such as I was, were no longer needed. This gave me a chance to enroll as a student again, and I thoroughly enjoyed taking courses in Ceramics and Art Appreciation, and in learning shorthand and typing. As a result of the latter training, Al Johnson asked me to be his "amanuensis" and I eventually had a part in all phases of his work in the Drama Department, as well as his own writing. I made a couple of his new plays "publisher-ready," carried on his personal correspondence with Broadway producers, typed his poetry, and helped at the house, too, even getting the meals when necessary.

Bertha and Al were second parents to George and Tommy, a bulwark of strength for me during this time, and dear friends now for more than forty years. When we brought Tommy home from the hospital after an appendicitis attack, Al carried him into the house in his arms, and I was one with whom they shared their joy in the anticipation of the arrival of their adopted daughter, Anne. Through their teaching, their writings, and their personal character, they have been a great influence for good, and we are proud and fortunate to have their love and friendship.

In many places in the country, the end of World War II was celebrated with wildly hysterical mob scenes, exuberance, and dancing in the streets – everything on an "anything goes" basis. Not so in Mount Vernon, where the boys and I were living at that time. There was rather solemn gathering of townspeople, Navy personnel, and faculty, hastily arranged in the college chapel. Everyone was thankful that the war was over, but sad because Harlan Nelson had been reported missing in action and presumed dead, just shortly before this. He was not the first casualty in town, but his family were very well known on the Cornell faculty and in town, and everyone thought of Harlan as one of the finest young men in the community. I always felt a special rapport with him, not only because I had known him since he was seven years old, but he was a Geology major in college and a Navigator. We were friends.

The last time I saw him, after a dinner in the Nelson home, he brought out a thick manuscript to show me. It was a research project report which he had just completed, and he said, "You're the only one who can appreciate this." When he went into the Air Force as a Navigator, he had been married only a few months. After his death, his wife went to England to do graduate study met and married a man who was on a social level that allowed them to be guests at Queen Elizabeth's wedding. The Nelsons always counted her children as their grandchildren, and one of her sons came back from England to graduate from Cornell College. I understand that he is the only Cornellian ever to have gotten his pre-college training on the "playing fields of Eton."

We had no personal association with the Korean War, except as it touched our friends, the Van Metre family, in Mount Vernon. Mary almost had a nervous breakdown because of worry over their son Douglas when he was sent to Korea. Shortly before his time there was up, he was allowed to come home because his father was dying of cancer. He got an emergency leave, but because of the circumstances he did not have to go back there and was soon out of service. However, by the time the Korean and Viet Nam Wars came along, our sons were old enough to be personally involved. George supplied this information at my request. When he started these experiences, he was seventeen years old, a freshman at Yale University.

"I joined the PLC (Platoon Leaders Class) program in May 1950, when I was unsure about my future career and wanted to keep open the option of a military career – not being old enough to go to one of the military academies and not having time enough for ROTC, I jumped at the opportunity to earn a Marine commission in 90 days of summer school. One month later the Korean war broke out, and was in full swing when I spent my first 45 days at Quantico. I was a corporal that summer, and a sergeant the next summer. All of us were planning to spend two years in Korea – not looking forward to it, but that was what we had ahead of us. But much to our surprise, we were called together and told that the government was asking us to sign new contracts, for an indefinite period of active duty, rather than the two years were had signed up for originally. I thought that was unreasonable, and refused to sign the new contract. Several of the others agreed, particularly those who were in the last year or two of college. (Since we were told that if we didn't sign the new contracts we would be draft eligible, as enlisted men.) I held firm, and was eventually was discharged, honorably, though I'm sure the Marine Corps was as disgusted with me as I was with the Corps at that point.

"As it turned out, of course, the war fizzled down to a stalemate, and it was over shortly after Eisenhower took office in 1952, so I wouldn't have had to stay in for more than the two years I originally agreed to. But none of us knew that at the time. There were a lot of promises broken by the government in the Korean War, men called back who had taken early discharges in good faith after World War II, Reservists who had not been counseled wisely before they signed up, and (worst of all among my friends) physicians in military residency programs who were pulled out and sent to Korea – their careers were never put back together, and it was a string of broken promises and broken contracts by all of the military medical services.

"Since I didn't serve on active duty in the Korean War, I was still draft eligible, and had to get it out of the way before I could be given a surgical residency position. Program directors were remembering the problems of the 50's when men were pulled out of residency in mid-year, and wouldn't take people who had a selective service obligation. But there was no war going on at the time, and the services didn't need doctors. So the only service I could get into was the Public Health Service, and I joined it simply for that reason, to get my draft obligation out of the way after failing to be accepted in the Army, Navy and Air Force. Of course, it turned out to be a wonderful opportunity, gave me a head start on a research career and a chance to travel to Mexico on a rather exciting mission. My book on leprosy was the culmination of that work in some respects, but it also gave me a taste for the problems of developing countries, particularly Latin America; and the semi-independent negotiations that I conducted were a valuable experience, preparing me for similar work in Colombia and Vietnam. I still don't talk very much about the details of that work, because I don't want it to limit my opportunities to be of possible service in the future.

"I was proud to be in Washington during the Kennedy years – they were exciting for all of us in my age group. Sarah was born at the Navy Hospital; the Chief of Surgery there, who I knew well – and still do – was one of the four men who performed the autopsy on President Kennedy at that hospital one and a half years later. I tried to be a part of the New Frontier, and enjoyed being with Lanie's and Babs' friends – Babs was either still in the CIA or had recently gotten out of it – and there were a lot of mysterious, interesting people around. I wanted to be as full of "vigah" as any of them, and a week after Bobby Kennedy took his 50-mile hike on the Chesapeake and Ohio towpath I took my 50-mile hike on the same path – except that I managed to pick the coldest day of the year (unfortunately) and had to do it alone. It was an experience I'll never forget.

"I was never satisfied with my 'service' rendered on active duty, particularly because there was no inactive duty Reserve program in which I could have some opportunity to contribute in some way to the public health, welfare or safety. I therefore began to look for some way to be in the Reserves or National Guard, and I discovered that – having served my active duty obligation – I was now welcome in any branch of service. I chose the Navy because I liked the approach I received from the recruiter in Denver, and the people I met who had been in the Navy Medical Corps and enjoyed it. It took a long time to get discharged from the Public Health Service, but I finally made the transfer in January 1968. I have two years of credit as an active Marine Corps Reservist and 9 years of credit as an active Navy Reservist. My 8 years of Public Heath Reserve time counts for nothing except in the Public Health Service, except that my 2 years of active duty satisfy the obligation which I had under the now extinct selective service act. [N.b.: Federal regulations have since changed since 1976, and my eight years in the Public Health Service Reserve now counts the same as other branches of service. I am credited with two years of active duty, and six years of inactive duty.]

"The Navy permits me to wear my Marine Corps Rifle Expert and other small arms marksmanship badges, and I was awarded the National Defense Service Medal for my time in the Marines. I received that medal in the mail. I also have had an opportunity to take in a lot of the world in the last 9 years with the Navy – San Diego, Camp Pendleton (including the Vietnam Refugee camps), Long Beach, Oakland, Great Lakes, Quantico, Fort Benning, Bethesda, Washington, Kodiak, Pearl Harbor, Manila, Subic Bay, and Vietnam. I became a Lieutenant Commander in 1968, a Commander in 1972, and a Captain in 1976, the latter promotion apparently being somewhat premature, but solid nevertheless. I am asked again this year to serve on a selection board, for promotion of officers to the rank of commander and captain in the medical corps reserve – this is the choicest duty one can get, as I understand it – they treat us very well, we serve in civvies, stay in a fine hotel, and have very personal treatment. The duty is performed in the Navy Annex, beside the Pentagon.

"Through my Navy connections with then Captain (now Rear Admiral) Ben Eiseman, a Professor of Surgery at the University of Colorado, I learned about the American Medical Association's Vietnam Medical School Project. The AMA had a contract from the Agency for International Development, an organization of the U.S. State Department, to assist in the development of an American-style medical school for South Vietnam. Although I had reservations about the goal, since I believed (and still do) that developing countries need individual programs of medical care designed for their specific problems, not simply carbon copies of our highly specialized medicine, I wanted to see the situation at first hand. And I also wanted to see what was going on there from a military point of view, experience combat medicine, and – if possible – get official Navy sanction for it, by offering service which no one else would be in a position to render. My unique position was that I was to be there as a fully accredited civilian professor, and able to travel widely with those credentials, but also a Navy physician, prepared to work and observe. And that I could bring together the thoughts and contributions of many people who otherwise would not have had contact with each other. I was one of the last Navy physicians to spend any length of time in South Vietnam. My report in 1972 was given to the Surgeon General in a major briefing at the Bureau of Medicine and Surgery, after I returned from my first tour of duty, which lasted six weeks, and took me to the front lines at Hue, and to the major military and civilian hospitals in Saigon, Nha Tranh and Cam Ranh Bay.

"I received the Navy Unit Commendation ribbon for this service, plus the Vietnam Service medal with one battle star, two Vietnamese Meritorious Unit Commendations (Gallantry Color and First Class Color), and a letter of commendation from the Chief of Naval Forces Vietnam. About one and a half years later, after the "cease fire,' I was invited to return for a second tour. I was terribly disappointed by what I found, for I then realized that our efforts had been almost totally wasted, that the Vietnamese that we worked with had been by and large lying to us about their activities and progress, that graft was siphoning off our equipment and supplies almost completely in the civilian hospitals, and the military effort which we had supported so vigorously had come to a standstill as soon as we had left the Vietnamese to carry it on with our dollars and advice.

"I wrote and spoke vigorously about this to all that I could contact at home and in Vietnam, including the Naval attaché, the Senior AMA representative, the Chief of the American Surgical program (who was based at the University of Pittsburgh), all without avail. I was forbidden to publish a greatly watered-down account of my observations – and, as of now, there is nothing in print about this debacle, which was misguided in its design, and cost tens of millions of dollars.[*] I wrote a very long report about my observations, including trips in the highlands, to Dalat, to the Montagnards, to the Delta, and other areas which had not been visited by Americans for more than a year. I was the last American to visit Le Hu Sanh, the major Vietnamese Marine Corps Hospital near Saigon. The military medical people were generally doing their jobs in a quiet efficient way; but the Vietnamese civilians were profiteering hugely. I paid substantial sums of money for "export taxes" to be able to ship home a lacquerware pot and coffee table, but couldn't get it validated on receipts – I think it was all graft, pocketed by the Vietnamese clerks. I think some people at the U.S. Embassy were involved in it, too – but that can't be proved, it just seems that way because of the circumstances.

My report was given verbally in in writing, with maps, to the CINCPAC Surgeon while I spent two weeks being debriefed in Pearl Harbor, and it also went to the Surgeon General and various other unspecified destinations in Washington. I was impressed with the interest and intelligent receipt of the report by the Navy, and thoroughly disgusted with the lack of perception of the AMA and USAID that their program was a washout. The young doctors we were training fled the country, by and large, when the Viet Cong took over, though many of the faculty, including those whom I thought were most sensible and conscientious, have stayed behind to continue to work in whatever way they can. Our problem was that we didn't realize that Vietnam needs sanitation, improvement in infant mortality, better management of trauma cases, better treatment of burns, tuberculosis, parasites, and so forth – including leprosy. It didn't need what we were setting up in our hospitals and training programs: pediatric cardiology, cancer chemotherapy, open heart surgery, kidney dialysis and kidney transplantation, etc. They never got a Department of Public Health established in the Vietnam Medical School; but that's what they needed most of all. I came away from my second tour of six weeks in November 1973, and I was certain that it would all fall apart before long. I was therefore not at all surprised with the event or its rapidity, though I was sad to see it all happen, nevertheless.

---

[*] I later published it anyway: George J. Hill, "Lerne and gladly teche": A view of the Vietnam Medical Education Project. *Military Medicine*. 1979;144:124-8.

98

"And now I continue to prepare for a future that I hope will never come to pass. I am qualified as an expert with the pistol, a sharpshooter with the new rifle, and have the medals for both, and as a Navy parachutist. I am physically in better health that I was ten years ago, and I am ready for anything the Navy might call upon me to do. I would like to go to the Antarctic, and I am preparing for that possibility by correspondence courses, interviews and an active research program – in the area of combat casualty management in the cold.* Perhaps it will all come together in a year of two – and even if it doesn't, I'll simply figure out something else to do." – end of George's writing.

In World War I, I felt I was doing my bit by rooty-tooting, in World War II, we were on the fringe of activity, but I had a personal patriotic project in the Vietnam War. (Tom was there.) He was not only in my mind, heart, and prayers very much of the time, but I also sent him many packages of books and magazines, curtains, rugs, tools, photographic materials, letters, and papers, to make the miserable places in which he had to live more comfortable. I even sent him, at his request, a plastic water bottle to carry in the plane in case he was shot down in the Vietnam forest. (Billions of dollars spent for supplies and no water bottle!) Thank God he got home safely. The most welcome sight we saw as we went around the world in 1970 was his smiling face and open arms when we got off the plane in Bangkok! A real surprise, arranged with the cooperation of his buddies!

As far as we know, the more than twenty years that our son Thomas D. Hill (Lt. Col., Ret.) spent in the Air Force is the longest time spent by anyone in the family in the active military service of our country, up to this time. In these later years, small boys have been inspired by the space exploration which culminated in the landings on the moon. They want to be astronauts when they grow up. Back in 1943, when Tom was eight years old, his friendship with Marc Pitts, the bombardier of the B-17 "Floozy," was undoubtedly the basis for his great desire to be a part of the Air Force. While I was teaching in the Navy Flight Preparatory School, that original spark of interest was kept alive, and later when he was in Navigation School in Harlingen, Texas, he wrote home, "I was the only fellow in the class who had an E-6-B as a plaything." An E-6-B is a small navigational instrument which we used in the Flight School.

---

* In 1977, I was appointed Consultant in Cold Weather Medicine by the Navy Surgeon General, and I served in that capacity until I retired in 1992. I gave many lectures on prevention of cold injuries, and I published " '...and some will have it cold'." *U.S. Naval Institute Proceedings.* 1983;109:125-7. I wrote NAVMEDCOMINST 6260.12, "Prevention of Cold Injuries" (19 February 1987).

After we moved to Sioux Falls, South Dakota, when he was in high school, he became active in the Civil Air Patrol Cadet program. I was the Commandant of the group of about twenty students. Tom and I went to the meetings together, dressed in our uniforms and ready for practice and instruction in military skills and ground school subjects related to flying know-how. Tom eventually won a trip to Washington, D.C., as an "Outstanding Cadet."

It was his determination to get into the AFROTC program that finally led to his going to the University of Colorado after he finished high school. He graduated from the University in June 1956, with a BS degree in Aeronautical Engineering, and was commissioned as a 2nd Lt. in the Air Force Reserves. While awaiting his entrance into active duty, Tom put his training to practical use with Pratt and Whitney Engine Company in Hartford, Connecticut. In February 1957 he began his career in the USAF at Lackland AFB, San Antonio, Texas. He received his basic training in Navigation at Harlingen AFB, Texas, and from there went to Randolph AFB, Texas, for training on the KC-97, a refueling tanker plane. The next move was to the Strategic Air Command (SAC) at Barksdale AFB, Shreveport, Louisiana.

During the next twenty years he lived on ten different military bases in the United States, plus several others located in Vietnam and Thailand. In addition to these he had short term assignments in Labrador, Alaska, Japan, and Spain, with stops in Hawaii, Guam, Okinawa, and flights to Rome, Marseilles, Stockholm, London, and Ireland. At my request Tom has written a detailed summary of the many different phases of this period of his life, the happenings, his frustrations, satisfactions, disillusionments, and his observations in theory and practice. He wrote about close friends, men of high character and integrity. He remembered tragic accidents, emotional times, and lucky times when his plane came back "on a wing and a prayer."

Typical of the many tense and frustrating situations he was to experience during his career, the first one came with the Lebanon crisis in 1957 when he was at Barksdale AFB. "On Alert," standing by to deploy, survival gear all ready, and nothing to do but wait. Then suddenly with no explanation, the alert was called off! However, there was much activity during the months he was there, and he flew nearly three times the normal amount during that first year, substituting whenever possible, with eight hours in the air at a time, landing, throwing his gear onto the next aircraft and then flying eight more. Flying was what he joined the Air Force to do!

The next step in his career was selection for the KC-135 in June 1959. This was the first jet-powered tanker plane, used for re-fueling the B-52 bombers. Although he was 13th on the priority list originally, he quickly moved to the top when it was announced that the assignment was to Minot, North Dakota. No one ahead of him wanted to go there, in fact most of them had never heard of the place, but to Tom it looked like a great assignment, only 300 miles from Aberdeen, and back near home.

After three months training in California and one month's vacation in Tokyo where he met and fell in love with Keiko, he arrived in Minot in October 1959, the same

100

week as the first KC-135 was ferried from the factory. The F-106 and the U-2 weather reconnaissance aircraft were there previously. This was a pleasant time. It was exciting to be flying in the newest Air Force planes. The crew consisted of four men, the pilot, co-pilot, Tom the navigator, and the boom operator, all of them equally responsible for the success of each refueling operation. Tom's job was to tell them where to go, the pilots got them there, and the boom operator made the contact with the B-52, skillfully maneuvering the gas hose into the bomber gas tanks while they flew along together at speeds of five or six hundred miles per hour. By this process the range of the bomber could be increased indefinitely. The crew was a close knit team, good friends as well as co-workers, and their record earned them the "Crew of the Quarter" award and special recognition by the Boeing Company, which had manufactured the aircraft.

Then changes began with the Kennedy election. There was less flying and more alert time, and Tom's enthusiasm for crew duty waned. He wanted an advanced academic degree, and arrangements for him were made to accomplish this in one year at the University of Colorado. Then the Berlin Wall crisis came in August 1961! Navigators were being recalled from retirement to meet the need, so Tom's application for leave of absence was turned down.

Alert was increased to one-half of the aircraft and one-third of the crews all the time, a grim existence, but necessary for the defense of the country in times of emergency. Times that not only "tried the souls of men" but were a great strain on the family and on family life. Most of the duty-time consisted of hours of "busy work," punctuated by meals and sleep. The men spent the time in the "ready-room," completely dressed to go, even while sleeping. When the siren sounded, they never knew whether it was the real thing, or just a test, so they bolted for the plane, overturning tables and chairs, spilling coffee, and ignoring everything except getting aboard the plane ready for take-off in the shortest possible time. They were ready to go anywhere, anytime, all the time – our silent defense.

During all this time, the desire for the advanced degree stayed with him, but he had to finish his five-year KC-135 tour with SAC before he was eligible. The height of frustration came with the Cuban crisis in October 1962. Keiko, Vicki, and Tommy came to Aberdeen to stay with us during this time, while Tom was on continuous alert, and the whole country wondered and worried. In Aberdeen we had food, candles, water, and bedding stored in the basement – our "bomb shelter" – and George, in Maryland, kept in mind the possibility of sending his family to Aberdeen in case of actual bombing along the east coast. The crisis was averted peacefully, as we now know, and Tom's ordeal ended with a surprise mission to Spain to support the Airborne Alert Force there.

On the day that Kennedy was assassinated, Tom was notified that he was eligible for a leave of absence to get his Master's degree at the Air Force Institute of Technology either in Aeronautical Engineering or in Reliability Engineering. Tom chose the latter, a comparatively new field, and he considers that that decision was the turning point of his life. He feels that promotion and success are often a matter of time and place, but "I've won more often than I've lost."

After he received his degree, his first assignment was to Edwards Air Force Base in California. He was to be responsible for the reliability evaluation of the new F-111 aircraft. Eventually he became the chief test engineer on that plane, with twenty-four engineers assigned to work under him. There were great pressures, many problems, and it was an emotional experience as well, to be involved with the preparing of this new, controversial plane for its fateful combat experiment. He feels that this was the high point of his career. His interest in flying had dropped "precipitously" and he recognized that his usefulness to the Air Force as a test engineer far exceeded that of a navigator. Also, he had much more self-satisfaction in the results of his work.

In October 1968 he was notified that he was to enter training for the AC-119K gunship and to plan for deployment to southeast Asia in March 1969. His job was to operate one of the infra-red sensors connected into the pilot's aiming system, a new type of navigation. The reliability of the sensors proved to be so low that they had to be re-designed, so his deployment was delayed until December 1969. The details of his experiences in SEA (South-East Asia) could be the basis for a book that Tom should write. For the present he does not discuss his work there, and he simply says that life on the airbase in Vietnam was "similar to being on an aircraft carrier, except the ship never came to port." He considers himself fortunate to have been reassigned to U-Dorn, Thailand, where, in between the duty flights over the Ho Chi Minh Trail, he made friends with the Thai people, especially the children, took language lessons, and became acquainted with as much of the culture as possible. He says he has mixed feelings about the SEA war, but the combat zone was not the place to consider them. Personal safety required total dedication and a closed mind to distractions. Among his associates and acquaintances, he saw little of the drug problem and other such evils.

After returning to the USA in December 1970, and six months at the Armed Forces Staff College in Norfolk, Virginia, he completed his more than twenty years in the Air Force at Andrews AFB, near Washington, D.C., where he was the Systems Command Manager of Reliability and Maintainability for all new Air Force development and production programs.

When he retired on May 31, 1977, his father and mother were proud members of the group which came to watch the ceremony, which was a formal occasion shared with a friend by mutual agreement. It was formal when Lt. General Robert C. Mathis entered the room with three ruffles and flourishes and the National Anthem was played with everyone standing at attention. It was informal in the way the General gave the traditional presentation of awards and Retirement Orders a warm personal effect. Tom was not only a fellow-officer but a faithful member of the General's weekly 6:00 A.M. Bible study class, and when Keiko came to the platform to receive an Air

Force Commendation as the wife of a retiring officer, the General was especially friendly and tender.

Tom's interest in the Air Force began with a crippled B-17 in an Iowa soybean field in World War II and lasted through the Vietnam War and beyond. Throughout the good times and the bad ones, I have heard him say that he always felt that his was a "life-saving job" for the people of the USA. And for his associates he says, "I can proudly say that with very few exceptions the Air Force officers with whom I was associated had impeccable moral character and were worthy of the trust of the country." His awards included the Air Force Commendation Medal, the Air Force Distinguished Flying Cross, the Distinguished Service Medal, and eleven Air Medals.

An important sustaining activity which goes with military life is the work of the Red Cross. The times which husband Gerald spent as a Field Director in that organization during WW II is another phase of our family's wartime experience. The Civil Air Patrol had whetted his appetite to have an active part in the war effort, but because of his eyesight he had to settle for the Red Cross. He got a leave of absence from the bank in Lisbon and went into training at American University in Washington, D.C. Eventually he was assigned to Camp Roberts, California, where he coordinated the work of the Red Cross between the Army's Divisions 76 and 89 on their maneuvers at Hunter Liggett Unit Military Reservation.

In June 1944 he was notified of his assignment to the 97th Division at Camp Cooke, California. During all the time he was in the Red Cross service, he was literally "with his men" all the time, doing whatever they were doing or helping them with their problems. Floods of telegrams, arranging emergency leaves involving deaths, births, or serious illnesses, counselling, making emergency loans, working out allotment problems, especially amount the colored troops, many of whom were almost illiterate, and to a limited extent providing "comfort items" such as cigarettes and writing supplies. He also went through amphibious training with the 97th, including landing from ships at various places along the California coast, scrambling down the nets which were thrown over the side, and practicing other ways of disembarking in the shortest time possible. They were being equipped and prepared for the invasion of Japan.

But plans were changed. In order to stay with the men in the 97th, Jerry, as he was now called instead of "Toot," had an emergency hernia repair. He went with the troops to Camp Kilmer, N.J., and boarded ship at Hoboken, joining a massive convoy to Europe. Although dates and places were classified information, I knew that he was on the high seas on February 22, when I received a letter saying, "I had cherry pie for dinner tonight."

The 97th Division landed at Le Havre, the first unit to go directly to Europe. Rain, mud, bone-chilling cold – this was Camp Lucky Strike! From the middle of April 1945, for several weeks, they moved back and forth across Germany wherever they were needed: Bonn, Bad Godesberg, Remagen, and Dusseldorf, which was a major

German command point for the Ruhr valley. The 97th was finally transferred to the 3rd Army under General Patton and they were in Marienbad, Czechoslovakia on VE Day.

His Red Cross training and prescribed duties did not include rounding up German prisoners, but at one point in the latter days of the war, German soldiers were surrendering in such numbers that his job was to supervise a group en route to a stockade. He "guarded" them in a jeep as they walked along the road. *Rauschmitt!!* In returning to Paris for deployment to the United States, he and his driver went the "long way 'round," so he saw Munich, Berchtesgaden, Hitler's "Eagle's Nest," Innsbruck, the Brenner Pass, and Lake Constance. On August 7, V-J Day, he resigned from the Red Cross and returned to civilian life. Several of the men have shown their appreciation of what he did for them, by continuing to send Christmas greetings for more than twenty-five years.

The Floozy Story

(I wrote this story in 1943 and sent it to *The Reader's Digest* hoping it would be printed. It wasn't. But I think it is still a significant story. Tom has the Floozy scrapbook with all the pictures and letters connected with the episode. I gave it to him because he and his friend Marc Pitts are the heroes of it all.)

One noon in the late fall of 1942, we heard the roar of a plane overhead. Because the "big ones" were still somewhat of a novelty in our quiet little village in eastern Iowa, the whole family dashed out into the back yard to see it. "Oh Daddy, it's a B17," cried nine-year old George, proud of his ability to identify aircraft. "And it's flying so low, I can see the pilot in it!" he added triumphantly. At this point, not wanting to be outdone by his older brother, seven-year old Tommy danced up and down and exclaimed, "Why I believe it's going to land!" The gap made by those recently pulled front teeth made him lisp just a little in his excitement.

"No, son, B17's don't land around here. You know it takes a lot of room for them to maneuver around in, "replied Daddy. Nevertheless, there was ill-concealed excitement in his voice too, for he had recently joined the Civil Air Patrol, had been doing a little flying himself, and the sight of that big bomber flying so low was really beautiful. As the plane disappeared into the west beyond the treetops, we all sighed a little, and went back into the house to finish lunch, and take up the humdrum existence of school, housecleaning, and the bank cashier's cage. The episode was over, but it had been nice while it lasted.

Little did we know! A couple of hours later, the phone rang. It was Daddy. "Say, Honey, that plane did land, after all . . . Emergency. They were out of gas, and came down in the country northwest of town about a mile and a half. Bye," and he hung up, without giving me a chance to caution him to get his heavy coat, for the wind had turned bitter cold. A few minutes later the boys rushed into the house, both talking at once almost incoherently, wanting their bicycles to "go and see the plane." I was left stranded at home, having neither car nor bicycle, and I saw nothing of the family for hours. The unaccustomed quiet of the house made the waiting seem endless. Then suddenly, everything began to happen. A great stamping and doorbell ringing on the front porch . . . many voices . . . I rushed to the door and when I opened it and looked out, it seemed to me that there were multitudes of smiling strangers, all dressed in helmets, and heavy fur-lined flying suits. Behind them I saw one tall civilian and a couple of youngsters – my family. "Come on in," boomed Daddy, and in they trooped. It was the crew of the B17 – "Floozy" as she was called. Introductions were made and then Daddy told me, "Do you think you could find places for six of these fellows to sleep here tonight? I took a hasty inventory of my resources, and said, "Of course."

Explanations followed. The plane was out of gas and by the time the high octane gas which was needed was trucked from Moline, the tires refilled, the batteries regenerated, and the whole plane ready, it would take several hours, so the crew were to stay all night with various townspeople and be all set for the take-off the next morning. "Floozy" had gotten off course when a cold front had suddenly moved in across their line of flight and with just fifteen minutes of gas left, the pilot had made a beautiful three-point emergency landing in a recently mowed soybean field.

Six of the boys slept at our house that night . . . twelve for breakfast the next morning at five o'clock! Daddy went back to the plane after all the arrangements were made, and spent the cold, bleak hours of the night as a Civil Air Patrol guard. We were all out there at six o'clock the next morning, after breakfast, to see it take off, but we were doomed to disappointment, for it was nearly two weeks before the plane got into the air again. Engine trouble developed and finally a ground crew and a new engine had to be sent out from the Base, before the final repairs could be made.

In the meantime, the news spread. People drove literally hundreds of miles to get their first close-up view of a big bomber. When it was evident that first morning that we wouldn't see it take off right away, I drove the children back to school. A few minutes later, a couple of the crew came to the house and said, "Do you suppose we could find something around here that we could use to keep the people back from the plane with?" The first guard fence was my clothes line stretched around bean poles which were hastily pulled up out of the garden.

It was midnight lunches for the fellows who were just finishing the "early watch," and five o'clock breakfasts for those on the "graveyard shift" . . . telephone calls to girl friends who waited back at the Base for dates which never appeared. My last supply of pre-war tooth brushes went into the "war effort" – just nine of them, so it happened. But what fun! And what wonderful guests those boys were! So appreciative, and so helpful. A timid knock on the kitchen door, after I'd shooed the last reluctant latecomer to bed. "What is it?" I asked, thinking maybe I should have put an extra cover on the bed in the north room. "I just didn't like to think of you doing those dishes all alone, so I thought maybe you'd let me help. The rest of the fellows are all asleep," he added apologetically, for that had been my instructions. He was the only

105

married man in the group – the co-pilot – and I've always thought that accounted for his offer. I was touched by their thoughtfulness . . . they were all wonderful, but the bombardier is the one who has a place all his own in our hearts. This is his story.

"This is Marc Pitts, the bombardier," Daddy said that first morning when I went with the others for my first, and what I thought would be my last, view of "Floozy." "He stayed to guard his bombsight last night while the others were in town. As a matter of fact, I was about to pull a gun on him about two o'clock last night. I saw someone running toward the plane in the dim light, and I challenged him a couple of times before I recognized him. He had gotten cold, and was just sprinting around for some exercise to warm up a little. I recognized him just in time." Daddy grinned rather sheepishly at the recollection.

Until officials came from a nearby military school to take the bombsight into protective custody, Marc stayed close to the plane, as his oath as a bombardier required him to do, but as soon as he was released from his responsibility he came into town to claim his toothbrush, freshen up, and become a member of our household. Later we learned that he had a little brother at home, just Tommy's age, but at the time, all we knew was that, left to his own devices, he went out into the back yard where Tommy was building a "Floozy Jr." out of orange crates. Those two boys, one just past twenty-one, the other only seven, talked over that conglomeration of string and rough boards, bent nails, and rusty wire, like a couple of test pilots discussing a new dive bomber. Tommy, ordinarily shy and reluctant to talk to strangers, opened his little heart and poured out all his dreams to his new friend, who listened and commented quietly in a "man to man" way. Tommy even drank his milk with relish when he found that Marc would really rather have milk than a cup of coffee, or even a coke.

Finally, word came that repairs on "Floozy" would be such an extensive job that a B17 would be flown from the Base in Kansas bringing a ground crew, and taking back the crew from "Floozy." My two boys and I were "elected" to take them to the airport about twenty-five miles away, where the incoming plane would land and take off. We arrived at the airport about seven o'clock in the evening, all set to see the take-off. More delays, the hours wore on. The men all dressed in their heavy flying suits ready for the trip and we civilians waited in a little smoke-filled eating shack.

Tommy, accustomed to early bedtime hours, grew restless and impatient. Marc took him on his lap, inconvenient as it was, trying to balance himself with his cumbersome gear on a high stool at the counter, and visited with Tommy about his own little brother and sister at home in Delaware. He showed him the ring his father had given him when he went into the Air Force, and told him how he hoped someday he could learn to be a pilot like his father had been in the other war. Finally, even that palled, and Tommy said with a sigh, "I'll be glad when I finally see that plane take off." Marc smiled understandingly, and then stiffened as a thought occurred to him.

"Why, Tommy, it has gotten so dark, and the plane is parked so far out on the field, you won't be able to see it take off after all." Tommy slumped in Marc's arms, in unspoken disappointment. "But, I tell you," Marc said, sensing intuitively the little boy's disappointment, "I'll be out in the Bombardier's bay, and I'll flip my lights to you to tell you good bye." A smile of eagerness came onto Tommy's tired little face. At last word came that everything was ready. Goodbye's were said, and we watched the men disappear into the darkness toward the roaring engines. But, nothing happened! The plane roared on, but nothing happened! Then out of the darkness we saw someone running toward us. "More delays," I thought in consternation. I saw Marc. Brushing past me, he went directly to Tommy, and putting his arm halfway around his shoulders he said breathlessly, "Tommy, I find that I've been assigned to a different place in the plane going back, so I won't be able to flip my lights to you after all, but I didn't want you to think I had broken my promise. Bye, Fellow," and with that he turned and disappeared into the darkness again.

We never saw Marc again, although he wrote to Tommy many times. His first letter, telling of the details of a practice flight was so interesting and Tommy was so thrilled that he took it to school, and the teacher let him read it aloud to all the children. The teacher wanted to give her pupils some practical training in letter writing, so she suggested that they each write a letter to Marc, as a Language assignment. She sent them all in a big envelope, with a note of explanation. Then Marc, with his infinite capacity for loving children, just "adopted" the whole grade. Individual letters came back from the airbase in Kansas to each one of the children. A basket of fruit from Florida when he was stationed there. One little third grade curly-haired girl collected paper napkins as a hobby. Marc sent paper napkins to her from all over the country.

But always there was Tommy, with extra confidences to him. Marc tried to get leave long enough to come back to Iowa and meet the teacher and the friends that he had come to know through letters, but he didn't quite make it. He was sent overseas. Tommy's last V-mail letter from him was dated June 13, 1943.

On June 15, Marc's plane was shot down over Germany. Nine parachutes were counted as they fluttered down. Marc and the co-pilot never got out. Marc couldn't break a promise, and Tommy has a private hero. Marc's father, back in Delaware, sends paper napkins to a little curly-headed girl in Iowa.

(Omitted from this story are other details, such as the children sending him a subscription to the *Reader's Digest* to show their love and appreciation to him, and then discovering that his father was an associate Editor of the magazine. His mother was a former newspaper woman, who wrote to me often, and appreciated what we had done for Marc.)

George J. Hill II
Captain
Medical Corps Reserve

Thomas D. Hill
Lt. Colonel (Ret.)
United States Air Force

Harris and Helen Thompson
Martha and Sally

United by Marriage

"Thy people
  shall be my people"

*Thomas D., Victoria, James, David, Sarah, George J.,
Kieko, Thomas D. Jr., Essie Mae, Gerald, Helena (Lana), Helene (Lanie)
'Fortieth Wedding Anniversary - 1970*

Lester, Harris, Jim High, Gerald
Helen Thompson, Helene Runkle, Essie Mae and Manly
Reunion 1972

"Runk"
1969

Harris, Jim, Tom, Jerry, George
Helen, Manly, Essie Mae, Helene and Lester
at 1974 Reunion

United by Marriage

If it is true that people are judged by the company they keep and "birds of a feather flock together" then it must follow that our family must be considered very special, because of the people with whom we are "united by marriage." Spouses are sometimes referred to as "my better half" and, if and when we say that (Heaven forbid), I think there may be "more truth than poetry" in it.

James, the oldest in our immediate family, married May Hoover, and the records of the early history of Lisbon, Iowa, are really the records of her family. Christian Hershey, who pulled away from his family's chocolate business in Pennsylvania and came to Iowa, bringing with him a group of about fifty people, founded a permanent colony in Linn County, Iowa. He built the first United Brethren Church west of the Mississippi River at his own expense, and was May's great-grandfather. Along with him were the Hoovers, Blessings, and others who intermarried and became her great aunts and uncles. Her family founded a town and thus made history. At present she is the only great-grandmother in our family, Edward, Jr., and William Bickford being James's and May's great-grandchildren, and also the first boys in their family line, after three generations of girls.

To single out one other person in that branch of the family, William Frederick May, Kathleen's husband, has been the recipient of many honors, the latest of which was The Family of Man Award, presented by the Council of Churches of the City of New York. He is Chairman and Chief Executive officer of the American Can Company and a member of the Johns-Manville Board of Directors. Previous recipients of this award include John F. Kennedy and John D. Rockefeller, III. That gives an idea about the level of the honor.

In Manly's family, his father-in-law, John Paul Simonton, was an outstanding person. When he retired after a lifetime career as an attorney in the United States government service, he was designated as the person who showed the sights of Washington, D.C., to distinguished visitors. He had the keys and the entre to buildings, offices, and rooms which were never open to the public. He had extensive knowledge about the history of them, and he was entrusted with responsibilities and privileges that few others have ever had.

He thought so much of Manly that because I was his sister, he gave me the VIP treatment when I went to Washington, D.C., in 1922, and I am sure he included some places in the tours that not even the highest officials and congressmen ever saw. For example, he took me down into the basement of the old Army-Navy Building (now offices) where the walls were about three feet thick, the windows small and barred, and the air close and stale. There he put into my hands a small box in which was a lock of Abraham Lincoln's hair, cut from his head as he lay dying in a bedroom in the house across the street from the Ford Theatre where he had been shot. There was also a small piece of bone from his skull, and a few other items. I was so overwhelmed by it all that I nearly fainted! I understand that those things and other memorabilia are now in a vault under the Lincoln Memorial, and well they should be. We also visited the room where Lincoln died, and Ford's Theatre long before its present restoration.

He took me into the room where President Harding met with his cabinet, and at Mr. Simonton's suggestion I sat in the President's chair. No one else was there, and no one questioned our presence. Forty years later, I asked Manly if my memory of those experiences was exaggeration or imagination, and he replied, "No, he had the keys to all those places, and I'm sure your recollections of those things are as they really happened." A personal guide to all the buildings, riding the streetcars from one stop to the next, day after day. He was nearing seventy then, but never seemed to get tired, always gallant, and handsome, the epitome of a "Southern gentleman."

Manly also said that because of research that Mr. Simonton did on the trial and execution of the people who were judged responsible for the assassination of Abraham Lincoln, the law was enacted which now prohibits a civilian from being tried in a military court. He was a devout Catholic and I think when he started his research he felt that there was some religious prejudice against them. He was the maternal grandfather of Manly's children.

Sister Rachel Edith's only son is named James Charles High, known as "Jim." His middle name, Charles, comes from his paternal grandfather, an intelligent, gentle, loving, soft-spoken man. Jim is the same kind of person, and only Mother Nature knows how much is the result of genes from his grandfather High. At any rate, he lives now on his grandfather's farm in Jones County, Iowa, north of Mechanicsville.

Gerald ("Jerry"/ "Toot"), my husband, is the ninth child of George J. Hill and Jessie Stockwell, both of whom were descendants of settlers who came from England in the early history of our country. The name Stockwell, through the efforts and work of Jessie's brother and his children and her sisters, has become well-known in the Orient and South America, as well as in many parts of the United States. Aunt Grace, a Methodist missionary, who never married, founded, supported, and taught in a school in Burma from the time she was a young woman until she fled from the Japanese troops in World War II. Gerald's cousin, Foster Stockwell, was a missionary College President in Buenos Aires, Argentina, for many years, and before his death was the Methodist Bishop of western South America.

However, if we had to choose just one of the Stockwells to include in this chapter, I am sure it would be Cousin Olin and his beautiful wife, Esther. Few people in my experience have the aura of goodness, love, spirituality, gentleness, tolerance, intelligence, and peace that they do. Suffering and grief have strengthened them, and thy have a special charisma that makes one want to be a better person just by being near them. His experiences as a prisoner of the Communists in China, the books that he wrote at that time, their attitude of love and forgiveness, give them a rating of "saints on earth."

Harris's son-in-law is Jim Montgomery, Sally's husband. No wonder four of their five children are red-haired, because ancestors on both sides of the family are "red heads." Jim's father is Verne Montgomery, who became interested in rocks and minerals because of his career with Johns-Manville (asbestos). He became known as one of the most outstanding Rockhounds in the Midwest. He has been President of the central division of the National Society of Earth Science Clubs, an outstanding mineral collector, and lecturer and promoter of the Koester archeological Indian excavation in southern Illinois. Jim's mother is Charlotte Bayne, whose father was Deputy Commissioner of Education in New York under Fiorella LaGuardia. He is also credited with establishing the first vocational school in New York City. Her brother was Bishop (Episcopal) Steven Bayne, one of the "great men" of the Church, whose service included a time spent in England when the "Red Dean" of Canterbury was making headlines.

Jim and Sally have been "one and only" since grade school days in Downers Grove, Illinois. The relationship survived through separation when Jim spent four years at Hamilton College in New York state, and Sally graduated from Iowa State University at Ames, Iowa. Jim now has a Doctor's degree in education from Loyola University and is the curriculum coordinator for Junior High schools in Arlington Heights, Illinois. More importantly, as far as Harris is concerned, is that Jim plays the kind of Bridge game that he likes . . . and that is not what is commonly called "conversational Bridge." Brains, both of them!

There are many other people who very deservedly could be mentioned to show how our family has been strengthened, enlivened, and enriched by those with whom we are "united by marriage." Mother's sister, Mattie, married Frank Runkle, who had great but unappreciated musical ability. His family history goes back to a castle-headquarters in Germany, which Lester and his wife Helene visited in 1971. Lester was so much a part of our family that the children were taught to call him "Uncle Lester." Manly's daughter Betty says that it was much more of a crushing blow to find out that he was not her real uncle than it was to learn that "there was no Santa Claus." Helene Runkle's ancestors in Germany include the world-famous Dr. Robert Koch, discoverer of tuberculosis bacilli, and contemporary of Dr. Louis Pasteur. He was the brother of Helene's grandfather, her great-uncle.

Does anyone doubt that our two sons are smart? Not if you know about the girls they married, the girls that they persuaded to join our family! Tom's wife, Keiko, who has a Master's degree from the University of Minnesota, is the daughter of Dr. Shigeru Nambara, who was the first post-war president of Tokyo University. He was so highly honored and respected in Japan that Tom reports that his father-in-law was the guest of the Emperor for lunch twice during one ten-day period when he was in Japan. When we were in Japan in 1970, Dr. Nambara gave us a lacquer bowl which had been given to him by the Emperor in appreciation for his help in handing out the awards in the annual poetry contest, sponsored by the Emperor.

George's wife, Helene ("Lanie") Zimmermann, is a most unusual person. "Let me count the ways." Her maternal grandfather was the head of a Department in the University of Pennsylvania Medical School; her father' father, an inventor who developed a machine in Philadelphia that revolutionized the weaving of wool carpets in this country. Lanie graduated from Smith College and has a Ph.D. degree in Biophysics. She is an author, a recipient of many honors, a teacher, lecturer, researcher, and she is truly George's partner in his research and writing. However, with all that, she surely hasn't neglected her "homework," because she is the mother of four children, a gourmet cook, an open-hearted and gracious hostess to the great and not-so-great, a collector and connoisseur of antiques, and does the family book-keeping. She helps George with his writing and research at home as well as at the office. Both she and Keiko make us very happy, especially because they make us feel so special, so welcome when we visit, and that we did a pretty good job in "training" their husbands to be good husbands and fathers.

Harris – Last but Not Least

The picture of our family would not be complete without telling about Harris. He was born March 14, 1907. He was the little "surprise" for my folks. Manly told me in one of his last letters that he thought that Harris inherited the best characteristics of both of our parents, and I am sure the rest of us agree. He started to school when he was less than four and a half years old, and sailed right through all twelve grades, ending at the top of his class in scholarship. He has musical ability – a voice range and an ear for harmony that got him a place in the Cornell Glee Club, and a lifetime of informal singing fun. He went two years to Cornell, and graduated from the University of Iowa with a chemistry major, and Sigma Xi honors. He spent almost all of his professional career with Nalco in Chicago, including two years in Europe, where he was expanding company offices and business.

After he returned from Europe in 1964 until his retirement in 1970, he was involved in various phases of the Nalco Metal Division in Indiana, as Director of Service and Assistant Vice President in the Research Department. He "grew up" with the company. And to think it all started when he went to a Methodist Epworth League Convention in Clinton, Iowa, when he was seventeen years old. He met a business man with influence and faith in his ability. He understands people and how to get along with others. He's a past master of hospitality, story-telling, diplomacy, and peace. Over the years he has had his physical problems – ulcers, tensions, surgery, and low vitality – probably the result of work and worry during the early years with the company. But thanks to his wife, Helen, and his own determination, he seems to be leveling off in good health.

I am thankful we have a good relationship now. I was mean and hateful to him when he was little. The green-eyed monster surely bit me hard when he was born!

During the nearly four years of my life up to that time, I had been the spoiled little darling of the household, and of Mattie's home, too, as Lester's playmate and companion. His "big sister." Then a new baby spoiled it all, "Two's company, three's a crowd." It was my fault, but we, Lester and I, really gave him a bad time. "Child Psychology" and "Sibling Rivalry" – modern terms. In those days "Spare the rod and spoil the child" was the rule, and Papa's razor strop or a switch hastily broken from the apple tree was supposed to keep me from being spoiled. The damage was already done, however, and punishment only made me more stubborn and resentful, and didn't improve Harris's position a bit.

Eventually, I am glad to say that I have come to appreciate him, and I hope and trust that he has forgiven me. The family cherishes his wife, Helen McKune Thompson, and gives her credit for getting them through some difficult early years to the health and comfort they enjoy now. They were married August 25,1929. Their branch of the family tree includes two daughters and eight grandchildren who are "chips off the old blocks" and a credit to us all. Helen and I have a lot of sisterly affection, and we are also sisters in P.E.O. as well as being sisters-in-law.

When the Time Comes That We Must Part

A long time ago, someone said that the only sure things in life are death and taxes. I don't want to inject too much sadness into this, but I don't feel that this writing would be complete without including some of my thoughts about this "sure thing": Death. For those of us who are still alive, the death of a loved one is an irreparable separation. It is terrible, hard to realize, to accept, and to go on living. In the course of my lifetime I have been exposed to thousands of sermons, many of which dealt with the life after death, and immortality, which is the philosophy and teaching of the New Testament. "God so loved the world that he gave his only begotten Son that whosoever believeth in Him shall not perish, but have everlasting life." The interpretation was each speaker's own. Some of the qualifications for getting into heaven which they set up were quite arbitrary, it seems to me, and open to question in my mind.

My family has tended to be quite independent of each other and everyone else in their religious beliefs and interpretations about life as it should be lived now, and what it will be in the hereafter. They have run the gamut from Grandfather Rundall's fiery Methodist fundamentalism to Manly's intellectual analysis. Quakers, Catholics, Congregationalists, Existentialists and Episcopalians, you'll find them all. All of them, no matter what their church or religious affiliation, succeeded in leading good, upright lives. And some were very confident that they knew what rewards and pleasures they would come into after they died. As for me, I am not greatly concerned about all that, although I do not think that all is ended when earthy life is done. I do not know the answers, and I am not worrying about them. However, wherever, and whatever

Heaven is, I would like to be reunited with my loved ones, and wherever they are, that's where I hope I will be.

On one of the Rundall grave monuments in the Norwich Cemetery this verse is carved:

"Remember this as you pass by
As you are now, so once was I.
As I am now, so you will be
Prepare for death and follow me.

When Clara Thompson (Manly's wife) read this, she said, "To follow you, I'd be content, if I just knew which way you went." Me too!

I like Toppy Tull's poem which was printed in a Methodist Church bulletin, April 8, 1928, and which I have saved for nearly fifty years. Toppy was a beloved English teacher at Cornell College for many years.

Afraid

Afraid to live? Nay, I would grow,
Triumph, conquer, fall, forego;
Not one whit of pain or bliss
In this Earth-life would I miss.
Life is marvelously good,
Full of Love and Brotherhood.

Afraid to die? Nay, Death to me
Would wondrous fine adventure be.
Beyond the narrow bonds of Sense
I would gain Experience.
What care I for mould'ring sod,
Death would bring me nearer <u>God</u>.

For the record, my father died in the University of Iowa Hospital at the age of seventy-two, of complications following a prostatectomy. The autopsy showed kidney infection and a blood clot. This is the last letter Dad ever wrote, and it shows two of the chief characteristics of his personality – his love for the family and his ability to "turn a phrase," to wisecrack:

"July 19 [1934]   [Iowa City, University Hospital]

I was operated on Tuesday afternoon. Since that time Ive been awful sick. Cant keep anything in my stomach. Today I am better. Doctor said I am all right. <u>Doc may Scrape out a horse and he may come through but the average man here feels the Effects</u>. [underlining added] Say to Mattie her and I are on our back. I think of her so much. But with me its all right if I go out this trip or any time. Love Pop"

Mattie was under heavy sedation at this time and died less than a week later. Dad recovered from the operation he mentioned, came home for a few weeks, and then had to go back to the hospital in Iowa City where he died September 12, 1934.

Mother died of a stroke at the age of eight-four years and nine months. She was living with Rachie at the time, and it happened early in the morning, December 28, 1949. Rachie was awakened by the cat clawing at her bedroom door. Kitty missed the usual morning attention and breakfast which Mother always gave here. Mother was unconscious and died a few minutes after Rachie found her.

Brother James, age 84, died of a stroke. Manly, 83, died from the after-effects of surgery for stomach cancer, and finally great weakness and a fall. When she was 68, Rachie had an inoperable brain tumor, and lived in a coma about a month after surgery.

My mother always thought that she was especially loved by her Heavenly Father because He never took any of her children away from her. She never had to experience the death of one of her children. She had five children, five in-laws, and ten grandchildren, and she loved them all, although she never really felt comfortable in the boys' homes. It was her own fault, I think, and not because she was not loved and welcome. She was shy, reticent, and did not communicate well. When the boys married they were "on their own" and she never made any effort to encourage them to feel that they were still part of the "nest."

In 1949, for the first time, we went to Mechanicsville to spend Christmas on the farm with Rachie, Jim, and Mother, who made her home with them. We had a very happy time, and when we started for home on December 26, I said to Mother, "We'll see you in April. You'll be 85 years old on your next birthday, and we'll come to help you celebrate." She just smiled and didn't make any reply. Two days later, Rachie phoned Gerald at the bank in Sac City, and he came home and told me that Mother had died that morning.

The funeral was in the Methodist Church in Lisbon, where she had been a member longer than anyone else at that time. My friend, Wilma Briggs, who had been my accompanist innumerable times, played the organ and in her special way brought comfort with her own arrangement of Mother's favorite hymns, modulating from one to another, without any music in front of her. Out of Mother's meager resources she left a U.S. Saving Bond to the church with which new collection plates were bought. She had thought for some time that her work on earth was done, and she couldn't understand why God didn't take her Home. Rachie reminded her of Jesus's saying, "I go to prepare a place for you, that where I am, there ye may be also." "So," said Rachie, "Evidently your place is not ready for you." Mother seemed satisfied with this explanation, and didn't question the Lord's plan for her life any more. Her place must be one of the "many mansions" in the Father's House, if they are built in ratio to Faith and the way life is lived on this planet.

Her wish to die at home, not in a hospital, came true. I hope I may be as fortunate as she and other members of the family have been, in not having a long final illness, which is so hard on everyone, the living and the dying.

From the time we left Lisbon and moved to Perry, I wrote to Mother every week, and after she went to live with Rachie, I wrote each of them each week. After Mother's death I continued to write my weekly letters to Rachie and she eagerly looked forward to them. This went on more than ten years. In 1961, however, I felt that we were due for a change. I was very busy with teaching and other activities, and I felt that I could not be as involved with her life and problems (she had quite a few) as I had been, so I began writing to her on a more indefinite schedule and casual basis. I am sorry now, for it was puzzling to her and hard to accept, and we did not know how little time she had left of her life. She died in September of that year, 1961, and I didn't even see her during the summer because we did not make our usual trip to Iowa. I still miss her very much even after fifteen years.

My brother, James, did lots of fine things for me when I was growing up, and we shared the same birthday. However, at the time of his death he had been away from home for a long time. It seems that his entire heart's love was given to his immediate family, his wife May and their two daughters and their families. I am glad that they appreciate and realize his complete and undiluted devotion to them. The last time I saw Jim was at Mother's funeral in 1942, twenty-seven years ago. We had very much "grown apart," but thanks to Harris's encouragement we did establish a good relationship in the last three or four years of his life, for which I am very glad. I have the highest regard for May and for their outstanding family. Kathleen was flower girl at our wedding. Since James's death, the fine letters I have had from May have told me more about the family than I have known for many years.

The reason I "fell apart" when Manly died was due, I think, to the fact that I had not prepared myself for the inevitable, in spite of all the information from Harris and his family about his deteriorating health. He died before he got my last letter, so it seemed to me that he passed away in the middle of a conversation about old times in Lisbon. To me, his death was sudden, and it has been very hard for me to become accustomed to the fact that our warm, compatible relationship is over.

Runk's death leaves a void that is incomparable. A lifetime of friendship with never a quarrel or angry word! When he and Helene left Arizona to go to California to their new home on November 11, 1975, it never occurred to us that he had so little time left of his earthly life. We had such a good time on his birthday, the day before, a picnic out at Thunderbird Park, with all his favorite foods. We visited about old times in Lisbon, and I took along and read aloud several of the humorous poems and articles that I had written, which he had never heard. I had a feeling, a premonition, if you please, that things would be different from then on, but little did I dream how different. He died December 30, 1976, of acute leukemia. His life, his love, his courage, his unselfishness, his generosity, and his philosophy of life, are all a comfort to those of us who are left . . . bereaved.

He Is Not Dead

I can not say, and I will not say
That he is dead, he is just away.
With a cheery smile, and a wave of his hand,
He has wandered into an unknown land
And left us dreaming how very fair
It must be since he lingers there.
– James Whitcomb Riley

This tribute written by a person who never knew Runk personally expresses the feelings of all of us who did know him. We, too, say "Amen."

"Recently, I had the opportunity, at the request of a friend, to serve as an usher at the memorial service of a man I did not know. However, in retrospect, I can see that the kind of man he <u>was</u> and the style of life he <u>led</u> continues to make a lasting impression even after his passing. And it was a <u>good</u> and <u>loving</u> impression. The service was brief but elegant. Members of his family participated by preparing artwork for the printed program of his memorial and by recording music for the service. A longtime friend in camping recounted precious memories of his and the families' lives around this man. Throughout, there was no sense of unmitigated grief – only the natural sorrow of losing someone very dear and assurance that he had lived a fruitful, rewarding, <u>Christian</u> life. Quite often there are valuable lessons to be learned from the experiences of others. I learned several lessons that Saturday afternoon. One was that it was obvious both from the service, which had been outlined ahead of time by the deceased, and from personal testimony, that this was a thoughtful man, thoughtful enough to plan for the eventual, so that part of the burden was already taken away from the bereaved. Another was that love freely given not only comes back, but flows outward to others like ripples on a pond. And still another was that there is no substitute for honest Christian living that has no need to apologize in any way for its actions. His friend concluded by saying 'God bless his memory.' To that I would add 'Thank you God for his life' and 'Amen.'"   – Joe Grady

The first break in our immediate family circle came when Keiko died in Tokyo on July 21, 1977. When we saw her in the latter part of May we were aware of the fact that she had gone "down hill" since we said goodbye to her a year ago. Perhaps we had become too accustomed to her constant suffering and were too aware of her determination to live, to realize that it would all be over so soon. Her death was a great, sad shock to us. It is always so very hard to part with loved ones, but we give thanks for the example of her life, and that she was spared to be a part of the family group until Vicki and Tommy reached a responsible maturity. We could not ask that she have to go on living in pain and hopelessness for relief. The belief that her spirit lives on is in our comfort. Jerry, father-in-law, wrote his personal tribute o Keiko, here reproduced in part:

A Tribute to
Keiko Nambara Hill

Born November 12, 1928   Died July 21, 1977

Devoted wife, loving mother, a life-long performer of the arts, Keiko Nambara Hill went to her Christian reward on July 21, 1977.

She had returned to her native land and birthplace where she died on the second evening in Tokyo at the home of her eldest sister. Her son, Thomas David, Jr., had accompanied her on this final visit to her Japanese family and friends.

Her husband, Lt. Col. Thomas D. Hill (ret.), starting a new career as a Reliability Engineer for Xerox Corp. at Rochester, N.Y., and daughter, Victoria Grace, completing summer school classes at Oxon Hill, Md., rushed to the side of Tommy and members of the Nambara family to plan and participate in the final traditional rites of Keiko's native land.

Reared by one of the early Christians of Japan, and noted educator, Dr. Shigeru Nambara, it was natural that the family looked for solace in those sorrowful days to her Episcopal Church for comfort. Funeral services were in Mejiro Episcopal Church followed by other traditional Japanese ceremonies. The Rev. Timothy S. Ogasawara conducted the Japanese Episcopal burial service. A host of classmates, friends and relatives attended the various ceremonies. According to Japanese custom, many flowers decorated the church, and numerous memorial gifts were proffered. In recognition of her great love for father and mother, part of her ashes will be interred beside their remains.

Keiko's life-long interest in the musical art was one of her profound pleasures. As a student she often served as church organist. Following her marriage, she continued her study of piano, and became a member of the American Association of Piano Teachers. Wherever she lived she was sought out as a teacher of the pianoforte.

One of her great delights was to practice and play her favorite classics on the grand piano she acquired in recent years. She constantly sacrificed to further the musical training of both Vicki and Tommy. Her interest in the arts was not confined to music. She had a natural sense of artistic arrangements and color combinations. This talent became known as she produced beautiful paintings of western desert scenes while living at Edwards Air Force Base in California.

Although a lover of peace and a practitioner of the arts, she served with distinction as the wife of a career Air Force officer. Shortly before her death she received the commendation of the United States Air Force for her devotion and assistance to her husband, Lt. Col. Thomas D. Hill, when he retired May 31, 1977, after 20 years of service to his country.

Keiko graduated from Tokyo's Women's Christian College. She was offered a scholarship to St. Olaf College, Northfield, Minn., where she received her BA degree in 1954. She received her MA at the University of Minnesota in 1956. She was then called home due to the serious heart attack suffered by her father. Following his recovery, she taught Industrial Relations at St. Paul's Episcopal University in Tokyo. The chance meeting of Keiko and Tom in Tokyo in September 1959 was a mater of love at "first sight." Tom barely returned to the States in time to report on October 1st for his Minot assignment.

In the absence of any of her family, Essie Mae and I provided the normal assistance in preparation for a wedding ceremony. It was held on December 25, 1959, the 29th anniversary of our wedding. The ceremony was performed by the rector of St. Andrew's Episcopal Church in Minot. I had the distinct honor of "giving away" the bride in the name of Dr. and Mrs. Nambara.

In addition to her husband, daughter and son, Keiko is survived by three sisters and two brothers in Tokyo. Other relatives, and a host of friends will live with the memory of a beautiful soul. Memorial services were held at St. John's Episcopal Church, Oxon Hill, Md., at 2:00 p.m., Sunday September 4, 1977, and her ashes were interred in the historic St. John's Cemetery.

The Thompson Genealogy

Joseph Scott Thompson   b. 1800   d. 1866   m. Ruth Archibald   b. 1806   d. 1866
      Buried, Union Cemetery, Brockton, Massachusetts
   Children (12, surname Thompson):
       1. Susan   b. 1826   m. William Muir
           Children (4, surname Muir): John, Franklin, Josephine, Hannah
       2. Hannah   b. 1827   m. Frank Graham
           Child (1, surname Graham):   Carrie m. George Ross
               Children (4, surname Ross): Graham, James, Allan,
               Marion m. McMahon. Children (2, surname McMahon):
                   Sheldon, Carol
       3. James   b. 1830   m. Jane Grant
           Children (7): Daniel
                  Harriett
                  Angie
                  Emily
                  William b. 1862 d. 1934 m. Sadie Rundall b. 1865 d. 1949
                     Children (5):
                        James
                        Manly
                        Rachel Edith
                        Essie Mae
                        Harris
                Frank
                Fred
       4. William b. 1832
Twins}   5. Sarah Thompson Geddis   b. 1835 (Laura Geddis Sheldon)
Twins}   6. Jane Thompson Broderick   b. 1835   d. 1916   m. William Broderick
           Children (7, surname Broderick):
              Laura Broderick Emery
              Everett Broderick
              Florence Broderick   m. Bernard Winslow
                 Children (3, surname Winslow):
                     Everett Winslow Chase, Jr.
                     Mildred Chase Bartlett
                     Phyliss
              Chandler Broderick   b. 1864   d. 1896
              Frank P. Broderick   b. 1866   d. 1883
              Alice G. Broderick   b. 1875   d. 1876
              Julia A. Broderick   b. 1876   d. 1876
                  (All Brodericks buried in Union Cemetery, Brockton, Mass.)
      7. Olive   b. 1836   m. William Bowen
          Children (4, surname Bowen): Roy, William

Susie m. James Strachan
Children (2, surname Strachan):
Earle (Children: Earl, Kenneth)
Ralph
Edward   m. Annie
Children (2, surname Bowen): Edna, Edward
8. Harriet   b. 1841   m. Frank Tremaine
Children (6, surname Tremaine): Grace m. George Fletcher; Edward, Lulie, Frances, Fred, Charles
9. Edward   b. 1843 (Buried in Blodgett Cemetery near Central City, Iowa)
Children (3): Benjamin, Joseph, Edna
10. Franklin Thompson   b. 1846
11. Charles Prescott Thompson   b. May 28, 1852   d. July 9, 1941
m. Cassie Calvin Rollins Ames   b. Aug. 27, 1863   d. Dec. 27, 1947
Children (6, surname Thompson):
Myrtle Olive   b. 1883   d. 1970
Howard Rollins   b. 1884   d. 1961
Edward Elmer   b. 1884   d. 1961
Joseph Archibald   b. 1893   d. 1919
Ruth Estelle   b. 1899   d. 1937
Priscilla Emma   b. 1903
12. Emma Frances Thompson   b. 1855   m. Joseph B. Steele   1883
Child (surname Steele):
Gladys Ruth   b. 1886   m. Albert F. Bolster
Child (surname Bolster):
Joseph Albert b. 1922   m. Audrey Mangrum
2 sons

The Family Record

William Henry Thompson married Sadie (Sarah) D. Rundall, September 3, 1889, in Central City, Iowa. Statistics: Five children, ten grandchildren, twenty-three great-grandchildren, and three great-great-grandchildren.

Their children:

    I. James Everett Thompson. b. June 29, 1890; d. November 14, 1974. Married May Hoover, June 15, 1916. [b. December 5, 1888; d. January 13, 1986]

    Their family:

        A. Harriet Elaine Thompson. b. August 26, 1918. [d. April 24, 2010]

        Married the Rev. Albert C. Ronander, October 10, 1944 [d. March 16, 2007]

        B. Kathleen Hoover Thompson. b. May 25, 1926.

        Married William Frederick May, June 14, 1947. [d. September 18, 2011]

            1. Katherine Hartwick May. b. August 22, 1948.

            Married Edward Watson Bickford, December 12, 1970.

                a. Edward Watson Bickford, Jr. b. October 30, 1972.

                b. William Thompson Bickford. b. February 27, 1975.

            2. Elizabeth Shaw May. b. July 15, 1951.

            Married Ralph Peter Alexander Jenssen, May 10, 1975.

    II. Manly Grant Thompson. b. September 18, 1892. Married Marie Simonton on September 19, 1914. [She d. April 14, 1952. He m. (2) Clara Louise Roth, Dec. 22, 1954; b. Aug. 19, 1908; d. abt Mar 21, 1964] He d. October 1975. Their children:

        A. William Manly Thompson. b. July 13, 1915. [d. aft 1976]

        Married Mary Meade, June 13, 1952. Their children:

            1. Donald William Thompson. b. December 3, 1951.

            Adopted April 25, 1956.

            2. Katherine Marie Thompson. b. November 29, 1954.

            Adopted November 1, 1957.

                a. Jason. b. January 12, 1974.

        B. John Paul Thompson. b. June 20, 1920. [d. November 14, 2002]

        Married Virginia White, May 22, 1943.

            [They divorced. She d. December 26, 2011]

            1. Margaret Ann (Peg). b. June 8, 1945.

            2. William Stephen. b. September 15, 1947.

            3. Robert Michael. b. April 25, 1950.

            Married Kathleen Young, May 10, 1975.

            4. Ellen. b. April 21, 1957. [m. Doug Audley; children: Eve, Collin]

        C. Elizabeth Ann (Betty). b. December 6, 1924. [d. March 4, 2001]

        Married Roy Haglund, August 23, 1946. Children (surname Haglund):

            1. Thomas Ray. b. September 14, 1947.

            2. Richard Manly. b. March 24, 1950.

            3. Jean Alice. b. July 2, 1953.

    III. Rachel Edith Thompson. b. November 13, 1894. d. October 2, 1961.

    Married Julius High on December 30, 1914. Divorced.

        A. James Charles High. b. November 6, 1917. [d. September 30, 2001]

        [m. Elizabeth Nadine Jack, January 24, 1983; she d. abt. Feb. 27, 2003]

120

IV. Essie Mae Thompson. b. June 29, 1903. [d. March 15, 1994]
   Married Gerald L. Hill on December 25, 1930. [b. Sep. 18, 1905; d. June 14, 1979]
   Their children:
   A. George James Hill, II. b. October 7, 1932.
        Married Helene Zimmermann Grover, July 14, 1960 [b. April 10, 1929]
        1. James [Grover] Hill. b. January 23, 1954 (adopted) [m. Uma Narayan, 18
           Oct. 2016].
        2. David Hedgcock [Grover] Hill. b. Aug. 29, 1955 (adopted) [d. Jan. 4, 2004;
           m. Sheri Wilson, Apr. 18, 1981; d. Feb. 11, 2003; child: Heather Dawn
           Hill, b. Oct. 4, 1982; m. Jason Haught (divorced); their children: Marcina,
           b. Dec. 27, 2005; Landon, b. Aug. 26, 2007; Christian, b. Jan. 5, 2009]
        3. Sarah Hill. b. January 5, 1962. [m. Megan Reynolds, Oct. 31, 2015;
           children, with anonymous sperm donor: Georgia Clare Hill, b. Sep. 19,
           2004 (by Sarah); Rosalie Mairead Hill, b. Feb. 14, 2008 (by Megan)]
        4. Helena Rundall Hill. b. May 1, 1964.
   B. Thomas David Hill. b. May 3, 1935. [d. July 3, 2003]
        Married Keiko Nambara, December 25, 1959. d. July 21, 1977.
        [m. Suzanne Margaret Eppley, M.D., November 29, 1986; b. Oct. 7, 1947]
        1. Victoria Grace Hill. b. September 6, 1960 [m. Mark Norfleet, Sep. 17, 1983]
        2. Thomas David Hill, Jr. b. September 18, 1962. [son with Julia Sheehy:
           Conor Patrick Desmond Sheehy, b. Aug. 29, 1993]
V. William Harris Thompson. b. March 14, 1907. [d. September 23, 1984]
   Married Helen Eliza McKune on August 25, 1929. [b. Oct. 4, 1904; d. Jan. 24, 1991]
   Their children:
   A. Martha Jane Thompson. b. July 18, 1930. Married Charles Rothery, March
      25, 1953. Divorced. Children: 1. Sarah Ann. b. November 22, 1953;
      2. Robert Winfield. b. March 29, 1955; 3. Norah Jane. b. June 5, 1958.
   B. Sarah Ann (Sally). b. May 20, 1933. Married Hugh James Montgomery,
      July 16, 1955. Children: 1. Janet Elizabeth. b. August 1, 1957; 2. Judith
      Ellen. b. May 22, 1959; 3. Joan Eileen. b. December 30, 1961; 4. Jill. b.
      September 15, 1969; 5. Peter. b. June 24, 1972.

Wedding Picture
Essie Mae Thompson and Gerald L. Hill
December 25, 1930

Left to right:
Lester Runkle,
Helene Runkle (bridesmaid),
Essie Mae and Gerald,
Judd Dean (best man),
Harris Thompson
Kathleen Thompson (flower girl)

A Last Word

"This is my story, this is my song," and I hope that this record of what I know about our family, and some of the details of what has been happening during my lifetime, will answer a few of the questions which may arise among future generations as to "Who Am I." It has been a "labor of love." I wish that someone had done this generations before me, but my hope is that someone will carry it on.

Reference Material and Sources of Information

Grace Mildred Ridings High, *Genealogy of the Manly Family*
Original letters written by W. H. Thompson and Silas Rundall
Copies of the obituaries of
    Silas Rundall
    William H. Thompson
    Sadie D. Rundall Thompson
Memorial Services and Eulogies for
    James E. Thompson
    Manly Grant Thompson
    Robert Lester Runkle
Letters written during World War II
The re-dedication of the Lisbon School, 1939
Copy of Al Floyd's speech at the dedication
Lisbon High School Alumni Directory, 1939
The Centennial issue of the *Mount Vernon Hawkeye*
    with the history and pictures of Lisbon
"A Centennial History of Mount Vernon, Iowa"
"The Lisbon Centennial Booklet"
George Sailor, "The Public Schools of Lisbon," 1939
Official Book of the Fair – A Century of Progress
"The History of Lisbon Sauerkraut Day"
Outstanding events at Cornell College, 1922-1926
E. M. T. H., Writings in prose and verse
Programs given by E. M. H.
Correspondence between Manly Thompson and E. M. H.
E. M. H., "Scrapbook of Participation"
Sears Roebuck Catalogue (1902)

Prairie Daughter's Sons

Tom

Tom and George

George

Lisbon, Iowa – 2012

Main Street

Mount Vernon, Iowa – 2012

Cornell College

Flapper
Fun
Other Poems
and Stories

by
Essie Mae
Thompson Hill

To George
with my appreciation for his inspiration, ideas, loyalty, and TLC,
without which this book never would
have been written

Introduction to the 2nd Edition of Flapper Fun
George J. Hill, M.D., Editor

The twentieth century has been a period of astounding changes in this world, and our Prairie Daughter has been both a witness and a participant in these events.

Born on the deep, black soil of Iowa, from a heritage of farmers, teachers and early American pioneers, she has seen her country pass through the turmoil of two world wars, and their aftermath, with changes in her own life that were beyond imagination at the time of her birth.

As a lively, beautiful young woman – the "Flapper" of this book's title – she has enjoyed the thrill of entry into work that had previously been impossible for women to consider. As a geologist and navigator, she competed with men and was more than their equal. As a singer and lecturer, she was respected and admired, moving her audiences to tears, always with perfect composure. A strong-willed but sensitive teacher for her own children and countless others – including those we now call "Special," because they are – she has enriched many lives. For the past decade, she has drawn on memories of events that touched us, with her visions of past and future.

Her poems and narratives are expressions of love and hope for us all.

Essie Mae Thompson – 1926

128

Prairie Daughter

A poet once told me
that each person has within himself
a well of water,
rich in the sights and sounds,
the mem'ries, emotions, and dreams of a lifetime.

This Prairie Daughter
now dips into her own well
of stored-up water,
and shares some of it
With you.

The Roaring Twenties

Favorite classes, unfavorite ones too,
Rumble-seat cars, and a sweet rendezvous
Chaperones watching each move that we make,
Learning hard lessons without a mistake.
Short flapper dresses, the Senior Class dance,
A sneaked cigarette – Oh, we took a big chance!
Dates and corsages, the friends that I met . . .
A big patchwork quilt of the times I can't forget.

– Essie Mae Thompson

The Roaring 20's

The years from 1920 to 1930 were indeed a very significant period in American history – a time of transition – and I feel fortunate to be able to share my memories of those times.

We had four Presidents during those years, one Democrat and three Republicans. Woodrow Wilson in frail mental and physical health occupied the White House only as far in 1920 as March 4, when he was succeeded by Warren C. Harding. His administration was marked by the Teapot Dome scandals, and rumors of a mistress (Ann Britton slipping in and out of the White House, and her illegitimate child), poker parties, hard liquor. President Harding died under mysterious circumstances while he was returning from a trip to Alaska in the summer of 1923.

I was working as a live-in baby sitter in Mount Vernon that summer, and I remember hearing the mournful wail of the whistle of the train bearing his body as it slowly passed through the town on the Chicago and Northwestern Railroad. Everyone who could be was at the depot that afternoon to watch it. Calvin Coolidge's cool, calm administration was a 180° turn from Harding's and it lasted until March 4, 1929, when he was succeeded by Herbert Hoover.

The composite emotions of the country had been sobered and suppressed by the events of the late 1800's – the first World War and the failure of the adoption of the League of Nations. With the advent of the 1920's, everything seemed to explode in wild excess, building up to such a peak that only a few months after Hoover's administration began came the stock market crash and the Great Depression, followed by FDR with all the changes and innovations which altered the course of American history forever.

What about life in Mount Vernon, Iowa, at the good, pious Methodist college of Cornell? Among sophisticated people – the "jet-set" of the 20's – their idol was F. Scott Fitzgerald, popular author of *The Great Gatsby*. He knew and wrote about the world of speak-easies, bootleg booze, and what is now known as "open marriages." The young people of the middle class hinterland were fascinated by it all.

However, in Professor Tull's English class when I was a freshman, it was not F. Scott Fitzgerald who was the recommended author, but Willa Cather, a beautiful writer who wrote about the Czech people in rural Nebraska (*My Antonia* and other novels), and eventually she authored *Death Comes to the Archbishop*, set in New Mexico.

My junior and senior years at Cornell were the happiest times of my life. I lived with the Runkles, so I didn't have to follow dormitory regulations, but of course, I missed out on all the camaraderie and fun that the girls in the dorms had. But what I didn't know about, I didn't miss.

Social life at Cornell was based on Literary Societies, five for men and five for women. Members were invited to join, after some mild rushing, and the societies varied in prestige. Initiations were very serious, formal occasions, and in some cases very close, lasting friendships developed. It was not until many, many years later that I found out that there were secret fraternities and sororities that crossed over Literary Society lines. In fact, Jerry belonged to the oldest fraternity of all of them – Delta Phi Rho, known simply as The Delts. As time passed, Literary Societies passed out of existence, and local fraternities and sororities are an important part of the contemporary social mores at Cornell.

I guess I could have been called "teachers' pet" – plural. As Assistant in the Geology Department, I had special privileges. Dr. Norton, the revered head of the department, used to invite me to his home to listen to his remarkable collection of classical records . . . because I was also very much into music. For John L. Conrad, my voice teacher and Director of the Girls Glee Club, I was the club soloist and sang on many trips through Illinois and Iowa, as well as at local concerts. Professor Syndey Chandler, Sociology teacher, excused me from his class exam during my senior year and then asked me to monitor the exam for the rest of the class. Unorthodox, but true. Gee Whiz!!

Next door to the Runkle house lived Ralph Kharas, a member of the faculty who was the boyfriend of my best girlfriend, Minnie Mohn. I never betrayed my friendship for Min, but Ralph and I developed a platonic friendship that lasted for more than forty years until his death.

The Roaring Twenties' girl is personified by the way we dressed, the way we acted, the songs we sang, and how we danced.

"Short flapper dresses." After the floor-sweeping and just-above-the-ankle dresses of all the previous years from colonial times to the end of the 1800's, the dresses of the 1920's seemed very short indeed. Actually, my dresses covered my knees – hardly a mini skirt of 1988! I made almost all of my own clothes, and the style was very simple . . . fortunately, because I didn't use or need a pattern. I could make a dress in less than a day. The front and back were the same, made from a single piece of cloth folded in two with the fold at the shoulders. A scoop neck, a little lower in the front, big enough to put my head through. The sides were curved in a little, to make cap sleeves, then straight down to the bottom. Sometimes I put a ruffle around the bottom. The sash-belt was tied around the hips, not at the waist. A long string of beads completed the outfit.

When Vicki was married in 1983, her wedding gown was a beautiful Laura Ashley original design in the style of the 1920's with elbow length sleeves, above-the-ankle length and dropped waist line. My own wedding dress in 1930 which I made myself was long-sleeved and floor length . . . the styles of the 1920's were over.

There were two all-college formal affairs when I was a student at Cornell – the faculty reception in the fall and the Sweetheart Ball in the spring. The dancing was the Virginia Reel. Dancing, of course, was forbidden by the Methodist church along with such evils as playing cards and anything stronger to drink than grape juice and lemonade.

Times change, however. At Gerald's 30th class reunion in 1957, he told his classmates that the proudest time in his college career was when "he broke the dance barrier" – his words – in his senior year. He masterminded the whole student revolt against dancing. It was nearing the end of the year, the orchestra was hired, President Updegraff had been notified, and when Gerald gave the signal, the crowd swarmed out onto the dance floor . . . and Cornell had moved into the modern age. That was 1927. Students were supposed to have written parental permission, but Gerald's mother absolutely refused to give her consent. Dancing was such a sin to her. It almost broke her heart when he went right ahead without her permission.

A typical flapper of the 1920's danced the Charleston, a very vigorous dance and a lot of fun. It was performed in a group or singly . . . hands crossed on thighs, and feet turned out. Then the dancer could move sideways by turning feet in and out and crossing and uncrossing the hands. Our exercise teacher told me that she uses that kind of movement in one of our "Seniorize" exercises. No wonder I'm so healthy!

A typical flapper of the 1920's danced not only the Charleston and the Shimmy, but also the old-time waltz. Irene Castle with her bobbed hair, beautifully marcel-waved, and her handsome husband Vernon were very much admired, and a favorite song was "When We Are Dancing Cheek to Cheek." The Fox Trot and the Two-Step were vigorous, fast dances, arms pumping up and down and a lot of foot activity.

The multi-colored, emotional pendulum of the era swung wildly. On one side were the pleasure-seekers in dance halls. On the other were the tents of convert-seeking Evangelists. Even Lisbon had one such visitor which drew big crowds and was endorsed by the ministers of the three Protestant churches. *Elmer Gantry*, Sinclair Lewis's titillating novel, and Amie Temple McPherson's real-life activities were part of the scene, countrywide. The story of the Roaring Twenties would not be complete without mentioning the Greats of the entertainment world whose names will never be forgotten. To name a few: Mary Pickford and Douglas Fairbanks, George and Ira Gershwin, Al Jolson, Irving Berlin, Norma Shearer, Rudy Vallee, Jeanette MacDonald, George Burns, Bing Crosby, and the Ziegfield Follies. They will always be associated with the glamor of the period, and I am glad that I was just the right age to enjoy it all.

Flapper Girls: Minnie Mohn and Essie Mae (L), and Minnie's portrait of Lisbon

Tommy drew this portrait of his mother while she was in the choir in the
Lisbon Methodist Church and he was sitting in the pew with his
grandmother. His "canvas" was the back of the church bulletin.

To Vicki

Last shimmering notes
of the violin
like breathless filaments of stardust
float through blue, eternal space,
terrestrial vibrations
left behind,
eternally charting an incandescent course
past moon and sun,
comets, and constellations,
toward Infinity.

Free Verse

Last notes seem
shimmering along
a path to join the comet out
in space.

Cinquain

Two poetry forms on the same subject – November 25, 1985

Victorian-isms

Vicki's first experience in a classroom was in the Fledgling School (Pre-pre-school) at the Wright-Patterson AFB near Columbus, Ohio. She was about four years old. One day when she was riding with Tom, she looked out at the sky which was criss-crossed with vapor trails. She remembered her experiences at school. Then thoughtfully she said, "Daddy, don't you think the sky is God's chalk board?" Out of the mouths of babes.

As long as Tom's family was in Minot, North Dakota, they spent Easter with us. A very happy time! One especially memorable Easter was when Vicki was only two years old. Dressed in a little bonnet, a fluffy pink dress, little white gloves, and little white purse, she was adorable.

When we got to church, she had to stand on the kneeling bench for prayers. With eyes closed, she said The Lord's Prayer very distinctly, along with everyone else, just as she did at home when she went to bed. The people around us were watching her quite surprised and amused. However, after the final Amen, she didn't stop. She continued to pray just as she did at home . . . and now came the real praying: "God bless Mommy, and Daddy, and Tommy, and Grandpa and Grandma . . . . . ." Then she began to realize that she was all alone. No other voices. She stopped in shy embarrassment and sat back with us. In the meantime, everyone else was smiling, and we were very proud of our Victoria.

Victoria Grace Hill (born 1960)
Birthplace of Essie Mae Thompson Hill (b. 1903)
– a farmhouse near Central City, Iowa

A Happy Birthday

I've seen the mountains and the seashore,
 orange groves and plains,
from buses and from horse-back,
 trucks, RVs, and trains.

But I had a new experience
 just the other day,
When I celebrated my birthday
 in a very special way.

I climbed into a bright balloon
 and floated all around,
Sometimes high up in the clouds,
 sometimes down near to the ground.

Arizona is so beautiful
 when you see it from the air,
That I took a lot of pictures
 to prove that I was there.

June 29, 1983

Royal Oak Road
at Six O'clock in the Morning

Palm leaves
whisper softly,
freight cars roar and rumble,
joggers' rhythmic footsteps salute
the dawn.

Sprinkler
fountains spurting,
Gambel quails parading,
rabbits scamper, dainty poodles
tiptoe.

Couples,
hand in hand, and
white-haired smiling housewives
nod and say, "Good morning, how're you
today?"

Then comes
dawn, and waiting
clouds, with soft white cheeks now
blush, grow red, with kisses from the sun.

Royal Oak Road at Dusk

A cloak
of darkness falls
on shoulders of the night.
Tall lamp-posts stand erect and tall
on guard.

Pale moon
looks down and smiles.
The day-time sounds are hushed
and one by one the house lights dim.
Good night.

Gems and Minerals of the Bible
Rockhound Fun

One of the first things that we did when we moved to the Valley of the Sun was to join the Sun City Rockhound Club. Everyone was very friendly and the programs were interesting, but it was when we went on our first field trip that we knew we had found a wonderful new activity.

We went in a caravan, following the lead car, driving across the desert, down through dry washes and flats, past all kinds of cacti . . . our introduction to the wonders of the wild Arizona. We finally reached the collecting area about thirty miles from Sun City, where we started looking for red jasper . . . climbing steep hills, finding specimens that looked interesting, making sure we didn't encounter any rattlesnakes, and enjoying the sunshine and camaraderie. No one waited until noontime to stop for lunch. Rockhounding gives one an appetite! After a couple of hours, we drifted back to where we had parked the cars, and out came TV tables, thermos bottles and our lunches. There were several four-wheel drive vehicles and station wagons. We had a two-door Cadillac at that time. Those who wanted to, did more rock hunting after lunch, and we found some "calico jasper" . . . speckled. We were very proud of our first specimens.

As time went on, we tried various other Sun City activities. Jerry went golfing a couple of times, and I joined some craft clubs, but Rockhounding activities always were our first love.

It was not long before my Geology experiences at Cornell became known, and I was nicknamed "Teach" by the club Vice President who was in charge of programs. During our second year, I consented to give a program on South Dakota geology. I put a lot of work into it. I made big colored posters showing the structure of the Black Hills, an eroded dome with concentric circles of rocks of various ages. I also made posters showing a cross section of the hills, and I had slides showing the Black Hills and the Badlands.

The next year, I was elected vice president and was in charge of programs. It was a very frustrating job . . . a lot of screw-ups. Things that never happened before or since that upset me. Such as the time that the speaker's wife sat smoking a pipe while her husband was setting up his materials. I had to tell her as diplomatically as possible that that was unacceptable.

Finally, I decided that it would be easier to do the last program myself than to find someone else. So I presented a program called "Gems and Minerals of the Bible," based on my two favorite subjects in college. This started a whole new phase of my life. I have no idea how many times I gave the lecture, but I gave it in churches of many denominations, including an Orthodox Jewish meeting, a half dozen different Masonic organizations, PEO, other Rockhound Clubs, Service Clubs, the Phoenix Mineralogical Association (at Phoenix College), and in Sedona before a large crowd in the Church of

138

the Red Rocks. I used slides, posters, a table-full of specimens, and autographed books showing the minerals in the Smithsonian collections which are "minerals of the Bible." Different translations of the Bible give different names to the minerals which are mentioned. I focused on those most frequently mentioned in the Bible . . . gold, silver, copper, and iron, and on the gems in Aaron's breastplate which represented descendants of Jacob, who became heads of the twelve tribes of Israel. The whole subject is an ever-fascinating study to me, and I never tire of it.

I sometimes included the following story:
The minister of a certain church decided to visit the teenage Sunday School Class to find out whether they were being taught the basics of the Bible. He pointed his finger at one boy and asked, "Who broke down the walls of Jericho?" The boy answered in a panic, "Oh, sir, it wasn't me!" The pastor then went around the whole class asking the same question and getting the same reply. The pastor met with the Official Board the next evening, told this "shocking" story, and asked what the Board thought should be done about it. One of the board members then said, "Well, if no one will admit to having knocked down those walls, then I move that we just have the wall fixed and forget about it."

I told that story to the Phoenix Mineralogical Society meeting and afterward a teenager from the audience came up to me and asked, "Mrs. Hill, did they ever find out who broke down those walls?"

————————

Ed: Photocopies of some of the newspaper articles about her lectures are in *Flapper Fun* (1st edition), with the following titles:

Gems and Minerals of the Bible
Publicity
"Geologist to tell Rockhounds of South Dakota Bad Lands"
"South Dakotans to hear talk on state's geology"
"Rockhound to speak on gems" (*Sun Citizen*, 14 May 1980)
"Talk due on gems of the Bible"
"Gems and Minerals of the Bible" "She was mentioned in the *Lapidary Journal* (February
        1978) as one of the outstanding lecturers in the area."
Lecture to Mineralogical Society of Arizona
"Geologist to speak on gems, minerals"
"Sundial Rock, Gem Club"
"Methodist Women to see Bible minerals" (*News Sun*, 23 May 1978)
"Talk due on gems of Bible" (*New Sun*, 8 October 1978)
"Gems, Bible Subjects of Talk to Sisterhood" (*Sun City Citizen*, 1 March 1978) – Big deal!
"St. Clements' Guild to see Bible minerals" (*News Sun*, 17 April 1978) –
        "Broke my right arm, PD books arrived – a Day to Remember"

A Day I'll Never Forget

I was scheduled to give the slide lecture, "Gems and Minerals of the Bible," in the big St. Clements' Catholic church to the general meeting of the Catholic women of the church. There had been a lot of publicity about it, and I had been told that a couple of priests would be present. I got up bright and early to get ready – the meeting was to be at nine-thirty in the morning. After I had finished my bath, I reached too far for a towel, lost my balance and fell over the side of the tub, pulling the iron towel rack off the wall, which hit my left shin and then I landed on my left arm and shoulder.

Jerry heard the commotion and rushed in, helped me up, and immediately said, "Oh, you can't give your program. I'll call them right away." "Hold it." I said, "You'll do no such thing. I'm going to give the program." And I did.

I got dressed, put my arm in a sling, and we went to the church, got my specimens out on a display table, and the slide equipment and screen set up, and went on with the show. The audience was very warm and appreciative when I told them what had happened.

I guess I had enough adrenaline in my system to carry me along until almost the end. By then my foot and leg were swollen and my arm and shoulder were hurting.

It happened, by an unusual coincidence, that our friends Julian and Florence Johnston from Mt. Vernon, and Paul and Caroline Bowman from Neenah, Wisconsin, were in the audience. Gerald had promised our old Aberdeen friends, the Albert Cornishes, to help them move into their new house that day, so he took off as soon as the lecture was over, leaving the Johnstons to take me to the doctor to have an examination and x-rays. They showed that the upper part of my left arm had been broken and jammed into the socket in my shoulder. Very painful! The doctor bound my arm, bent at the elbow, securely to my chest.

At last we went to lunch, with me wearing only one shoe! My left foot was swollen. Finally, we got home to relax. But that wasn't the most exciting part of the day. As we sat talking, we saw a strange man hauling big cardboard boxes up our front sidewalk. He was bringing my 500 copies of *Prairie Daughter*. The Johnstons and Bowmans got the first autographed copies of the book. And we had a great celebration.

I wish I had kept enough copies for "posterity," but if anyone wants one, Tom made copies on a Xerox machine.

The Ojo de Dios
(Eye of God)

In ancient Indian ruins are found
Rude frames with natural fibers wound.

They were made long ago
In faith and in love,
For protection and blessing
From the Great Spirit above.

The name which was given
Was Ojo de Dios,
Which means, "Eye of God"
As you probably know.

The center was dark
And around it were seen
Nature's own colors –
Orange, brown, red, blue, and green.

Woven with care and with prayer
By the Medicine Man,
It was hung on the wall
Of cave or hogan.

Within this old talisman
All these traditions still lie,
We give them, cherish,
And offer the blessings

That
go
With the ancient
Indian's
God's
eye.

Note: Borrowed from ancient traditions of the Pueblo and Mexican Indians, an Ojo de Dios (o-ho-day-dee-os) or Eye of God, is a message of warmth and hospitality. It brings wishes for good health, good fortune, and long life and happiness. (December 1978)

141

Some Philosophical Ideas
Expressed in Poetry

Enigma Solved

Along
a starry path
across the endless space
where all creation's mystery
awaits.

Perhaps
a time will come
when moonbeams will disclose
the secrets of the universe
at last.

Cinquaine

_____

The Path of Life

My rough and rocky pathway led along
an ancient pine-clad ridge where fog and mist
obscured my view, and I was overcome
with doubt and dread. Just then I saw a ray
of sparkling sunshine light the road ahead.
My fears were gone . . . I knew that I was nearing home
at last.

Blank Verse
Iambic Pentameter

Was My Face Red!

When Tom, Vicki, and I visited the Hill Tree Farm in 1980, Lanie went all out to give us a fresh lobster dinner. While she was putting the lobsters into the big vat of boiling water and steaming the clams, the rest of us were setting the table – she had special placemats and lobster bibs – and generally trying to do the other necessary jobs. She suddenly asked, "Do we have any lobster crackers?" At home no meal was complete without some kind of bread. I knew there wasn't any bread but remembered having seen some little fish-shaped cocktail crackers. So I said, "No I don't think we have any lobster crackers, but there are some Triscuits." Everyone began to laugh and laugh! Then they told me what lobster crackers were! WAS MY FACE RED!

In the spring, romance blossomed among the eighth-graders at the School for the Blind in Aberdeen. Love is not blind! Ever on the alert to notice the distracting signs, I distinctly saw a girl pass a note to the tall, handsome Indian boy who sat beside her. Before he had time to open it, I said to him very sternly, "What would you say if I asked you to read that note out loud to the whole room?" He grinned at me and said, "I wouldn't care. It wasn't for me!" Then I realized that he was only the go-between. WAS MY FACE RED! I APOLOGIZED, AND DROPPED THE WHOLE THING. Actually, I hadn't altogether forgotten how wonderful spring heart-throbs can be, so I was sort of amused by it all.

When Tom and Suzanne came back from their honeymoon at the Grand Canyon, I was very pleased when Tom said they had brought back to me a specimen of the granite at the bottom of the canyon. It was quite a large piece, and obviously very heavy from the way Tom handled it, and he warned me about being careful not to drop it. I was all braced to take it, but when I took it into my hands they almost flew up to the ceiling. The granite was made of GRAY PLASTIC FOAM! WAS MY FACE RED!

Ojo de Dios, woven by Essie Mae Thompson Hill

143

Child Labor
Minimum Wage?

The Industrial Revolution spawned the horrors of child labor, but George and Tom suffered the experiences of child labor in the twentieth century. <u>DELIVERING NEWSPAPERS</u>.

In the Lisbon and Mt. Vernon areas, it was the delivering of the *Cedar Rapids Gazette* which was supposed to provide extra money for hard-working teenagers, or even younger children. The work involved collecting the papers when they came from Cedar Rapids, then folding them and packing them into big canvas bags which were carried on foot or on their bikes. Like the mailmen, they had to go through snow, sleet, cold, or rain. Go as fast as possible, and throw them toward the customer's house as accurately as possible . . . not to land on the roof or in a puddle of water. In that case, they'd probably have to make a return visit and lose a paper.

The worst part was yet to come. This was collecting the money due the carrier. This had to be done on Saturdays. People could gripe bitterly about a missing paper, but when it came to paying for it, that was a different matter. They could find all kinds of excuses not to be at home, or not to have the money. I could help the boys with the deliveries when they needed it, but it broke my heart to see the frustrations of collecting their money.

When we were in Perry, Tommy took his turn at paper delivering. We were strangers in the community, but I remember going out with him in the evening darkness on foot trying to find the addresses. It was cold, snowy, and very discouraging. "Character-building" . . . NO! Gerald always remembered his delivering the *Des Moines Register* in Clarion with some pride and fondness, but it was not "inherited." <u>Child Labor</u> – awful, at any point in time.

After we moved to Lisbon, both George and Tom pulled weeds in Bish Stahl's commercial garden for about ten cents an hour. George said (February 8, 1988) that the wages for high school kids who went out to detassel corn in Mount Vernon in 1944 and 1945 were sixty cents an hour. It was hard work and he came home with an infection on his face and neck from the pollen and cuts from the corn leaves. George said, "Pulling weeds taught me two things: that truck garden farm labor such as the migrant workers do is very, very hard and pays very poorly; and that I'd rather do almost anything else, such as selling *Saturday Evening Posts*, even if I didn't make much more per day than pulling weeds. We should be prepared to pay more for garden vegetables, if the price paid was somehow passed along to the people who work those long, back-breaking, terribly hot or terribly cold hours to do it by hand."

Bish Stahl was actually a very generous family friend, and I was welcome to gather all the vegetables I could use without charge. I remember the wonderful asparagus and cabbage we gleaned, and I made quarts of beautiful white sauerkraut in the basement of the Lisbon house.

144

Haiku

soft snowflakes flutter,
earth sleeps, quietly waiting
the spring's kiss-waking

tiny humming bird
rests quietly in sunshine
on swinging clothes line

snow on the mesa
slender spires dark silhouette
lonely coyote howls

little gray kittens
scamper, play and sham battle,
then quietly sleep

A traditional Haiku is a form of Japanese poetry,
unrhymed, untitled, three lines, seventeen syllables: 5, 7, 5.

Haiku

blue pansy faces
look up, give hope, cheery smiles . . .
ignore cold and rain

cold rain
chicks nestle under mother hen's warm breast
spider web in dusty window

lightning
flashes across black tumbling clouds
thunder claps

memories stirring . . .
jingling sleigh bells, rusty cowbells
tolling church bell

quail in single file
scamper across the busy street
seeking food

wild geese formation
honking as they settle down
among dried corn stalks

Modern Haiku is a nature poem in three lines: short, long, short.

The Quest
My Bell Collection

During the summer before Gerald and I were married, we took a two-week trip to Washington, D.C., to visit Grandma Hill's beloved sister, Aunt Emma Price. As we were leaving, she gave me an interesting brass "bell" with which she had called her servants to the dining room during the many years she had been in India as a missionary and as the wife of the publisher of the *Indian Witness*. It was in the form of a mortar and pestle and around the bowl were Indian characters which meant Good Wishes, Blessing, Happiness, etc. When the bowl was struck with the pestle, it made a beautiful sound. This was the beginning of my bell collection.

While I was teaching in the Navy Pre-flight School in Mt. Vernon during World War II, I was a kind of surrogate mother to the cadets. One of those fellows had brought with him a footlocker which was too large to be allowed in his room at the school, so I stored it for him at our house. When it came time for him to ship out, he wanted to pay me, and when I refused, he said, "I notice that you have a bell collection. Here, buy a bell," and he handed me a five dollar bill.

That started my quest for "the perfect bell" which finally resulted in quite a respectable and interesting collection. I kept saving his five dollars for the perfect bell, and of course there is no such thing. I wish I could say I still have the money, but if I ever find the perfect bell, I am sure that the five dollars will miraculously appear. The criteria for perfection in a bell include appearance – beauty of shape and form, color, decorations, and embellishments. It must also have a beautiful tone – pleasing to the ear as well as to the eye. A hand bell must feel good in the hand – not awkward to hold and ring. No bell ever fulfilled all the requirements for perfection, but I finally accumulated an assortment of several hundred, and I organized a lecture and display which I presented numerous times. A free program is always welcome! But I am sure every collector knows the pleasure of sharing a hobby, and I enjoyed the trips around the county and to various clubs and groups locally. (That's the ham in me!)

The bell which personifies the worst features a bell could have is the one I made myself in pottery class at Cornell College. It is an ugly color, has a terrible tone, and it is just terribly crude. The only redeeming trait is that the handle feels good in my hands . . . it is easy to ring, although it "thuds" rather than rings.

Most of my collection has been given away, but I like to remember that at one time I had various authentic animal bells, such as a camel, elephant, and little bird bells. There were church bells, sleigh bells, bells made of Mexican clay, ordinary clay, and a bell carved from a piece of anthracite coal. Brass, glass, and silver, lava dust, tin, and iron. Many different countries were represented. The quest for the perfect bell grew into a fascinating hobby. A fringe benefit was learning a lot of geography and native customs. I recommend the hobby although I never found the ultimate perfect bell.

Father's Day

1. This is Father's Day you see
    And we'll be good as we can be
    For that's the way you all will know
    What makes us love our Daddy so.

Chorus

Daddy, Daddy, you're the best
We love you more than all the rest
We think you're great in every way
And we hope you have a happy day.

2. You are big and tall and strong
    And you plan for us the whole day long
    It always makes the day seem right
    When we see you coming home at night.

3. He teaches us things that we don't know
    And that's one reason we love him so
    He laughs and plays and works and sings
    And often brings us very nice things.

Written by Essie Mae Hill, June 1958

We were guests of the Harry Burrishes at Pickerel Lake on Father's Day weekend.
Margaret asked me to write the words of a song that the youngsters in the Sunday
School might sing as a tribute to their Daddies. These verses are the result. They are
sung to the tune of "Yankee Doodle" and one of the strongest traditions of the Sunday
School is the annual observance of Father's Day by singing this song.

148

Family Reunion

Fiddledy, diddledy, fiddledy, dee,
I know the place where I'd like to be.
Way down on the farm
on Thanksgiving Days
folks came one by one, in couples, and flurries
in brand new Chevrolets
and old-fashioned surreys.
Parents, brothers, and sisters,
aunts, uncles, and cousins,
with in-laws included, there were
two or three dozens.

The men sat at the table,
kids parked here and there,
women in the kitchen . . .
food their special care.
Lots of love and good feelin'
when the folks got together
talking crops, corn, and hogs,
and especially the weather.

The day always ended with a sing-sing-along,
the sopranos squeaking slightly,
the bass loud and strong.

But when it was finally nearing the end,
we sang soft and tenderly
"Dear God be with us
till we meet again."

August 1985

149

Grandma Thompson Won the Battle for Education
Family Graduations

When George graduated from Sac City High School (at age sixteen), my friend Tudy Irwin, whose daughter was also in the graduating class, and I sat in the audience crying all the time. Especially when the band played the *1812 Overture* and *Land of Hope and Glory*. Boo! Hoo! Nothing will ever be the same again! So true. One of their classmates died of Rocky Mountain Spotted Fever a few weeks later.

However, when George graduated from Yale in 1953, it was all sunshine, pride, and some giggles. George and Tom were leading the procession – George playing the bass drum and Tom playing the tuba – in the band which preceded the whole distinguished procession, and they continued playing while all the VIP's were being seated. I was watching George through binoculars. He was standing, arms outstretched in full swing. Then I saw a stricken look come over his face. He never missed a swing, but the end of one of his drumsticks had flown out into space! That is when I giggled. As soon as everyone was seated, George went around back of the platform to don his cap and gown for the rest of the ceremonies. He was one of the class representatives. His duty was to collect diplomas for the rest of his classmates and take them to the courtyard of Jonathan Edwards College where the Master presented them personally to each graduate. Tom snapped a picture at the exact moment when Dr. Robert Dudley French presented George his diploma. In fact, each of them had his hand on it. This was the first of many diplomas and certificates which hang on the walls of his office. A happy day indeed!

When Tom graduated from the University of Colorado in 1952, the ceremonies were held on the football field. George came out to Boulder to attend the ceremonies. (We later attended his graduation exercises from Harvard Medical School in 1957.) The unique part of Tom's graduation was when he received his commission in the USAF. I had the privilege of pinning on his wings and the gold bars which marked him as a Second Lieutenant, the first step in a twenty-year career. It was a proud moment for his Dad and me! After that, the four of us took a trip up into the mountains past the university's summer camp where I spent a very happy time studying "in the field" in 1927. I climbed Long's Peak at that time.

Graduations among the family at this date (1988) include those which I have personally attended (college and university): George at Yale and Harvard; Tom at the University of Colorado; Vicki at Nazareth College at Pittsford, New York, and the University of Michigan, Ann Arbor; Tom Jr., also from the University of Michigan and Mather Air Force Base at Sacramento, California. Altogether there have been twenty-five of "Grandma Thompson's" immediate family members who have graduated from higher institutions of learning, not counting their spouses and at least three who are currently enrolled in graduate programs. I think she would have considered her fight for the education of her children worthwhile!

In Another World

Oh, I love to curl up in my over-stuffed chair
with a book and a sandwich, a glass of iced tea.
Of weather or time I am scarcely aware,
Because I'm in the spot where I like most to be.

In my chair I can travel where ever I please,
 or enjoy a romance with a handsome young man . . .
I can go out in space with the greatest of ease
and come back as easily right where I began.

October 21, 1985

The Path of Life

My rough and rocky pathway led along
an ancient pine-clad ridge where fog and mist
obscured my view, and I was over come
with doubt and dread. Just then I saw a ray
of sparking sunshine light the road ahead.
My fears were gone. . . . I knew that I was nearing home at last.

November 4, 1985

Address to the Lisbon High School Alumni Association

Lisbon, Iowa, May 12, 1944*

Dear Alumni,

Alumni banquet night in the old home town! And perhaps you are thinking how much has happened to you, since you sat here as one of the guests of honor, one year ago, or perhaps two or three or more! Tonight we are honoring another class of graduates, some of whom will soon be sharing your experiences. In reality, however, you are sharing honors with them, for you are very much on our minds tonight as we see your star on the service flag above our heads. Our theme for the toast program is "When the Lights Come on Again All Over the World," and you won't mind if we dream a bit of that day "When the Boys Are Home Again from All Over the World," for we know you dream of that too, even while you sing, "Anchors aweigh my boys, Anchors aweigh," or "The caissons go rolling along." We have no qualms or doubts about the way you are taking your new responsibilities. We just want you to know, that those of us who can't possibly do what you are doing tonight are making new resolutions to make our small part of the world the kind of place you'll want to find when you do come home. We know that down in your hearts you don't expect to find people and things unchanged from what they were when you went away, just as we know that the experiences you have will have left their imprint upon you. All that we hope for, and what we are working for, is that you won't be disappointed in us, and what we have done, but will be as proud and happy, as we are and will be, of you.

As the years roll along, after we leave school, much of the detailed information, which we crammed into our heads just before the final examinations, either slips away from us entirely, or is buried beneath things for which we have more immediate need. That is true of the multitudes of admonition and advice which is poured out especially for the benefit of those who are graduating. The person, who out of all the wisdom of the philosophers, and the writings of the poets and sages, to which the average student is exposed in his four years of high school, that person who has retained even a handful of all this, but who has grasped it so tightly that it has never been lost, is fortunate indeed. I say "fortunate" or "lucky," because if it is retained it is usually, I think, due to no credit or fault of his own, but either because he had the

---

* Explanation: The Lisbon High School Alumni banquet is the social high point of the year. Individual classes don't have reunions. It is a mass meeting, with special honors going to the current graduating class and to the Golden anniversary class of fifty years. There were songs, greetings, and usually a "speech," which I have perhaps given more often than any other person – a result of program chairman desperation, and an easy "mark." This was the talk that I gave in 1944, when the President of the Alumni Association was Dr. Gaylord André, serving in Europe, and whom Gerald, by good luck and arrangement, got together with over there. [Ed.: At the time Essie Mae spoke, her audience was waiting to hear that the Allies had landed in France. D-Day for the invasion was about three weeks later, on June 6, 1944.]

privilege of having an inspiring and devoted teacher, or that the chain of circumstances of his life emphasized the truth of the idea until it has never been forgotten.

Now, perhaps you are asking, "What does all this have to do with the time "When the lights come on again, all over the world?" Just this, my friend. I am one of those biological curiosities, whose early educational roots go back to the day when Virgil's *Aenead* was part of the Lisbon High School curriculum. And not only that, but one of the things which I have remembered all these years is that line written in Latin by the poet Virgil, *Forsan haec olim meminisse juvabit*, which means, "Someday you will be glad to remember these things."

Now do you see? Most of us are working harder than we ever did in our lives before. We have to fight off loneliness, and longing, while every day brings new problems to face and solve, which we have never had to work out before. We look ahead and dream of the day when our children will have their Daddies home again, when our families will be reunited, and when brothers, wives and husbands will gather round the table like it used to be. But in the meantime, IN THE MEANTIME, to paraphrase what the Italian poet said a couple of thousand years ago, "there is so much, even in these trying experiences, that we will be glad to remember," . . . for we wouldn't feel that we had a right to share in the world of light that will come if we hadn't had our part in making it possible.

There is a well-known story in a very old book – a book which many of you are probably appreciating more now than you ever did before. It is the story of a group of girls who were waiting for the time to come when they could "light their lamps," or in the words of today, "when the lights come on again all over the world." Of course, some of the girls in the story weren't ready, but we here pledge ourselves to be "wise" and not "foolish." This is the time of waiting, but also of preparation. It isn't easy, I can tell you, but the girls back home are doing a swell job. You'd be proud of them – "They're right on the beam" – some of them are even going on to school, and it's no fun, either, without the fellows around. But I think you'll give them due credit for realizing that no matter what field of activity they choose, you're going to expect the girls to be well-trained, mentally alert, and ready to take their places beside you, in helping solve the problems of the postwar years. The Lisbon High School graduates are doing all right, too. For example, I recently heard from Peggy Frink, whom many of you will remember as an outstanding graduate of four years ago. She has carried on her high school background, and with her own ability and personality graduated "with distinction" at the University of Iowa last month, won Phi Beta Kappa honors, honors in English, and an A in Voice. Don't worry about the girls – like "Johnny" they'll "be waiting for you."

Again, please allow me the privilege of going back into the "I remember" of my own high school days. The motto of my graduating class was a mathematical formula, A + O = R. Like all formulas of that kind, unless you know what the letters stand for, it doesn't mean a thing, so this is the key. A stands for "Ability," O stands for

"Opportunity," and R for "Responsibility." That's a lot of big words, but translated, the formula means that each person's responsibility toward himself, his family, and society, is based directly on his ability and his opportunities. This is his Responsibility, with a capital R. Each person's ability differs from another's and so do his opportunities, but whatever they add up to, then THAT is his responsibility . . . his duty.

Since the first of August last year, I have been teaching aviation cadets, first in the Army and later in the Navy at Cornell. And needless to say, the old adage "that a teacher must be prepared for anything" is especially true in the armed forces. One of the Aerology teachers at Cornell started out by telling the cadets that she was going to teach them how to tell weather. One of the cadets spoke up and said, "Why, Ma'am, you don't need to teach us that, we can just LOOK at a girl and tell weather."

Well, maybe he can, but I maintain that there are lots of things that a person can't tell about another just by looking, and one of those is an individual's responsibility in these times. You see, it all goes back to the formula, and THAT says that Responsibility is the result of one's ability and opportunities. An individual's responsibility in these times is something each person must determine for himself. For myself, I am not so sure about my teaching ability (that's for the Navy to decide) but I know the Opportunity came like a bolt out of a clear sky. Not all of us can wear the uniform of a WAC or a WAVE, but if our wartime work – whether it is on the farm or in the factory, at home or in the schoolroom – allows someone else to go into active service, then our Responsibility becomes a privilege and a <u>pleasure</u>, as well. Which just goes to show that even "when the lights are out all over the world" there are little spots of brightness in the dark.

I have noticed another thing which applies to us at home as well as to you who are far away. These cadets which I have been teaching have come from all over the country, some of them fresh off the farms of the middle west, some of them from the crowded foreign sections of New York City and San Francisco. Some of them are old-time, seasoned fleet men, who represent the war's activities all over the world – the South Pacific, Attu in the Aleutians, Brazil, Iceland, and Europe, and some are just out of high school with little background of experience, except a little "book-larnin'." Which would you guess gets the most out of their experiences at Pre-flight school? Which are the most eager to learn – which ones are going to retain the most of what they do learn, and which ones have the most practical point of view? You have guessed it. Yes, it is the ones who have been through the most, and the ones who have had the most experiences.

Doesn't that give us who are at home, a clue as to the smart thing for us to do, while you boys are away? It means that the more we know, the wider our background of knowledge and experience, the more we get out of life. It means that although we can't follow you to the places where you are, fly the planes, drive the tanks, and all the rest, we can work, read, study, and plan at home so that you won't be disappointed and ashamed of us when you come back. So that we can at least know what you are talking

154

about, when you tell us of your experiences. (I was going to say, "speak your language," but maybe you'd rather we wouldn't do that literally.) The things that we'll be "glad to remember" are not the backaches, headaches, and heartaches, but, that while you were carrying your heavy pack, we were really shoulder to shoulder with you, although we were in different "service commands."

I hope you don't mind my reading this to the Alumni Association. We are having a grand time – the fellows and girls all look wonderful, and so do the "poppas and mommas" . . . but we miss you. We are wishing you all success, and we pledge ourselves to carry on the responsibilities here at home, to the full limit of our ability and opportunities.

School Days

I hear
the school bell ring.
The children's laughter dies,
the trampling of their feet now sounds
instead.

Memorial Day

We hear
the mournful sound
of taps across the hills
re-echoing in hearts that beat
in grief.

Memories

In dreams
I walk again
with friends of long ago.
We laugh, we love, and then in tears,
I wake.

Amore

Their love
is like a bond
invisible, and yet
so strong it lasts forevermore.
Amen.

(To Bertha and Al Johnson)

The Alamo

They chose
to fight till death.
The blood of sacrifice has sanctified this place for all
mankind.

Monument Valley

I see
tall spires, pale moon.
A lonely coyote howls.
The mesa shines with snow's bright dust tonight.

Faith Conquers All

The path
led out beyond
the misty hills . . . but I
had faith that I would reach my goal at last.

156

Heartstrings

Do you not know that you are always in our thoughts
and ever in our love?
The day, the weeks, the months
drag by on weary feet;
The mailman comes, and never stopping,
on he goes without a sign that you care at all.
Old memories fill our hearts – your baby smile,
your hair so soft;
The years went flying, flying, flying,
all too fast. Then off you go
into a wider world.
We severed early ties, but we were glad and proud.
Roles changed.
When we were sick or were in need, you came.
Sometimes we were the anchor in your life,
or buoy when times were low.
Then life changed in ways we could not foresee. . . .
more cares and burdens now for you,
and we are many miles apart,
but never for a moment doubt
that we still care,
and you are always and forever in our hearts.

The Day That President Kennedy Died

November 23, 1963, was a typical Friday afternoon at the School for the Blind in Aberdeen. My twelve fifth and sixth graders were in the special typing room having class together. The routine was abruptly broken about 2:30 p.m. by the voice of the Superintendent of the school on the intercom. He said, "We have just heard over the radio that President Kennedy has been shot!" He added that he and Mrs. Kennedy were in Dallas, Texas, and were riding in an open car when he was shot. He also added that he did not know any of the details, but if he heard anything more, he would let us all know. We were stunned . . . as we later realized, everyone in the world was. Everyone began talking at once, and there was confusion, as you can imagine. Time passed. It seemed long.

When we heard nothing more, each of us was hoping that it had all been a mistake and everything would be all right. However, when the afternoon was almost over, the Superintendent came on the intercom again with the news that the President died. I went home as soon as I could get away, and the children went back to their dormitory rooms and the lounge. All of us spent the weekend glued to the radio and TV watching the horrendous events which followed.

When we came back to school, I asked my pupils whether they would like to write letters of sympathy to Mrs. Kennedy. Would they!! Of course. They did write very touching, sincere letters. All of them were in Braille. One of the boys who was not only blind, but was not able to stand without crutches, invited Mrs. Kennedy to come out to South Dakota and ride horseback. Braille lines were always written far enough apart for me to "translate" (called "interline") so that they could be read by sighted people. This I did and then I sent them to Mrs. Kennedy at the White House.

The following newspaper article tells "the rest of the story":
"Mrs. G. L. Hill's fifth and sixth grade classes at the School for the Blind have something to cherish. Soon after the assassination of John F. Kennedy, the classes sent letters of sympathy to Mrs. Kennedy. They were written in Braille and Mrs. Hill translated them between the lines before they were sent. There was excitement and pleasure in the room a week ago when Mrs. Kennedy's acknowledgement arrived. The beautifully addressed envelope had Mrs. Kennedy's frank on it instead of a stamp. Inside was a formal acknowledgment of the receipt of the class letters. The card was bordered in black. 'The nicest thing about it,' Mrs. Hill said, 'is that the card was engraved, so the children could actually feel that there was something written on it.' "

Later I read that all sympathy cards were put into the Kennedy Library in Boston. The children were happy about that.

About ten years later, Gerald and I visited the "eternal flame" in Arlington Cemetery. I wish I could have had those young blind youngsters with me. Their hands and hearts would have been warmed.

158

Around the World in Eighty Days – More or Less

In 1970 the annual Alumni banquet in Lisbon honored the graduating class of that year and also the fifty-year class of 1920. I had been president of the Class of 1920, so it fell to my lot to give a toast. In addressing the graduating class, I predicted that they would be holding their fiftieth reunion on the moon! I based that on the fact that when I graduated I had not been outside the state of Iowa; and now, fifty years later, I was going on a trip around the world in just two weeks. This is an account of that trip, written by Gerald as part of his tribute to Keiko.

"One of the highlights of Essie Mae's and my life came in the year 1970 when Tom was in Vietnam. We booked a flight around the world in July 1970. Starting from Aberdeen, we stopped briefly in Denver and had a short visit with George and Lanie. Continuing to Seattle, we began our non-stop flight to Tokyo where we were greeted by Keiko, Vicki, and Tommy (at midnight).

"Keiko and her family made our days in **Japan** something special, a truly memorable experience. We were regally received and entertained by Keiko's father, Dr. Shigeru Nambara, at the University Club, of which he was president in recognition of his role as President Emeritus of Tokyo University, one of the largest universities in the world. His car and chauffeur, provided by the Japanese Emperor, were placed at our disposal for the rest of our stay in Tokyo. A lunch with Keiko's sister, Aiko, at the Hotel Okuro, and a typical Japanese family dinner in the Nambara compound were other highlights.

"Though the good efforts of Akira Nambara, a brother, we were received as special guests at the headquarters of the Bank of Japan and given the unusual privilege of a visit to the highly secret and secure museum in the lower vaults in which priceless examples of Japanese coins and mediums of exchange are stored. Hours following our visit to the Bank of Japan, Akira, a bright and rising young officer of the bank, departed for an assignment with the branch of the bank in New York City. Since then, he has represented his country and bank in numerous monetary posts.

"Also in recognition of my long banking experiences in the U.S.A., we were favored by a high tea at the Fugi Bank on Saturday afternoon, by an officer who had been a classmate of Akira's at Yale University. We were given special passes to the Fugi Bank building at Expo '70, which we visited the following day with Keiko and the children.

"Following the family dinner at the Nambara home, Dr. Nambara presented Essie Mae and me with treasured gifts. Essie Mae was given a lovely incense burner, and I received a beautiful red lacquer bowl which had been presented to Dr Nambara by Emperor Hirohito in recognition of his work with a national poetry contest, and his personal esteem for the internationally famous educator.

159

"In departing from Tokyo, we joined a tour group to several famous Japanese landmarks, including a popular lake front awash with humanity. The group was then taken to a lovely mountain resort for a day of relaxation.

"A ride on the famous Japanese railroad from Nagoya to Kyoto gave us a touch of their phenomenal mechanical engineering and efficiency. Keiko and the children, on another fast train from Tokyo, joined us in Kyoto for the balance of our visit to the island of the Nipponese.

"In Kyoto, we experienced many Japanese ceremonies including a dinner served by geisha girls, an entertainment consisting of a display of flower arranging, art, music, and a full performance of the tea ceremony.

"Farewells to us were given by Keiko, Vicki, and Tommy as we departed from the Osaka airport. A brief stop was made in Taipei, Taiwan, before our plane flew nonstop over South Vietnam to Bangkok, **Thailand**.

"The great surprise of the world-circling trip came at our landing there. We knew that Tom was located hundreds of miles north of Bangkok at U Dorn, BUT THERE WAS TOM TO GREET US!!"

This is as far as Jerry went in describing our trip around the world.

Our headquarters in Bangkok were at the Manora Hotel. The first night that Tom was with us, he slept on a cot in our room . . . the second night in a room of his own. Among the very special paces that we visited was the emperor's palace, the site of *The King and I*. This musical was never allowed to be shown in Thailand. It was considered degrading. Tom and I had our pictures taken in front of the palace.

Bangkok is known as the "city of canals." We took a boat trip through the canals, called a "floating market," with boats filled with vegetables and food of all kinds for sale to the people who lived alongside. The canals furnished water for everything that water is used for – from bathrooms to cooking.

Bangkok is also known as the City of Temples. The roofs of the temples are always edged with distinctive bells, and as gifts from Tom, I added several strings of these bells to my collection. Jerry finally said, "I have taken off my shoes in order to get into these temples for the last time! I'm going to sit outside from now on!" So he missed seeing the most famous of all, the Temple of the Emerald Buddha, which is made of jade rather than emerald.

After we left Bangkok, our next stop was the fascinating city of **Hong Kong**. Very busy days! Among the places we visited were Victoria Peak, Repulse Bay, and the floating restaurant at Aberdeen, reached by a boat which was propelled by a woman who was one of the "boat people," who lived on boats their entire lives.

We bought tailor-made clothes which were completed in three days from the time we picked out the material, fitting and all. I bought a wool suit and a blue and silver cocktail dress, oriental style, which I still wear. Jerry bought two sports jackets and slacks . . . beautiful wool, silk lined.

160

On our "free" day, the little girl who was adopted and supported by the Pickerel Lake Sunday School in Aberdeen, South Dakota, was brought to our hotel, the Hong Kong Hyatt, on Nathan Road, Kowloon. She was brought by limousine from her school to visit with us. She was very shy, and we talked through an interpreter who accompanied her. But we took pictures, and when we got home the Sunday School was thrilled to hear about our visit.

We celebrated the Fourth of July dining and dancing on the twenty-seventh floor of the Mandarin Hotel. Everyone in the dining room applauded as we sang very lustily "God Bless America."

Sampans and junks, typhoon shelters, children clustering around us begging for handouts, the Suzie Wong district, Tiger Balm Gardens (a kind of oriental Disneyland), lunch at the famous Mandarin Hotel, and much more, were all part of our stay in Hong Kong.

Then on to Calcutta (Benares) in **India**.

Although our hotel was supposed to be the best in the city, we really didn't enjoy it. The poverty and filth! We really could not enjoy the luxury because everything around us was so awful. All the water we used had to be "purified," but in spite of that, I picked up an intestinal infection which made me so sick I have never been the same since. Lomotil, the prescription anti-diarrhea medicine, was sold over the counter like aspirin. Along the streets sacred cattle wandered freely, and we passed many hovels which were sided with the "holy" dried dung. We saw naked children relieving themselves in the gutters. I saw a bare-breasted woman begging as she held a starving child . . . her breast look like a brown, wrinkled old potato at the bottom of the winter barrel!

Calcutta is a sacred city to the Hindus and the goal is to reach the banks of the Ganges, bathe in it, and have their ashes scattered into it. The banks of the river are lined with ghats where bodies of the dead were being burned and the ashes are scattered into the water, adding to its filth. You may get the idea that I don't think much of the Hindu Holy City!

But the rest of our time in India was a different story. First Agra, and the beautiful Taj Mahal. The wife in whose memory that mausoleum was erected must have been "quite a gal" because she was the favorite over about sixteen other wives. It really is indescribably beautiful. Our next stop was at Delhi where we visited the site of Mahatma Ghandi's assassination and cremation. The spot is marked by a marble Samadhi (as it is called) surrounded by a beautiful garden. Our guide here had been one of Ghandi's secretaries. We were told that every Friday night a prayer service is held. The movie *Mahatma Ghandi* (when it came out) had a special interest for me.

There were many other interesting things and places to see in Delhi. The Red Fort was the most magnificent of all the royal palaces, and when it was in use in the seventeenth century, it was filled with all kinds of luxuries . . . jewels, furniture . . .

161

harems, princes, and potentates. Delhi was the site of the famous Peacock throne which was inlaid with every known gem and jewel.

Our next destination was New Delhi. Quite a modern city. We drove past the India Gate built in memory of the Indian soldiers who died in World War I. Lots of other interesting places . . . both ancient and modern. We stayed at the Hotel Oberoi. Behind the walls we knew there were estates of great luxury and people of wealth beyond our imagination, but all that was well hidden from the tourists' milieu.

From there we went to **Pakistan** where our stay was very special because the Minister of Education had been a visiting Professor at South Dakota State College in Aberdeen the year before. He arranged visits for each of us in private homes. Our hosts were a banker and his wife, a Montessori teacher. The pair couldn't have been more perfect. We were interested to hear that their marriage had been "arranged," according to Muslim custom. It seemed very successful. They had four sons and were very eager for them to come to the United States. We really had the V.I.P. treatment in Pakistan.

On to **Nepal** where we stayed at the Karachi International Hotel in Kathmandu. We toured the city and took a bus trip through the beautiful countryside. In the hotel lobby was a huge board covered with prayer wheels which one could spin and get a plethora of petitions offered with very little effort. I have a tiny gold prayer wheel on my charm bracelet "just in case." Our experiences in Nepal were brief and superficial, but when George and Lanie went on their trek up Mount Everest, we had the satisfaction of having flown into the same airport.

I bought a beautiful bell here with money which my lifelong friend Ella Johnson Miller gave me before we started our trip. It is the most nearly PERFECT BELL – the answer to my QUEST – that I probably will ever find. It is beautiful to the eye, the ear, and to hold and to ring.

Egypt. We stayed at the Nile Hilton overlooking the Nile River. Our experiences there started with an evening boat ride on the river.

Highlights included a camel ride to the Ginza to see the pyramids (close-up). I stayed behind to take a picture of Jerry on his "steed" and then missed joining the caravan and had a scary trip in a horse-drawn cart, clutching my purse so tightly my knuckles were white, while the driver begged a prepayment for the ride (our guide had warned us about that). Jerry climbed up into one of the pyramids, but I didn't try that. We were told that in one place the tunnel was so low that one could hardly get through . . . not for one who has claustrophobia!!! We saw the Sphynx, of course, and I thought about the fact that it was old even when Moses lived there in Egypt!

Back in Cairo we went to the National Cairo Museum, which was fascinating. Among the precious things which we saw were the treasures which had been taken from the tomb of Tutankhamen. These included the golden mask inlaid with carnelian and lapis lazuli which was found on the mummy of King Tut. The exhibit which toured the major cities of the United States in 1978 did not include a great many things which we saw in Cairo in 1970.

Out in the desert away from Cairo, we saw many relics of the past . . . the head of Ramesses, the historic step pyramid which predates the pyramids on the Ginza by many years, and many more interesting examples of the earliest stone architecture.

Greece. When we landed at the Athens airport, it was so clean and efficient that it seemed like we were really home at last. We looked out at the Acropolis from the balcony of our hotel, and I could hardly wait until the next morning when we were to go up there. It is built on a rocky hill 156 m. above sea level about 500 B.C. As we sat on the steps and looked out over the city, and while our guide was giving us a lecture about the structure, I picked up some small pieces of the marble and put them into my pocket. After we got home, I polished them and made them into precious keepsakes. Nearby were the little temple of Nike and the south portico of the Caryatides with its six statues of beautiful girls. Unfortunately, Jerry sprained his ankle on the way down the hill, and he spent the next several days with wheelchair and cane. In our tour of the city, the spot where St. Paul stood when he said, "I found an altar with this inscription 'To an unknown god' whom therefore ye ignorantly worship declare I unto you." Acts 17:23 was very significant to me.

Italy. More wonderful, interesting sight-seeing in Rome. The first place was St. Paul's Basilica (Jerry in a wheelchair), then historic churches, the Coliseum, the Forum, Spanish steps, and Capitol Square, where Mussolini addressed hundreds of thousands, Michael Angelo's statues of Moses, David, the Pieta, and famous fountains.

And now, **Home** again. From Rome we flew nonstop to Kennedy International Airport in New York City, went through Customs and then on to Minneapolis and Aberdeen, all in one day!

The limitations of time did not allow us lengthy stops anywhere. We knew that there were many, many places which we would like to have seen and which we didn't; but our lives were enriched and changed forever. I have read, read, read, and studied since we came home and I'll always be thankful for the wonderful experiences.

More Traveling

Gerald was more honored among national banking groups than he was among the bankers of Aberdeen. During the years that he was president of the Dacotah Bank Holding Company (DBHC), his counsel and advice were especially sought and respected among the membership of the Bank Administration Institute (BAI). This group of veteran bankers were responsible for educational programs offered, and often required, to younger and less experienced men. He was a member of the Board of Directors and Chairman of the Small Banks Commission. He was awarded a beautiful large plaque indicating that he was a "Director at Large."

The Board of Directors met at least once a year in various cities throughout the United States and in conjunction with these business meetings, conventions were also held. Our expenses were paid, the Board members were honored, friendships developed, and entertainment was par excellence. Sad to say, the "Big Wheels" in the Dacotah Bank Holding Company of Aberdeen never recognized Jerry's expertise and vision, and the possibility of becoming a nationally known institution. However, we had the opportunity to travel and enjoy luxurious life-styles in a way that otherwise would not have been possible for us. We always sat at the head table, and when we marched in, formally dressed, and were introduced, the others at the convention were standing and clapping and clapping . . . everybody happy!

Among the cities were the meetings were held were Seattle (the Space Needle), San Antonio (the River Walk and the Alamo), Pointe Verde Resort (near Jacksonville and St. Augustine, Florida), Miami Beach (Fontainebleau Hotel), twice Memphis, Cleveland and Atlantic City. Also, two weeks in the Hawaiian Islands attending the American Bankers Convention.

The most elaborate convention we ever attended was held in Williamsburg, Virginia. This was a convention to which only the presidents of bank holding companies throughout the country were invited. Jerry represented the smallest of the holding companies present, but that didn't affect the quality of our entertainment, nor deter him from speaking out in the business meetings (I was told).

Enroute from Aberdeen by car, we stayed overnight in the exclusive Minneapolis Athletic Club. Our next stop was Richmond, the capitol city of Virginia. The capitol itself was designed by Thomas Jefferson. There's a statue of Washington in the rotunda, and around the walls are statues of the seven presidents born in Virginia. We were entertained at an elaborate banquet that evening, and I had a chance to sample shad roe for the first time. Among those seated at our table were the Sheplers, who had recently bought George and Lanie's big house in Denver. (They acted pretty snobbish!)

Our headquarters were at the Williamsburg Inn. Since the Inn opened in 1937, sovereigns and statesmen from many nations have been guests there. These have included both Presidents Truman and Eisenhower, Queen Elizabeth II and Price Philip,

164

Winston Churchill, the heads of state of Japan, Germany, Thailand, Nepal, Norway and many others. We stayed in one of the most luxurious and historic places in America!

While the men were attending their meetings, there was very special entertainment planned for the ladies. This included a trip to Jamestown. We traveled by buses, with several stops at interesting historical places. Separately and together, I think Gerald and I saw all the shops and historical buildings in Williamsburg, and I made a scrap book with pictures and photographs and postal cards showing many of them, as well as menus and souvenirs. The entertainment for the evenings included places and famous historical homes, privately owned, but opened for this prestigious group. One of these was a reception at Carter's Grove Planation, which has been described as "the most beautiful colonial house in America." "King Carter" originally owned 300,000 acres of choice Virginia land. The present house is made of red brick, a three-story Georgian house, where legends say that both Washington and Jefferson proposed to early loves in the southwest parlor, and were turned down. Now it is called "The Refusal Room." There are noticeable deep gouges in the staircase which spiral up from the hall. They are said to have been made by a British cavalry man who rode his horse up the stairway, hacking the balustrade with his sabre as he came down.

Another evening we had the unique privilege of being invited to the house which now stands on the land where the first settlers from England landed on December 4, 1719, almost a full year before the Pilgrims landed in New England. It was here, and not in Plymouth, that the first Thanksgiving feast was held. [Ed.: It is not clear what Essie Mae had in mind. The first English settlers arrived at Jamestown on May 14, 1607, and the *Mayflower* landed on Cape Cod on November 11, 1620.]

The present house, a Georgian three-story mansion, was built by Benjamin Harrison, and named Berkeley. His son, Colonel Benjamin Harrison, was elected governor of Virginia three times and was a close friend of George Washington, who was often entertained there. For us, it truly was a fabulous experience to walk back through time and see, feel, touch and share all the grandeur of the past. Next in the Harrison line to make Berkeley his home was the colonel's younger son, Benjamin. However, as a young man, he migrated to Ohio, married, reared a family and completely changed his life-style. When he ran for president of the United States in 1893, his logo was a log cabin, and his motto was "Tippecanoe and Tyler too." However, when he was elected president, he came back to Berkeley and wrote his inaugural address in the room in which he had been born. He was sixty-eight years old and in frail health. However, he insisted on standing out in the cold and dampness to give his two-hour inaugural address. He contracted pneumonia and died exactly one month later. Benjamin Harrison was succeeded by Grover Cleveland and he was followed by William McKinley. His assassination opened the door to Roosevelt's presidency . . . and we're back to the time when I was born.

We went back through Washington, D.C., where we had dinner at the Mayflower Hotel with Congressman and Mrs. Ben Reifel, our friends from Aberdeen.

165

Faith

The gods of Olympus are out of control!
The children of Zeus are at war again.
My cabin walls shake with Aeolian fury,
And rain streams down the dark window pane.

But I'm calm, snug and warm in my bunkbed inside,
Because I'm sure that this will soon pass.

Nature's pendulum swings from the foul to the fair,
We're all buoyed and borne in the strong arms of Atlas.

A Prayer

Just what my mother thinks I am
I pray thee, Father, help me to be
Sweet, living, innocent, and good,
As when I knelt beside her knee.

This poem was chosen to be published in the *Cornell Mother's Day Book*, when I was a freshman in 1921. Everyone in Freshman English had to write a "tribute" to Mother, and I was very much surprised to have this little verse chosen for the annual booklet put out by the English Department. I always suspected that it was used to "fill a page," but it was pleasant to see my name in print on a creative writing, anyway.

166

Season's Greetings – The Hills of South Dakota

Christmas 1956

A warm fire burns at the Hillsite,
And warm hearts dwelling there too,
Our thoughts reaching out, spanning the space,
To wish Merry Christmas to you.

> They say that the way to keep moss off a rock,
> Is to make sure that it doesn't stand still,
> So we try to keep bustling . . . even moved once again,
> In order to fulfill the bill.

We had a grand time at our 25th anniversary,
And appreciate the nice things that were said;
Then some kind of "bug" caught up with E. M.,
She had a short time in a hospital bed.

> But all that is past . . . feeling better than ever,
> Housekeeping is easy in Hillsite, Number Two.
> Every morning at eight, with <u>School</u> there's a date,
> Too busy to ever feel blue.

In June the four Hills met in fair Colorado,
And we had a most wonderful time,
Saw Tom get his sheepskin and AF commission . . .
To say we're "bursting with pride" is surely no crime.

> 'Twas a short vacation for George, the young Medic,
> But with Tom now in Harford, they often spend time together.
> Working, playing, climbing mountains, or dancing . . .
> Everything's fine . . . even New England weather!

A trip back to Iowa in the middle of summer,
And many friends and relations were seen;
It gladdened our hearts . . . Now we hope they will come
Here to see us in Aberdeen.

Jerry is looking and feeling "on top of the world" . . .
Works hard (bank's doing fine), but has fun,
And you know that at last he's a real Pheasant State guy,
For this fall he bought his own gun.

And now in the freezer are birds, ducks, and geese,
Tho' I've heard some of his pals question the shot;
But it's a whole lot of fun, and we're thankful 'bove all,
For the ol' "Toot" pep that he's got.

Now, if you've had time to read this long verse,
We repeat, "Merry Christmas" to you.
We're thankful for many good things come to us,
And we hope that that's true for you too.

Christmas 1957

We're old fashioned folks at THE HILLSITE,
For in spite of rockets and such,
We think that the words
"MERRY CHRISTMAS TO YOU"
Can't be improved very much.

We've thought of you often throughout the year
(And how fast this year has flown by!)
But
"A HAPPY NEW YEAR"
Is the best wish we can send you
No matter how hard we try.

We've a great many things for which to give thanks,
And we hope that that's true for you too.
The blessing of busy-ness, health, and good friends,
Give strength and meaning to all that we do.

The high point of the year, as we look back upon it,
Was our trip to New England last June;
Saw our son George get his M.D. from Harvard –
Now we should have a "family doctor" real soon!

168

But with son Tom in the Air Force in Texas,
We think of that old childhood rhyme,
"'Twas the night before Christmas and all through the house"
And hope that there'll soon come a time

When bombers, and warships, and missiles are gone,
When fears and suspicion shall cease,
When young folks, as well as we oldsters, too,
Can live out their lives in a world of quiet and peace.

And now, once again, may we repeat
Our good wishes, sincere and true.

MAY YOUR CHRISTMAS BE MERRY
YOUR HOLIDAYS GAY
AND THE NEW YEAR BE HAPPY
ALL THROUGH!

Christmas 1961

A star of hope,
A baby's smile
Love all divine,
God's radiance.

Man was not planning trips to outer space,
        Nor flying faster than the speed of sound,
Machines to do the work of many hands,
        Mass media, with all that implies,
All, all then quite unknown

And yet, somehow it came to earth.
        They knew it then – the Wisemen and the Shepherds,
We know it now. Through Time and Space,
        The greatest miracle of all!
GOD'S LOVE TO ALL MANKIND

169

Christmas 1984

The stars
in the desert sky
shine brightly Christmas eve.
My memories fill mind and heart
with joy.

These sounds
I hear, can they
be angels' serenade
or children's voices echoing
the songs?

As through
the ages ring
those precious words again,
"To all mankind good will and peace."
Amen.

Anatomy of a Poem
Doorways

(Onomatopoeia)	There are <u>creak</u>ing, rusty hinges (Enjambment)
	on old castle doors.
	My lady's boudoir has a door (Enjambment)
(Personification)	dressed in pearly pink. (Alliteration)
	The moldy <u>dungeon door</u> (Alliteration)
	is reinforced with iron bands.
(Alliteration)	And strong <u>bars block</u> the doorways (Alliteration)
	of the tyrant's prison. (Enjambment)
	An angel in Gethsemane opened
	a stone-blocked tomb,
(Caesura)	and we are told . . . that Heaven's golden doors
	will be opened to the faithful
	on the final Judgment Day.

Free Verse
March 12, 1988

The Cure

I give a time-tried remedy
when you feel bored, distraut, or blue,
please don't feel sorry for yourself,
just look around, try something new

Although perhaps you live to be
an even hundred years or more,
don't let yourself get in a rut,
Reach out, learn something new, explore.

Frustration

My mother had a way with plants,
although her garden was a mess.
It mattered not how hot or cold
the things she grew were limitless

The hollyhocks and sweetcorn stood
beside a thorny yellow rose.
She scatted seeds prolifically . . .
They all came up, she could not
                lose.
I must confess I lack her knack.
Although I hoe and plant the seeds,
the only things that come on strong
are crab-grass, thorns, and loco
                weed.

Essie Mae and Gerald Hill, 1955

*At the opening of the Farmers and
Merchants Bank, Aberdeen,
South Dakota.*

Let
Thy Handmaidens
Speak

Essie Mae Thompson Hill

Dedication

To my sons

George J. Hill
and
Thomas D. Hill

Whose love and encouragement
have made the dark times lighter
and the good times brighter.

Handmaidens of the Bible

Did you ever wonder what Bible women thought
As they went about the work they did
And the life they led each day?

Let them speak out, and tell us how they felt.
Some loved in vain, or knew regret –
Love, sorrow, joy and pain,
As have all women through the ages,
      They were the same.

Many were great heroines, whose names are inspiration,
Others, just as truly great, are hardly known by name,
But they all had emotions, heart and soul;
Let them speak out, and tell us how they felt,
As in faith and prayer they played the game
      Fate dealt.

A mother's sacrifice. She gave away her baby. She dedicated him to Jehovah; and he became one of the greatest men in Jewish history – he was the high priest Samuel. From the time he was weaned Hannah only saw him once a year, when she made the annual visit to the temple and each time she took him a coat which she had made with loving care. Her prayer of thanksgiving has been called the fore-runner of Mary's Magnificat – "My heart exults in the Lord; My strengths exults in the Lord."

Revised Standard Version

I Samuel 2:1,2

From the Heart of Hannah

Forgive me, great Jehovah, for these tears that flow unchecked.
You knew my longing for a child,
The anguish that I suffered through all those barren years,
And my great joy when at last my prayers were answered.

Those precious times we've had with baby Samuel
Today came to an end.
My arms are empty and my heart is heavy
With the longing that I have
To see his dear, sweet face against my breast.

Three years old! And today we left him at the temple
As I promised I would do.

For many years we made our annual visit
To give our sacrifices and our offerings to you,
            All-knowing God.
You knew the taunts and jeers which I endured
Because I stood alone, praying for a child
To make my life worth while
Even Eli saw my lips moving and my tears,
As I stood apart in prayer.

Until I told him all my sorrow, he misunderstood
And reproved me very sternly.
But when he heard, O great Jehovah, that I'd promised
That if I bore a child, that I would give him back to you
For service all his life, and that
His life would be to your great glory, not my own,
Then Eli blessed me, and he told me
That my covenant had been accepted.

But I told no one.
My husband, Elkhanah, knew my sorrow
And he tried to comfort me.
When we returned home we made tender love together
And my heart was lightened.
My baby Samuel was born, and my whole world turned
From darkness into light.

I always knew the time would come
When I must give him back to you,
And that is what I've done this day,
In all humility and great thankfulness.

But parting with him, I do now confess,
Was almost more than I could ever bear.
And I'll remember always through my tears,
His tiny form, the brightness of his hair,
And his small hands outstretched toward me
As we left the temple gate.

Disbelief

The Lord rained down fire and flaming tar from Heaven upon Sodom and Gomorrah and utterly destroyed them.   But Lot's wife looked back as she was following along behind him, and became a pillar of salt.

The Living Bible

Genesis 19:1-26
Luke 17:32

I was told by Lot
The world's going to pot,
But I just thought
'Twas a dastardly plot
To lure us from the city.
What a pity!

I was warned as we fled
To look straight ahead,
"Or you'll soon be dead,"
He said

No backward glance?
Well, I just took a chance!

O, my!
So dry!
Want to cry!
I'm salt –
His fault.

Sarah and Rebecca

Sarah was a beautiful woman, of great character, faith, and love – the
"Mother of Nations." The fact that she is the only woman in the Bible
whose age at the time of her death was recorded, shows the high esteem
in which she was held. She was one hundred and twenty-seven years old
according to the record. Abraham paid 400 shekels of silver for her
burying place and "came to mourn and weep for her." She was the mother
of Isaac, grandmother of Jacob, and great-grandmother of the men who were
the heads of the twelve tribes of Israel.

Genesis 23:2-20

Swan Song

Please come close to me, Rebecca
And sit here by my side,
I'd like to get acquainted
With Isaac's lovely bride.

I want you to know me, too,
And tell you of your great mission,
Because Jehovah has chosen me and you
To be the mothers of a great nation.

Although my life has not been easy
It's been better than most women's in this day,
Because Abraham loves and respects me as a partner
And does not insist that he always have his way.

There have been many happy times, and sad ones in between;
Sometimes my faith was weak and his was strong,
But at other times I was in the right
And he was very wrong.

177

For instance, many years ago,
You may be surprised to know,
I could have lived in Pharaohs' royal court
A most luxurious and pampered life,
If I hadn't told him that I was already Abram's wife.

We were traveling through the desert,
When we were captured and detained,
Abraham turned coward and said I was his sister,
but Pharaoh knew I told the truth
And my honesty touched his heart;
In the end he gave us many gifts
And allowed us to depart.
Although it was my loyalty that had set us free,
It was a very frightening and unhappy experience
              for me.

There came a time, however,
When I was the one who faltered and
I want to tell you about that, too.

Jehovah promised Abraham
That his descendants would become a mighty race,
Impossible to count them
As the sand upon the shore, or any place.

But I was barren – the years went by, no children came,
And finally, I gave up hope – I lost my faith,
And with reluctance, I made the decision
To let my maid, Hagar, take my place.

Her son was born, and for many years
I cared for him as my own,
But this was not what God had planned,
As the miracle of Isaac's birth has shown.

Time had not diminished our love and desire for each other,
But I was far beyond the age when women can conceive,
So when I heard the heaven-sent messengers
Tell my husband I would bear a son,
I laughed and could not let myself believe.

But I was wrong – it all came true – I bore a son,
And now your life with Isaac has begun.
I am very old and tired now,
And I think my life is almost done.

Always keep this in mind, my dear,
Isaac loves you, and you have great destiny ahead of you,
This is what I am asking you to do,
Never forget that it's been promised that our family
            will become a mighty race,
So when the history is written, you will have a
        special place.

                SHALOM

Jacob worked seven years so that he could have Rachel . . . Laban gave a wedding feast . . . but that night instead of Rachel, he took Leah to Jacob . . . not until the next morning did Jacob discover that it was Leah. He went to Laban and said, "Why have you tricked me?" . . . Laban answered, "It is not the custom here to give the younger daughter in marriage before the older" . . . then he worked for Laban another seven years . . . When Rachel died, she was buried beside the road to Ephrath, now known as Bethlehem. Jacob set up a memorial stone there, and it still marks Rachel's grave to this day.

From the Good News Bible

Genesis 35:16-20

Leah's Lament

This is a day of mourning . . . my beautiful sister is dead;
Now I must comfort Jacob, and care for her newborn son,
I weep because it's too late now to ask her
To forgive the mean and jealous thoughts
That I have carried in my heart
Through many, many years.

It's too late now.

I never have forgotten the look on Jacob's face
And his anger when he realized
That instead of having Rachel as his bride
It had been I, all swathed in veils,
Who, during the wedding ceremony,
Had been standing at his side
And then, according to our father's plan,
I went into the marriage tent to take her place.

It was too late then.

He had slaved for seven years to win her,
But he never had been told
That the eldest sister in a family must always be married first.
I knew this all the time
And I was glad, because I loved him,

And I hoped that he would learn to care for me,
But this was not to be,
And if he ever does,

It's too late now.

I know that I was wrong.
I did my best to please him,
And bore him many tall, handsome sons, and strong,
But when Rebecca finally bore her son, Joseph,
It was he who was his father's pride and joy.

She had always envied me my family,
Almost gave up hope for herself,
Now she has died in giving birth to her second boy.

It's too late now.

He will be called Benjamin, "Child of grief"
And through my tears,
I'm thinking of the household that we shared,
Our girlhood, the deceptions, and troubles,
And why and how,

It's too late now.

Father cared for us, but he did us all great wrong.
Although he made Jacob work for fourteen long and awful years,
The first seven were in vain . . .
He came here with nothing, fleeing from his brother's wrath.
Now he returns with wealth, a retinue of servants,
Great flocks, and herds, a daughter, and twelve sons,
But Rachel is dead!

It's too late now.

My heart is heavy with memories and sad regrets,
But I have faith, and I must dry my eyes,
Try to forgive myself, and put the past behind me.

It's not too late for that.

When Noah was 601 years old, on the first day of the first month, the water
was gone. God said to Noah, "Go out of the boat with your wife, your sons
and their wives." All the animals and the birds went out of the boat in groups
and pairs of their own kind.

The Living Bible

Genesis 7:1-24
Genesis 8:1-19

Mrs. Noah's Confession

Noah saw a rainbow and he said
        that was a sign
God was telling us that from now on
        we would be just fine.

Believe me, when I tell you
        I am might glad,
Because this is the worst time
        that I have ever had.

For forty days and forty nights
        I was nauseated ev'ry minute –
The ark smelled awful and so did the beasts
        that were living in it

I couldn't sleep, I couldn't eat . . .
        Oh! the rocking deck beneath my feet!
And now that I see land ahead
        That's where I'll stay until I'm dead!

The daughters of Zelophehad stood before Moses and the whole community at the
entrance of the tent of the Lord's presence and said,

> *"Our father died in the wilderness without leaving any sons. Just because*
he had no sons, why should our father's name disappear from Israel? Give us
property among our father's relatives."

Good News Bible
Today's English Version

Numbers 26:33; 27:1; 36:11
Joshua 17:3

Father: Zelophehad. Tribe of Manassas
Daughters: Mahlah, Noah, Haglah, Melcah, Tirzah

Equal Rights Amendment

When our father died without a son,
All his land would have been lost,
    Even his name.

But he did have other children, we five girls,
So we went to Moses to protest,
    And make a claim.

After he heard our story and consulted with the Lord,
He made a ruling in our favor, and justice has been done.
It took a lot of courage, but we had nothing to lose,
    and much to gain,
At last women have rights as human beings,
And a new day has begun.

The judgment which he rendered will become a law,
And women will have some rights equal to the men.
This is only one step in that direction,
But nothing will ever be the same again.

Job's Wife –

His wife said to him, "Are you still trying to be godly,
when God has done all this to you? Curse Him and die!"
                              The Living Bible   *Job 2:9*

Patience Tested

Job, this is a hard thing for me to do,
But I want to say I'm sorry for what I said to you.

You've always been so kind and good,
We were happy and in complete accord.
We had friends, and wealth, and children,
It seemed you were especially favored by the Lord

Indeed you were, and He knew that
You'd be faithful, come what may,
But Satan laughed, and said to God one day,
"Of course he loves you, when You're so good to him,
But wait!
Just take away his treasures, make him suffer,
And you'll see his love will turn to hate."

I should have helped you through those awful times,
When you lost all you cherished –
Your flocks and herds destroyed, our children dead,
Your strong body wracked by sores and pain –

But you bore it all, although I became an ugly, nagging wife,
I urged you to give up, but all in vain,
Finally I lost my temper and shouted,
"Curse God, and die, you fool!"

But Bless you, dear, you bore that too – I don't know why –
We know now God knew your patience, and
That your trust in Him would never fail,
So Satan's daring challenge went down in dire defeat,
Although we still don't know why good people have to suffer,
Our lives are once more happy and complete.

184

Should an innocent daughter have to give up her life to fulfill a bargain which her father made with Jehovah at a time when he felt inadequate to do a task which he had been called upon to do? The Bible does not give her name, but she did not question the sacrifice he asked. All that she asked was that he allow her to go up into the mountains with her girl friends for two months "to bewail mu virginity."

Jephthah made a vow that if Jehovah gave him the victory he would show his thankfulness in the form of a burnt offering. But to ask a daughter to give up her life in that awful way! Although human sacrifice was a common custom among ancient peoples, that was never the custom among the Israelites. Even Abraham's son Isaac was saved from that fate by a voice from Jehovah just before the sacrifice was to be made. Some Biblical scholars think that the daughter of Jephthah spent the rest of her life at the temple, denied the joys and fulfillment of being a wife and mother.

Judges 11:29-40
Hebrews 11:32

Jephthah's Daughter

I've come here to the mountains to mourn what lies ahead
To think about my father, and wonder what will happen now.
I must prepare myself to be the living sacrifice
Which my father promised when he made a sacred vow.

He was an outcast, but his name well known and feared
Because he was a fighter, fierce and wild,
The leader of a band of faithful reckless men, but when
Israel called him to defend them from an enemy threatening to destroy,
He had self-doubts, they were too many and too strong.

But Israel said, "We need you and we'll make you king of Gilead."
He knew it was his duty, so he made a bargain with the Lord;
"I need you, God, to insure the victory. This is my pledge,
Whatever living creature first comes through the gate when I return,
Will be a sacrifice to you in thankfulness, this I do swear."

I knew nothing of this, but we all prayed and waited,
And when at last we heard the joyous sounds, the laughing and the shouts,
We knew that they had won, our people saved.

On dancing feet, with arms outstretched I dashed to meet him,
            ahead of all the rest;
But when he saw me, a stricken look came over his dear face,
And his men bowed their heads in silence as he told me of his vow.

The usual sacrificial offering was a dove, a ram, a ewe;
Jehovah had told Moses exactly what to do.
Abraham was tested when he was told to slay his son,
But never in all our history had human sacrifice been done.

Perhaps this is the time.

I am a child no longer and I understand that I must be ready
To pay the price of father's honor and the saving of our race,
My life will be the price and I am ready . . . what will it be?

Death, quick and merciful, upon the altar,
Or Life, virgin forever, spent in service at the temple,
Denied the joy of being wife and mother, a lingering sacrifice
To you, Jehovah, for my father's victory and for my people
Now I must go back and try to comfort my father and my friends.

Babel Babble

Our men were building a tower
       that they said would reach to the sky,
When suddenly all was confusion
       and we can't understand why.

Now everyone talks in gibberish
       that makes no sense, head nor tail,
The work on the tower has stopped, and
       I think the project is doomed to fail.

I'm sorry because I'll never know the rest of the
       gossip my neighbor has just started to tell,
'Cause I can't understand a word that she says –
       but perhaps it's just as well!

I'll just look on the brighter side.
       Our family will move to a new place,
Where we won't worry about neighbors,
       And we'll have plenty of breathing space.

In the third year of his reign King Ahasu-erus (Xerxes) gave a great celebration. The climax was a banquet which lasted for a week, amid couches of gold and silver, and drinks served in golden goblets. On the seventh day "when the heart of the King was merry with wine" he ordered his wife, Queen Vashti, to come to the hall, in order that his friends might see how beautiful she was. She had the personal integrity and courage to refuse, and it made him so angry that he banished her. This paved the way for Esther, another beautiful woman, to become his queen.

Esther 1:10-11

Proud Queen

Banished from the palace in disgrace,
Another has been chosen to take my place.
Wives are always required to obey,
But I didn't see it quite that way.

Although I was his queen, I had no more freedom than a slave.
I was subject to his wishes, and expected to behave.
I never had refused before, to obey his every whim,
But that really was not hard to do, because I was quite fond of him.

During the week of revelry, he had bragged about my beauty
But when he summoned me to come
To that room full of drunken men
I felt that went far beyond the wifely call of duty.

I refused and he was irate because
Before his friends he had lost face.
He told me to get out, and
I was banished from the palace in disgrace.

I knew what I was doing, and
I took an awful chance;
I lost, but I have kept my pride.
I went with head held high, without a backward glance.

Courageous Abigail

When David came to the large estate
of Nabal and asked for food for himself
and his little band of men, Nabal
drunk as usual, refused to help,
although David had helped him at one
time. Abigail then took it upon herself
to try to make amends. She arrived just
in time to hear David say, "may God
strike me dead if I don't kill every one
of these men before morning."

Later David said, "Praise the Lord who
sent you this day to meet me. Thank God
for your good sense and for what you have
done this day in keeping me from the
crime of murder."

The Living Bible

I Samuel 25:2-42

Courageous Abigail

David loves me, I am his wife,
And I am happy now at last.
He calls me beautiful,
And I have borne his child.

How well do I remember the fateful day we met.
David and his little army were starving in the desert
And he sent messengers to Nabal to ask for food,
But drunk as usual, he refused him with contempt and scorn.

When I heard this, I knew what I must do
And quickly called the servants and the kitchen slaves.
We loaded up a caravan with bread and meat and wine,
And with fear and trembling I set out for David's camp.

As we approached, I heard him say in rousing angry voice
That by morning Nabal's flocks and herds, his household
And all that he possessed would be destroyed. I breathed
A prayer for courage to present my offering and to beg for his forgiveness.

When David saw me and our eyes met,
I felt a surge of confidence rush through me.
He accepted what I'd brought and my apology for the wrong,
And as we talked that night, I caught a vision of his greatness.

I shared it with him, and when I was free to wed
He asked me to be his wife; I felt unworthy of this great man,
But now all I have, and all I am – my future is with him
And I will remember all my days.

The joy he brought me when he said,
"Blest be the great Lord God of Israel which sent thee
That fateful day to meet me. Abigail, my Love,
I cherish all thy words and all thy ways."

Rizpah is the little-known heroine of a terrible tragedy. Saul broke a treaty of peace between Israel and a neighbor country. To meet the demand for retribution for the massacre which followed, David gave in and hanged seven of Saul's descendants, including two of Rizpah's own sons. By her courage, her compassion, and selflessness, she shows herself to be a person of integrity, honor, and strong character, deserving of recognition.

II Samuel 21:8-14

Rizpah's Vigil

Seven innocent men, slain in atonement
For the guilt of others, not their own.
At last the rains have come, the years of famine over,
And my long lonely vigil now is done.

Once I was Saul's beloved, and the mother of his sons,
His sons who had to give their lives to satisfy his sins.
He broke a sacred covenant made long years ago,
And for that Jehovah sent a drought upon this place.

For three long years we all suffered,
Until the sacrifice was made,
And after their death, until rain came,
Alone I guarded their dear bodies
Protecting them from desecration and disgrace.

Sack cloth I spread upon the ground and
Night and day for weeks and months
I fought off beasts and birds of prey.
But now the sacrifice has been accepted
And I praise the Lord this day.

Now they are reunited in honor, though in death,
With Saul and Jonathan, the seven who were slain,
All buried now, and so I am at peace at last,
With no more pain.

Naomi and Ruth

After Naomi's husband and two sons died in the land of Moab where they had fled to escape a terrible drought in the Land of Israel, she decided to return to her native village of Bethlehem. Ruth, the wife of one of her sons, loved her enough to leave her native land and accompany her. With Naomi as a kind of 'match-maker,' Ruth found new happiness as the wife of Boaz. Their baby was named Obed, who became the grandfather of David. An old prophecy was fulfilled when "Jesus was born of the lineage of David."

Ruth said to Naomi, "for where you go, I will go; and where you lodge, I will lodge: your people shall be my people, and your God will be my God."

II Samuel 1:20, 4:14-22
Ruth 1:16

Naomi Dreams

Sometimes I thought that Jehovah gave me
More of sorrow and of woe
Than I could ever bear.
But now I know
The Lord is good, I sing His praise
And I will bless Him all my days.
For Ruth has born a son.

She is not of our own people,
But I knew that it was right
When I sent her to the threshing floor
To lie at Boaz' feet that night.
Perhaps their baby is the One.

When in my arms I hold this child
I feel blest beyond compare.
And I wonder if Jehovah's planning for his people,
Could possibly be nestled there.

Martha and Mary

Martha had a sister named Mary who took a seat at Jesus' feet and listened to him talk. Martha finally complained to Jesus about all the work she was doing without any help from her sister, but Jesus answered, "Martha you are anxious about many matters, Mary has chosen the better portion."

Modern Language Bible

Luke 10:40-42

Apology to Martha

I'm sorry, Martha dear, because I didn't help you
with the work that day, when there was so much to do.
I just sat listening to what He had to say,
and Jesus told you I had chosen the better way.

I know that you were hurt, but think of this –
He comes here to rest, relax, and
to regain strength for His great task.

We know He loves us, and our brother Lazarus, too,
 so please remember, dear, it was to you
He gave the greatest thought of all His teaching.

I was not there when he raised Lazarus from the dead,
but you said He told you He was the Resurrection and the Life.
That if we truly trust Him, and believe that this is true
then we shall live forever! This is what He told to you.

So who can say which has the better part,
I think we each have a special place in His dear heart.

"He looked up and saw the rich putting their gifts into the treasury, and he saw a poor widow drop in two copper coins. And He said, 'Truly I tell you, this poor widow has put in more than all of them, for they all contributed out of their abundance, but she out of her poverty put in all the living that she had'."

Revised Standard Version

Luke 21:1-4

A Widow Wonders

My two small coins were everything I had.
      The temple court was crowded and
I hoped no one would see,
      When I put them in the off'ring box,
Because it was such a small gift
      For all the good things that God had done for me.

I thought no one had taken notice,
      But when I turned to leave the place,
I saw the man called Jesus look at me
      With kindly eyes and a smile upon his face.

Then He spoke a few words in a serious way
      To a group of friends who stood nearby.
Did He know that I had given everything I could?
      I don't know why, but suddenly I felt warm and happy,
And although my gift was poor, I think He understood.

Dorcas was a woman who truly gave of herself to others, and "She stretched out her hand to the poor; yea, she reacheth for her hand to the needy."   *Prov. 31:13, 20*
She was the patron "saint" of those who love to sew, and she used her talent as a seamstress and her home as a workshop to help the poor of her home town of Joppa.   *Acts 9:36-42*

Testimony

I must tell you the wonderful story of what happened here today.
Our tears and wails of sorrow were changed to smiles and shouts of joy,
When our friend Dorcas was brought back from death to life again,
In a most miraculous way.

No one has done more than she for the people of this town.
The way she sewed for needy folks, the poor, the old, and sick,
Brought warmth and self respect to them, and to her, love and wide renown.

Four days ago, our friend was stricken, and her life came to an end.
With aching hearts and streaming eyes, the final preparations all were made.
But Peter had heard about her goodness, and he hastened here on foot –
And he raised her from the dead!

He knelt down in prayer beside her,
            and laid his big rough hands upon her head
Then "Tabitha Dorcas, arise!" is what he said.
As people watched, her eyes opened and
When she saw him, she sat straight up;
He helped her stand, and all the wailing turned to shouts of joy.
"God has restored her to us. Blest be the Lord."

We have resolved to make sure that she will never be forgotten.
We'll tell our children and those who come after
            how she helped all those in need and was risen from the dead.
Some people use their wealth and property,
            but all she had was a needle and some thread.

THANK YOU, GOD, FOR DORCAS

What did a woman of Samaria, who was practically an outcast, think after a chance meeting with a strange man at an ancient well dug many years before in land that had once belonged to Jacob? The man was Jesus, and what He told her about Himself is one of the most significant stories in the New Testament.   *John 4:7-42*

Woman of Samaria

It was hot. I was tired, dispirited, and thirsty,
Because I'd come a long and weary way,
But as I approached the well to refresh myself that day,
A man was already sitting there and asked me for a drink.

I was so surprised that I answered him sarcastically before
            I took time to think,
"You Jews hate us in Samaria, so how can you ask this of me?"
But he ignored this and answered quietly,
"If you knew who I am, you would ask me for a drink,
Not from the well, but from the Fountain of Life Eternal."

I didn't understand this, but as we talked,
I found out that he was no ordinary traveler.
He knew my past, my sins, my heartache.
My tiredness slipped away, I felt refreshed, uplifted,
As if indeed I had drunk of some kind of Living Water.

Finally I told him I believed that a Messiah, called the Christ,
Would come and tell us everything, and then
He answered with calm certainty,
"I, the man who's speaking to you now, am He."

Strangely enough, I truly believed him as he spoke,
He forgave my sins, and we talked some more.
Then I hurried away on joyful feet to spread the word.
Even strangers believed when I told them what I'd heard.

They came in great numbers to hear and see, and all of
            them eager to hear what he had to say.
When they heard him they too, called Him the Christ,
            Who'd come to save the world.

Lydia was the first Christian convert in Europe. One Sabbath day, Paul found a group of women praying to a river in Joppa, among whom was the well-known, influential business-woman of the town, Lydia. She heard his message about Jesus, believed, and was baptized. Her home thereafter became the headquarters from which Paul carried on his mission. Acts 16:14

[Ed.: Essie Mae was mistaken when she wrote "in Europe." Joppa is in Asia; it is on the Mediterranean seacoast, about 30 miles north-west of Jerusalem. Nevertheless, Lydia was an important early convert to Christianity.]

Royal Purple – Pure Gold – First Convert

Please let me introduce myself –
My name is Lydia. Most people know me
     for my family business which is
Selling the distinctive purple dye
Which aristocrats in Rome and elsewhere
Covet and pay for dearly, when they buy.

I know that people say I'm rich, and they call me
     beautiful and generous,
But the happiness that fills my heart, and
Makes my life worthwhile
Is the knowledge that I have found the Truth.

How well do I remember when and where it happened.
My friends and I beside a river met and knelt for prayers.
Then Paul came by and told us about Jesus Christ, the
     Son of God.
Who gave His life to save us from our sins.
Suddenly I felt as One with all the Universe.

This was the answer!
Right then and there, I asked to be baptized.
And forever more, I'll be proud, though humble,
In doing what I can to spread this message.

Don't hurry off! I'd like to share some of Paul's
letters which he sends from time to time. They
give us hope, and confidence, and inspiration.
But they're for everyone.

So Peter left the cell, following the angel . . .
When Peter finally realized what had happened . . .
he went to the home of the mother of John Mark
where many had gathered for a prayer meeting . . .
He knocked at the door in the gate and a girl
named Rhoda came to open it.

The Living Bible

Acts 12:6-16

Rhoda Remembers

I was just a working woman in this house,
And I spoke when I was spoken to, and not much more,
So that's why when Peter's friends thought I had lost my mind
When I got excited and behaved as I had never done before.

Peter was in prison and condemned to die.
A large crowd of his friends were praying
In an upper room, and that is the reason why
They didn't hear him knocking at the gate, as luckily did I.

Herod had sentenced him to a sure and awful death,
And it truly was a miracle, the way that he escaped at last.
He said an angel came, and released him from the chains,
Then opened up the prison doors which had held him fast.

Through the years that I had waited on my mistress and the rest,
I had listened to folks talk about Christ, the risen Lord,
And I knew how His disciples went abroad to spread the Word.
So when Peter was arrested, I too was anxious and distressed.

I prepared their supper, then they went upstairs to pray;
My work was finished but I stayed on to pray and wait.
The hour was late, and no one else heard the knocking
And pounding at the garden gate.

In my heart I knew that it was Peter,
And I raced upstairs to tell them he was here.
It made them angry and they called me mad, but then
They too heard the knocking loud and clear.

And so to me, a humble servant, came the joy
Of being the first to know that Peter'd been set free.
It was a blessed happiness for me. I only did what I felt I had to do,
But I knew that my prayers were answered too.

Many things have happened since that night,
Peter is dead, and I am old and blind.
But I'll always remember when he came knocking at our door
And when I think of all that he endured, my hardships I don't mind.

He wrote a special letter to us before he died,
And we often talk about the things he said.
He strengthened our faith, and he told us how to live . . .
We almost memorized it, because 'twas so often read.

But the words that mean the most to me
Are that our gifts are not all the same – some great, some small.
And if we believe in Christ and do the best we can
That's all He asks, and He loves us one and all.

Essie Mae's Cook Book
with Recipes from
Family and Friends

Recipes from Essie Mae's kith 'n' kin

Editor's Note: *Essie Mae's Cookbook* is a comb-bound book with 168 numbered pages, plus two additional unnumbered pages; one blank page to be used for Notes and the other is a handwritten Index which she compiled. The 120 recipes in this *Cookbook* are copies of handwritten pages or typed from notes made by 30 members of her family – the Thompsons – and 19 in her husband's family – the Hills; and 27 of her friends. Interspersed are photocopies of old magazine and newspaper articles, showing kitchen stoves and other items used in food preparation; poems by Essie Mae and her family; and quotations about food from the Bible and other authors. I have reproduced below a few representative pages from *Essie Mae's Cookbook*. All of the recipes and text can be seen in the original *Cookbook* in the library of the Genealogical Society of Linn County, Iowa. P.O Box 175, Cedar Rapids, Ia. 52406. (319) 369-0022. gensoclinncoia@aol.com

Who's Who

Mother - "Grandma" - Cassie - Sarah
Rachel Edith - Rachie - (High) - sister
George and Carrie - Son and daughter-in-law
Sarah - Granddaughter   Jim - grandson
Lena (Helena) - Granddaughter
Vicki and Mark - Granddaughter and husband
Tom Jr. (Tommy) - Grandson
Suzanne Eppley - Tom Sr.'s fiance
Keiko - Mother of Vicki and Tommy
Harris - Brother and husband of Helen Thompson

Nieces and nephews and spouses

Harriett Thompson Runander -
Kathleen Thompson May- daughters of brother James
Katherine (Koko) May Bickford
Elizabeth (Fluffy) May- Kathleen's daughters
John Thompson - son of brother Manly
Ellen Thompson Audley - John's daughter
Virginia Thompson - Ellen's mother
Betty Haglund - Manly's daughter
Sally Thompson Montgomery - daughter of brother Harris

Nieces - Continued

Sarah Rothery - Granddaughter of Harris (Sally's daughter)
Elizabeth Fitch - Jim Jr.'s wife

Cousin

Priscilla Thompson
Aunt Cassie (Mother of Priscilla)

Sisters-in-law

May Hoover Thompson - deceased
Marie Thompson - deceased
Clara Thompson - deceased
Helen McCune Thompson - wife of Harris

*Essie Mae in
June 1977, age 74*

201

When I started planning this book,
my purpose was to preserve and share some
old family recipes which I have saved.
They are keepsakes from the era of "Good
eating before the era of microwave ovens,
mixes, and frozen dinners."

These include Grandma Thompson's
recipe for her soft sugar cookes, and
Grandma Hill's instructions for making
homemade soap, both of them in their own
handwriting.

However, I have enlarged the project
to include recipes from other members of
the family and special friends. It has
become a memory book of occasions where
good food was part of the good times we
had together.

I have a modest collection of cook-
books whick I treasure. Every one of them
has a special meaning for me, so I have
included recipes from them in this book.

Putting this book together has been
one of the great joys of my life. My
thanks go to all of you who have shared
your recipes. This is your book, a leg-
acy to the future.
ENJOY ENJOY ENJOY ENOY ENJOY ENJOY ENJOY

My Kitchen Prayer

Bless my little kitchen, Lord,
I love its every nook,
And bless me as I do my work,
Wash pots and pans and cook.

May the meals that I prepare
Be seasoned from above
With thy blessing and thy grace,
But most of all, thy love.

As we partake of earthly food,
The table thour hast spread,
We'll not forget to thank thee, Lord,
For all our daily bread.

So bless my little kitchen, Lord,
And those who enter in,
May they find naught but joy and love,
And happiness, therein.

                              Amen

I copied this poem from a copper-toned
plate which hangs in my kitchen. It was
given to me many years ago by one of my
fifth-grand "mother's"....I cherish it.
                              EMTH

203

Thompson Family Recipes

Mother's Sugar Cookies

Sugar Cookies.
2 eggs, well beaten.
2 cup (scant) sugar.
½ " shortening. butter is best,
beat all together well.
add three teaspoons, (rounded up a little) baking powder,
sifted with flour to make a "soft"
dough (a little less than 3 pt.)
alternately with one cup
of canned milk, or thin cream.
Roll out sprinkle with sugar
cut out and bake in hot oven
I like 500° Farenhite. best.

This is Mother Thompson's recipe for her
prize-winning soft sugar cookies' in her
own hand-writing. It is a very soft dough
and hard to handle. I have tried to make
them and they are 'passable' but not as good
as hers. She sometimes made a filling of
raisins and nuts cooked together, put it on
half the cookie and folded the other half
over it. They were delicious, but the
plain ones won the prizes.

Keiko's Beef Burgundy

Keiko's Beef Burgandy

½ C bacon grease
1¼ lb small white onions
4 lbs chuck beef cut into cubes
¼ C flour
1 tsp meat extract paste or
    1 C beef bullion
3 C Burgandy
¼ tsp pepper 2 bay leaves
½ tsp thyme 1½ tsp marjoram
¾ lb. fresh mushrooms

Fry onions. Remove. Brow beef a little at a time. Add seasonings and wine. Either bake or simmer 3 hours. Then add onions and mushrooms. Cook 3/4 hours more.

Serve over rice or noodles or gnocchi.

Suzanne's Mocha Cheese Cake

MOCHA CHEESE CAKE

in a small bowl mix 3/4 C gram cracker crumbs.
        1 1/2 T sugar
        4 T butter (melted)
press into bottom of spring form set aside.

in a large bowl mix 3 8oz cream cheeses
        1 C sugar
        2 large eggs.

melt 8oz package semi sweet chocolate bits
    with 2T heavy cream + add to large bowl

then add 8oz sour cream
       1/2 cup coffee (made 1 cup strong)
       1 tsp. vanilla.

Pour into the pan and bake 58 – 75 min
Comes out soft in the middle
Let set for a day or two.

SUZANNE

207

The Hill Family

Who's Who

Mother - Grandmother - Jessie
Ruby (Woodin) - daughter
Adelia (Hemenway McBeth) - daughter
Essie Mae - daughter-in-law
Jessie (Woodin) Kent - granddaughter
Lela (Hill) Odlund - granddaughter
Bonnie (Hill) Treloar - granddaughter
George Hill - grandson
Lanie Hill - granddaughter-in-law
Betti Woodin - granddaughter-in-law
Agnes Hemenway - granddaughter-in-law
Marie Hill - granddaughter-in-law
Mildred Hill - granddaughter-in-law
Avis Hill - granddaughter-in-law
Dorla Hill - granddaughter-in-law
"Gerry" Hill - Granddaughter-in-law

Julia Woodin Hill - daughter-in-law

A Hill Family Reunion
"Give us this day."

Parents, brothers and sisters
Aunts, uncles, and cousins,
With in-laws included
There were two or three dozen

To appreciate these occasions, I think a brief history of the Hill family in Iowa should be included in this book. Here is what I remember of what has been told to me.

Great-grandfather Charles W. Hill, born August 31, 1831, and his wife, Adelia Riley, came to Wright County, Iowa, with their three children, George J., William, and Adella, from Elmira [Caton], New York in 1887. When they were crossing the river near Rowan, 9-year-old William slipped off the horse he was riding and was drowned. His was the first grave in the Rowan cemetery where many of the Hills and Stockwells are now buried.

George J. married Jessie Stockwell and they were the parents of nine children, five boys and four girls, two of whom died very young of the dreaded "Black Diphtheria." The Hills were farmers and eventually acquired a great many acres of fertile Wright County land among the various members of the family. When George was about fifty years old, he retired, left the farm, and moved to Clarion. The original domicile was a log cabin, long gone, but when I came into the family in 1930, the "home place" was a large white house with a big porch across the front. There was a huge red barn where work horses and a stallion had been kept, fruit trees, an apple orchard, chicken yard, vegetable garden, and flowering bushes and peonies around the house.

An unusual circumstance made these family reunion dinners very large affairs. Not only were there seven Hill families, but a brother (Myron) and a sister (Ruby) married a sister (Julia) and a brother (Howard) of the Woodin family. There were six children in that family and they all lived nearby. There is now a sixth generation of Hills living in Wright County on land that was originally bought by great-grandfather Charles for $10 an acre. Deep roots!

In "my time," the reunions centered around Mother Hill's supervision, but in later years, Ruby's home was the focus of these gatherings. The reunions are now a thing of the past, but on the following pages are recipes from the "Hill girls" of the present generation. They are indeed carrying on the tradition of being great cooks.

(Note about the big white house on the "home place." In the mid-thirties, it was a sad sacrifice on the altar of Cookery, when it burned to the ground because of an over-heated stove pipe, fired up to bake some pumpkin pies. Now there is nothing but the memories of the good times we had there.)

209

Hill Family Recipes

Mocha Cakes Gerry Hill

1 cup sugar
1½ cups flour
2 scant tsp baking powder
1 cup boiling water
3 tsp butter melted in the water
2 well beaten eggs
Bake in loaf pan 350° 20-25 min
when cold cut in 1 inch squares
& ice with icing
½ cup butter & approximately 2 cups
of powdered sugar to make stiff
dough. Add cream till thin enough
to spread all around cakes and
roll in 1# peanuts (jumbo salted peanuts)

Jerry Hill's Mocha Cake

210

Mother Hill's Soap Recipe

Soap

Dissolve 1 can of lye in
6 quarts warm, soft water
Add to this 4 lbs. clear
grease. Let stand 5 days
stirring twice daily, then
boil 25 minutes. Before
its is done add 2 tables/
borax and $\frac{2}{3}$ cup ammonia

These are Mother (Jessie) Hill's
instructions for making home-made
soap. During WW II I made several
batches of soap, using grease that I
got from the Bowman Hall (Cornell College)
kitchen. It was as white as Ivory, but
considerably stronger. Using Lewis Lye
is always a little scary, but it was
one step up from the way the pioneer
housewives made lye by leaching wood
ashes.

Essie Mae

Jessie (Woodin) Kent's *Tarte Tatin*

Tarte Tatin
upside down apple tart

Pastry
1 C flour
1 T sugar
½ tsp salt
4 T butter
1½ T margarine

} Blend dry ingredie[?]
with a pastry
fork. Add 2-3 T[?]
cold water, mix an[?]
form in a ball.
Chill.

(For cooking the apples I use a
deep dish 7 inch diameter copper [?]
Any flameproof or ceramic [?]
round pan will work)
Smear copper pan with 2T but[?]
Peel and slice 6 Granny Smith
apples in ⅛ in. slices. Toss apple[?]
with ⅔ C white sugar and ⅓ C
brown sugar and ½ tsp cinnam[?]
Arrange slices in concentric rin[?]
in pan and drizzle ¼ C melted
butter over the top. Cook on to[?]
of the stove til sugar begins [?]
Caramelize

Roll out dough to circle slight[?]
larger than pan. Cut holes for
steam and put on top of apple[?]
Tuck dough in around edges
with a wooden spoon.

Bake at 400° about 30 min til
crust is brown. Remove and
invert on a serving dish. Serve
warm with ice cream.

Jessie Woodin Kent

93

Essie Mae's Angel Cake Dessert

Angel Cake Dessert

1 small angel cake broken into small
pieces. Put into a 9x12 cake pan.
3 egg yolks   1 Can crushed pineapple.
1 C sugar   Nuts 1 C cream, whipped

Mix beaten egg yolks, sugar, and
pineapple. Bring to a rolling boil. Set
off the fire. Soak 1 pkg. geletin ½ C
cold water. Stir into hot mixture, be-
fore it cools.
Let cool. Add 3 beaten egg whites
and the whipped cream to the cooled
mixture. Pour this over the angel
food pieces. Let stand at least ½
day before serving. Serve with whipped
cream. Nuts on top or red and
green cherries at Christmas.
(Howard-Hedger School
   refreshments – Aberdeen)

Essie Mae

George Hill's Pancake Recipe

<u>Pancakes</u>
(George Hill)

3 cups pancake mix flour ("Bisquick," etc.)
   or make your own "scratch" mix
   from 3 C flour, 1½ tsp. salt,
   6 tsp. baking powder, 3 TBSP sugar
3 cups milk (skim milk is best)
3 TBSP liquid shortening (corn oil, etc.)
3 eggs

1. Use cast metal skillets, medium heat.
2. Mix flour and milk, then oil, then eggs,
   and beat until nearly smooth.
3. When water drops will dance on the
   skillets, start frying, and fry them
   fast so the skillets won't overheat.
4. Makes about 36 pancakes, each with
   2 TBSP of batter. Serves 6 adults
   or hungry kids.

Lanie Hill's Never-Fail Hollandaise

Never Fail Hollandaise
from
the Waring Blendor Cookbook
with
modifications

<u>3</u> egg yolks   or 2 whole eggs
<u>2</u> Tablespoons lemon juice

<u>1</u> ¼ lb butter
pinch of cayenne. salt to taste.
Put all butter in Waring Blendor well
ahead of time to bring to room temperature.

Melt butter until it starts to bubble.

Turn blendor on full and slowly add
melted butter. Continue blending for a minute
or two.

Use <u>immediately</u> (that's the trick)

Lanie Hill.

Recipes from Friends

Recipes from Friends

Some times there is some one
who takes
Time enough
to listen
Some one who cares
about us
when we lose
And who loves us
even when
we're wrong

Scripsit EMTH

Magic Fire

An eternal flame burns like a candle
lit by the spark of love,
brightening dark corners of the heart,
where memories of the past are stored away, fanned
by thoughts of times almost forgotten,
the fire brings a glow into the soul
as did the embers on the heart at home,
bring warmth into the body long ago.

EMTH

Barbara Johnson's Hummus

Hummus

2 c. cooked or canned chick peas, drained

2/3 c. Sesame tahini paste (available in health food stores).

3/4 c. lemon juice

2 cloves garlic

1 tsp. salt

Parsley

Place all the ingredients in a food processor, blender, or food mill and blend until smooth. Pile into a small bowl and garnish with parsley leaves. Serve with Arab or Pita bread as an appetizer. 8-10 servings.

Barbara Johnson (Lanie Hill's Sister)

137

217

Tudy Irwin's Ham Casserole

Tudy Irwin's Ham Casserole

3 C ground ham
1 C peas
3 C cooked rice
1 T onion
1 T parsley
1½ C milk
¼ C melted butter
1 C grated cheese
3 eggs beaten
Grease pan. Bake 1¼ hr.
    in 325° oven.
Serve with mushroom soup
    for sauce.

Tudy was my best friend in Sac City.
She was very popular with the young
folks. She played piano by ear and
kept her grand piano busy with all the
latest popular music. I mourn her pre-
mature death.

153

218

Essie Mae and Her Family

Essie Mae Thompson Hill, center, in front row; her husband, Gerald "Jerry" Hill is beside her; her son Tom is at L rear; his wife, Keiko, is at L front. Tom and Keiko's children Victoria and Tommy are beside them. Essie Mae's son George is at R rear; his wife, Helene "Lanie" is at R front. Their children are Jim, David, and Sarah from L to R at rear, and Helena in front, between Jerry and Lanie

This picture was taken at Christmas time in 1970 in Aberdeen, S.D.

Chicken Feed

A thoughtful farm wife found a ten cent piece
In an old hen that she was cleaning,
And like a priestess at the Greek Delphic Oracle,
She pondered upon its meaning.

At last she made her pronouncement,
"Inflation is here to stay.
Because it is very obvious
That a dime is just chicken feed today."

E.M.T.H.

Memories

In dreams
I walk again
with friends of long ago
We laugh, we love, and then I wake
in tears

Sun City   Essie Mae Thompson Hill

Bistro

The glass
Glare-gold and green,
Clear crystal   silver glaze,
Crimson grey colors   glancing dance
and fade

Paris   Helene Zimmermann Hill

220

Annotated Bibliography

The four books published by Essie Mae Thompson Hill are the basis for this work, which is entitled *Prairie Daughter: Stories and Poems from Iowa (2nd Edition).* The 1st edition of *Prairie Daughter* is presented here with very few changes. Most of these are changes in spelling or grammar, re-formatting the paragraphs, and correcting a few minor factual errors. The second book of her memoirs, *Flapper Fun*, included some stories that previously appeared in *Prairie Daughter*, and they are omitted. The selections from *Let Thy Handmaidens Speak* includes all of the poems in the first edition, but it has been reformatted for the larger page size in the present book. I made an editorial decision to reproduce all of the poetry and much of the text in *Essie Mae's Cookbook*, but to select only a few illustrative recipes from the 120 in the first edition.

Hill, Essie Mae Thompson. *Prairie Daughter*. Phoenix, Ariz.: C. O. L. Publishing, Inc., with O'Sullivan , Woodside & Co., 1978.

_____. *Let Thy Handmaidens Speak*. Chatham, N.J.: Minuteman Press of Chatham, 1983.

 _____. *Flapper Fun: Other Poems and Stories*. Phoenix, Ariz.: O'Sullivan , Woodside & Co., 1988.

 _____. *Essie Mae's Cookbook with Recipes from Family and Friends*. Sun City, Arizona: Essie Mae Thompson Hill, c. 1990.

The genealogy and family history of Essie Mae Thompson's family was previously published in two books, and some of the illustrations from those books are reproduced here. They are:

Hill, George J. *Fundy to Chesapeake: The Thompson, Rundall and Allied Families. Ancestors and Descendants of William Henry Thompson and Sarah D. Rundall, Who Were Married in Linn County, Iowa, in 1889*. Berwyn Heights, Maryland: Heritage Books, 2016 (2 vols.).

_____. *Four Families: A Tetralogy. Reader's Guide to* Western Pilgrims, Quakers and Puritans, Fundy to Chesapeake, and American Dreams. *Synopsis of 481 Immigrants and First Known Ancestors in America from Northern Europe in the Families of George J. Hill and Jessie F. Stockwell, William T. Shoemaker and Mabel Warren, William H. Thompson and Sarah D. Rundall, and John Zimmermann and Eva K. Kellenbenz, with Outlines of their Descent from the Immigrants*. Berwyn Heights, Maryland: Heritage Books, 2017.

Extensive bibliographies for the many known and suspected branches of Essie Mae's ancestral families – the Thompson and Rundall families – are in the two books shown above. Her mother, Sarah (Sadie) Rundall was a descendant of Rundall, Manly, Ogden, Tompkins, and Sharples/ss, and she was a collateral relative of Varina Howell Davis, wife of Jefferson Davis. Her father was an Archibald from Nova Scotia, and his ancestry includes Prescott, Putnam, and Rebecca (Towne) Nurse, who was hanged as a witch in Salem. Some of the most important sources are:

Anderson, Bart. *The Sharples-Sharpless Family*. 3 vols. West Chester, Penn.: Bart Anderson, 1971. Documents the beginnings of the Sharples/Sharpless Family in America, and continues with paternal line descendants to the 1970s.

Anderson, Robert Charles. *The Great Migration Begins* and *The Great Migration*. Online database. Several of the ancestors of Essie Mae Thompson arrived in the Great Migration to Massachusetts.

Cannon, LeGrand, Jr. *Look to the Mountain*. New York: Holt, Rinehart [1942] 1983. The fictional young couple, Whit Livingston and Melissa Butler, who settled in Sandwich, N.H., could have been Essie Mae's ancestor Joseph Prescott and his second wife.

Cather, Willa. *My Ántonia*. Boston: Houghton Mifflin, 1918. This book was mentioned by Essie Mae as being a good description of her students at Valley Chapel School. They and their parents, like Ántonia, were immigrants from Bohemia – known later as Czechoslovakia, and now as the Czech Republic. They didn't speak English when they came to school, and their habits were very different from her classmates and friends.

Cope, Gilbert, comp. *Genealogy of the Sharpless Family, Descended from John and Jane Sharples, Settlers Near Chester, Pennsylvania, 1682: Together with Some Account of the English Ancestry of the Family ... and a Full Report of the Bi-Centennial Reunion of 1882*. Philadelphia: Published for the family, 1887. The descent from John Sharples, the emigrant, to Essie Mae's ancestors, Rachel Manly and her daughter, Sarah D. Rundall, is shown in this book.

Eagan, Timothy. *The Worst Hard Time: The Untold Story of Those Who Survived the Great American Dust Bowl*. New York: Houghton Mifflin, 2006. Iowa was not actually in the Dust Bowl, but Iowans could imagine the suffering of those who were in it. The dust blew across Iowa when Essie Mae was a young bride, and her sons can remember it.

Fisher, David Hackett. *Albion's Seed: Four British Folkways in America*. New York: Oxford University Press, 1989. Essie Mae's ancestry includes all four of the folkways: Scots-

Irish (to Nova Scotia), Puritans of New England, Quakers of Pennsylvania, and Cavaliers of the Chesapeake.

Fitzgerald, F. Scott. *The Great Gatsby*. New York: Wisehouse Classics, [1925] 2018. Essie Mae mentions this book, in contrast to her life in middle America in the 1920s.

Franklin, Benjamin. *The Autobiography of Benjamin Franklin*. Paris: Buisson, 1791. Benjamin Franklin is Essie Mae's first cousin, 7x removed, although she didn't know about this. It was one of the pieces of the puzzle of her Nova Scotia ancestry.

Frazier, Charles. *Varina: A Novel*. New York: Harper Collins, 2018. An interesting novel about Essie Mae's fourth cousin, 3x removed.

High, Grace Mildred Ridings. *The Manly Genealogy: The Manly Family. A Record of the Descendants of William Manly and Rachel Jackson Manly, His Wife, of Cecil County, Maryland*. Claflin, Kansas: The Claflin Clarion, 1962. The line of descent from William Manly and Rachel Jackson to Essie Mae (Thompson) Hill is shown in this book, and some of William Manly's ancestors appear here, too.

Holmes, Marjorie. *Two From Galilee*. New York: Bantam Books, 1972. She was the most famous of Essie Mae's students. Her copy of this book, with EMH's bookplate, is inscribed on the flyleaf, "For Essie may & 'Toot' Hill, who both brightened my days at Cornell College. With love blessings and happy memories. Marjorie Holmes."

Hoover, Dwight W. *A Good Day's Work: An Iowa Farm in the Great Depression*. Chicago: Ivan R. Dee, 2007. Another very typical story of Iowa in the Great Depression.

Kalish, Mildred Armstrong. *Little Heathens: Hard Times and High Spirits on an Iowa Farm During the Great Depression*. New York: Bantam Books, 2007. Praised by reviewers.

Kantor, MacKinlay. *Andersonville*. New York: Penguin, 1955. Famous author, born in Webster City, Ia., won the Pulitzer Prize for this book. Mentioned by EMTH.

Lewis, Sinclair. *Elmer Gantry*. New York: Harcourt, 1927. A reference cited by Essie Mae in her books.

Michener, James A. *Chesapeake: A Novel*. New York: Random House, 1978. A good account of the settlements along Chesapeake Bay. Essie Mae read and re-read Michener's novels, especially *Hawaii*.

Miller, Arthur. *The Crucible*. 1953. A fictional account of the Salem witch delusion, written to attack Senator Joseph McCarthy, but with fictional changes to make the plot salable to audiences (titillating sex). Miller's "Goody" Nurse is, however, accurate.

Montgomery, Lucy Maud. *Anne of Green Gables*. L. C. Page & Co., 1908. A good story of life in the English settlements in eastern Canada in the late 19th century.

Pope, Charles Henry. *Pioneers of Massachusetts*. 1901; reprint by Heritage Books, Bowie, Md., 1991. A useful reference for some of Essie Mae's ancestors.

Prescott, William. *The Prescott Memorial*. Part 1. *A Genealogical Memoir of John Prescott, of 1640, and His Descendants*. Part 2. *A Genealogical Memoir of James Prescott, of 1665, and His Descendants*. Concord, N.H.: William Prescott, 1890. Essie Mae's Nova Scotia ancestors include Dorothy Prescott, known as "Dolly," who appears in this book.

Putnam, Eben. *A History of the Putnam Family in England and America: Recording the Ancestry and Descendants of John Putnam of Danvers, Mass., Jan Poutman of Albany, N.Y., and Thomas Putnam of Hartford, Conn.* 2 vols. Salem, Mass.: Salem, Mass: Salem Press Publishing and Printing Co., Vol. 1, 1892; Vol. 2, 1908. Essie Mae's family is here.

_____. *The Putnam Lineage: Historical-Genealogical Notes Concerning the Puttenham Family in England, Together with Lines of Royal Descent, and Showing the Ancestors of John Putnam of Salem and His Descendants through Five Generations, Together with Some Account of Other Families of the Name and of the Putmans of the Mohawk Valley.* Salem, Mass.: Salem Press, 1907. The English ancestry of the Putnams is given here, along with their conflicted involvement in the Salem witch trials.

Reid, Jennie. *Musquodoboit Pioneers: A Record of Seventy Families, Their Homesteads and Genealogies, 1780-1980*. Hantsport, N.S.: Lancelot Press, 1980. Essie Mae's Thompson and Archibald ancestors are recorded here.

Rundall, George Ardel, and others. *The Rundle, Rundel, Randle, Randol, Randall, Rundall, Rundell, Runnell Family Ancestry of Long Island and Greenwich, 1667-1992*. Decorah, Ia.: Anundsen Publishing Co., 1991. This book shows the descent of Essie Mae and her siblings from the Rundall Family (spelled variously), from Long Island and Greenwich, Connecticut.

Seton, Anya. *The Winthrop Woman*. 1958. Elizabeth (née Fones) Winthrop Feake Hallett, who is fictionalized in Seton's book, was known as the "Winthrop Woman." She is related by marriage to Essie Mae, unbeknownst to her. She was a daughter-in-law of

James Feake, and a mother-in-law of the first wife of Thomas Lyon. Both of them appear in this novel.

Tapley, Charles Sutherland. *Rebecca Nurse: Saint but Witch Victim*. Boston: Marshall Jones Co., 1930. Essie Mae's most famous ancestor is Rebecca Nurse, known as "Goody" or "Goodwife" Nurse.

Tate, Allen. *Jefferson Davis: His Rise and Fall. A Biographical Narrative*. Nashville: Sanders & Co., 1998. Essie Mae's fourth cousin (3 removes), Varina Burr Howell, married Jefferson Davis, who became President of the Confederacy.

Tompkins, Robert A., and Clare F. Tompkins, *The Tomkins-Tompkins Geneology* [sic]. 1942. Essie Mae's great-great grandmother Rachel (Tompkins) Rundall came to Iowa from Putnam Co., N.Y. She was the illegitimate daughter of Bartholomew Tompkins, whose genealogy appears in this book. It is ironic that Sadie Rundall (Essie Mae's mother) was unaware of the circumstances of her birth, for she was very strongly opposed to sex out-of-wedlock. The story is told in the chapter about the Tompkins family in *Fundy to Chesapeake*.

Wallace, Anthony F. C. *Rockdale: The Growth of an American Village in the Early Industrial Revolution*. 1980. The story is a fictionalized version of life in Chester County, Pennsylvania, which mentions mills owned and operated by the Sharpless family and others who are related to Essie Mae.

Waller, Robert James. *The Bridges of Madison County*. New York: Warner Books, 1992. Shows how rural life continues in Iowa.

Wilder, Laura Ingalls. *Little House on the Prairie*. New York: Harper & Brothers, 1932. She captures the story of the life that was typical of Essie Mae's grandparents, James and Jane (Grant) Thompson, and their children – who grew up in a house on the prairie.

Wile, Jane (Currie). *The Archibald Family: Ireland, New England, Nova Scotia*. Belmont, N.S.: GeneJane, November 1998. The Archibald family is said to be the "first family of Nova Scotia" or of Colchester Co., N.S. Essie Mae's great-grandmother was Ruth (Archibald) Thompson, who came back to the United States with her husband, Joseph Scott Thompson. They settled in Brockton, Mass., and their son – Essie Mae's grandfather, James E. Thompson – came to Iowa with his wife, Jane Grant, who was also from Nova Scotia.

_____. With Arthur Putnam, Doug Putnam, and Nan (Parker) Harvey. *The Putnam Family: England to Nova Scotia*. Belmont, N.S.: GeneJane, November 1999.

Willey, George F. *Willey's Book of Nutfield: A History of that Part of New Hampshire Comprised within the Limits of the Old Township of Londonderry from its Settlement in 1719 to the Present Time.* Derry Depot, N.H.: George F. Willey, 1895. Reprint, Salem, Mass.: Higginson Books, 2002. Essie Mae's Prescott ancestors appear in this book.

Wilson, Meredith. *The Music Man: The Musical.* 1957. Set in "River City" and based on his home town of Mason City, Iowa.

Wood, Grant. *American Gothic* and *Stone City.* 1930. The mysterious, iconic, paintings were of scenes in eastern Iowa. He was born in northern Linn County, Iowa, only a few miles from where Essie Mae was born. Stone City (now the summer headquarters of the Iowa Writers' Workshop) is on the Wapsipinicon River, near her birth place.

Woodward, W. Elliott, ed. *Records of Salem Witchcraft, Copied from the Original Documents.* Vol. 1. Roxbury, Mass.: W. Elliott Woodward, 1864. Includes transcripts of the original testimony of "Goody" Nurse, and those who condemned her and those who testified for her. Quoted in *The Crucible.*

Yool, George Malcolm. *1692 Witch Hunt: The Layman's Guide to the Salem Witchcraft Trials.* Bowie, Md.: Heritage Books, 1992. A good description of the witchcraft episode. At the time she wrote her memoirs, Essie Mae was only dimly aware of the involvement and suffering of her ancestors and other members of the Nurse and Putnam families in this awful episode of American history.

Internet Sources

Essie Mae's obituary was published in *The [Cedar Rapids-Iowa City] Gazette* (17 March 1994). A copy can be seen on the Wright County Iowa IAGenWebProject site, at: http://iagenweb.org/boards/wright/obituaries/index.cgi?read=143249, posted 1/29/2007 by Sarah Thorson Little (viewed 10/3/18)

Curriculum Vitae

ESSIE MAE THOMPSON HILL
    10030A Royal Oak Road
    Sun City, AZ 85351
    (602) 977-8026

Occupation: Writer, Retired teacher and housewife

Birth: June 29, 1903, at Paris (Linn County), Iowa. The fourth of five children, and the second daughter, of William Henry Thompson, a creamery operator, and Sadie D. Rundall, a Methodist laywoman and weaver.

[Death: March 15, 1994, at Sun City (Maricopa County), Arizona. Burial: July 30, 1994, Hill Family Cemetery, Rowan, Iowa]

Education: 1909-1920 Lisbon, Iowa, public schools. Graduated from Lisbon High School, 1920. President of the Class of '20.
    1920-1926 Cornell College, Mount Vernon, Iowa. B.A., 1926.
    1927   Field studies in Geology, University of Iowa, Black Hills, South Dakota
    1928   Field and graduate studies in Geology, University of Colorado, Boulder, Colorado
    1944-45   Shorthand and typing classes, Mount Vernon, Iowa
    1969   Braille studies
    1980-1989 Poetry classes at Arizona State University, Sun City, Ariz.

Marriage: December 25, 1930, in Mount Vernon, Iowa, to Gerald Leslie Hill of Clarion, Iowa; publicity director of Cornell College, and later President, Dacotah Bank Holding Company, Aberdeen, South Dakota [deceased June 14, 1979 at Payson, Arizona. Burial, Hill Family Cemetery, Rowan, Iowa]

Employment:
  1918   Teacher, Second Grade, Lisbon School
  1921-22 Teacher, Valley Chapel School, near Lisbon, Iowa (one room)
  1923-24 Teacher, DeWitt, Iowa, Public School (third grade)
  1924-26 Assistant in Geology, Cornell College, Mt. Vernon, Iowa
  1926-30 Instructor in Geology, Cornell College, Mt. Vernon, Iowa
  1926-43 Self-employed (part time) alto soloist and teacher of vocal music. Cornell College Baccalaureate soloist, 1926 and 1927.

National radio soloist for American Legion Auxiliary.

1939-43 Choir Director, Methodist Church, Lisbon, Iowa.

1944 Instructor in Civil Air Regulations, U.S. Army Air Corps School, Coe
College, Cedar Rapids, Iowa; and Instructor in Meteorology, Civil Air Patrol,
Cedar Rapids, with rank of Master Sergeant, C.A.P.

1944-45 Instructor in Navigation, and Instructor in Engines, U.S. Naval Flight
Preparatory School, Cornell College, Mt. Vernon, Iowa

1945 Executive Secretary for Prof. Albert Johnson, Cornell College, Mt. Vernon, Ia.

1950-52 Teacher, Sioux Falls, South Dakota, Junior High School

1969-73 Teacher, South Dakota School for the Visually Handicapped, Aberdeen,
South Dakota

1973- Author and lecturer, Sun City, Arizona. Topics include "Gems and Minerals
of the Bible," "Women of the Bible," and poetry readings.

Honors and Certificates:

Permanent President, Class of 1920, Lisbon, Iowa, High School

President, Lisbon High School Alumni Association, 1939

Linn County, Iowa, Teachers Certificate, by examination, 1922

Iowa State Teachers Certificate, 1926

Scholarship awarded for graduate study in geology at Clark University,
Worcester, Mass., 1930 (award declined)

President, Mt. Vernon, Iowa, Chapter, American Association of University
Women, 1934-35

Instructor rating in Navigation, Meteorology, and Civil Air Regulations, by
Civil Aeronautics Administration (now F.A.A.), 1944

Second Lieutenant, Civil Air Patrol; and Commander, C.A.P. Cadet Program,
Sioux Falls, S.D., 1951-52

South Dakota State Teachers Certificate, 1953

"Ambassador of the Diplomatic Corps of South Dakota," 1968

Vice President, Sun City (Arizona) Rockhound Club, 1973-74

[Resident of the Month, Brighton Gardens, Sun City, Arizona, March 1994]

Memberships:

American Association of University Women

Phi Beta Kappa

P.E.O. Sisterhood

Sun City (Arizona) Rockhound Club, Historian, 1974-84; Vice President, 1973

Sun City Poetry Club

Arizona State Poetry Club

University Club, Sun City, Arizona

All Saints of the Desert Episcopal Church, Sun City, Arizona

228

Publications:

        Hill, E. M. T., *Prairie Daughter* (Phoenix: O'Sullivan, Woodside and Company, 1978)

        Hill, E. M. T., *Let Thy Handmaidens Speak* (Chatham, N.J.: Minuteman Press, 1983)

        Hill, E. M. T., *Flapper Fun: Other Poems and Stories* (Phoenix: O'Sullivan, Woodside and Company, 1988)

        Hill, E. M. T., *Essie Mae's Cook Book, with Recipes from Family and Friends* (privately printed, n.d., c. 1990)

Personal:

        Her grandmother, Rachel (Manly) Rundall, is said to have been a teacher at Cornell College prior to her marriage in 1856. Her mother, Sadie Rundall held a Teacher's Certificate by examination at age 19 from Linn County, Iowa. Her husband, Gerald, received the annual Alumni Award from Cornell College's Alumni Association in 1974. She was the first female faculty member in Cornell's history to be permitted to continue teaching after she was married, except for the wife of the head of the geology department, a decade earlier.

        Her two sons, her daughters-in-law, and six grandchildren have earned fifteen college and university degrees, including five doctorates and five master's degrees. In 1976, three of her grandchildren were currently degree candidates; two had married, and she had one great-grandchild.

Many careers – She has been a teacher, in grade school, in junior high school, in the South Dakota school for the deaf and blind, and in college; a geologist and lecturer; a performing artist as vocalist and character actress; a wife and mother; and a writer of poetry and family history.

To Century Oaks

Humpty Hil-upy
Had a great fall
The worst in my life
As I recall

I may be down
But I'm still ahead
And I quote Mrs. Noah
When she said

"Noah saw a rainbow
And he said that was a sign
That from now on
Everything would be just fine."

Believe me when I say
That when comes the day
I can see Royal Oak Road ahead
That's where I'll stay until I'm dead.

In the Eye of the Beholder

My hair is white,
and I walk with a cane
It's hard to stand straight,
'Cause my back is in pain.

But when I look in the mirror,
Do you know what I see?
Not the way I look now,
but the way I used to be.

I don't see the wrinkles,
my hair's soft and brown,
And my ragged old house-coat
is a lovely ball gown.

Essie Mae and Gerald Hill's sons
Thomas D. Hill and George J. Hill
1949

ABOUT THE AUTHOR

ESSIE MAE THOMPSON HILL was an Iowa girl of the early 20th century. She was born in 1903 in a farmhouse in Linn County, Iowa, on land that her paternal grandfather had homesteaded after emigrating from Nova Scotia. Her father was a creamery operator, skilled in making sweet butter, and known for  his absolute integrity. Her maternal grandfather was a carpenter and inn keeper. He came to Iowa as a young man with his parents from Putnam Co., N.Y. He built a Select School building, and he dedicated himself to educating children. Essie Mae's mother and her maternal grandmother were teachers before they were married.

Essie Mae's three brothers worked their way through college and were successful – the oldest in education; the second, in law; and the youngest, in chemistry and business. Essie Mae entered grade school at age 4 and she was president of her high school class. She worked her way through Cornell College, majoring in geology and vocal music, and graduated with honors, as a member of Phi Beta Kappa. She chose to stay at Cornell College, where she was the first female faculty member in Cornell's history to continue teaching after she was married. Essie Mae married Gerald L. "Jerry" Hill, also a farm boy and Cornellian, who became a banker in Iowa and South Dakota.

During World War II, while her husband was in service, she returned to teach Navy students at Cornell College. Essie Mae was also a teacher in grade school, in junior high school, and in the South Dakota School for the Visually Handicapped; a geologist and lecturer; a performing artist, as vocalist and character actress; a wife and mother; and a writer of poetry and family history. Her two sons, her daughters-in-law, and her six grandchildren have earned fifteen college degrees, including five doctorates and five master's degrees.

Essie Mae's four books have been edited and combined into one volume by her son, George J. Hill, M.D., D.Litt.

Heritage Books by George J. Hill:

American Dreams: Ancestors and Descendants of John Zimmermann and Eva Katherine Kellenbenz, Who Were Married in Philadelphia in 1885

"Dearest Barb": From Karachi, 1943–1945, Letters and Photographs in the World War II Papers of a Naval Intelligence Officer, Lieutenant Albert Zimmermann, USNR

Edison's Environment: The Great Inventor Was Also a Great Polluter

Four Families: A Tetralogy Reader's Guide to Western Pilgrims, Quakers and Puritans, Fundy to Chesapeake, *and* American Dreams; *Synopsis of 481 Immigrants and First Known Ancestors in America from Northern Europe in the Families of George J. Hill and Jessie F. Stockwell, William T. Shoemaker and Mabel Warren, William H. Thompson and Sarah D. Rundall, John Zimmermann and Eva K. Kellenbenz, with Outlines of Their Descent from the Immigrants*

Fundy to Chesapeake; The Thompson, Rundall and Allied Families: Ancestors and Descendants of William Henry Thompson and Sarah D. Rundall, Who Were Married in Linn County, Iowa, in 1889

Hill: The Ferry Keeper's Family, Luke Hill and Mary Hout, Who Were Married in Windsor, Connecticut, in 1651 and Fourteen Generations of Their Known and Possible Descendants

John Saxe, Loyalist (1732–1808) and His Descendants for Five Generations

Prairie Daughter: Stories and Poems from Iowa by Essie Mae Thompson Hill

Quakers and Puritans: The Shoemaker, Warren and Allied Families; Ancestors and Descendants of William Toy Shoemaker and Mabel Warren, Who Were Married in Philadelphia in 1895

Three Men in a Jeep Called "Ma Kabul," Script for a Movie: A True Story of High Adventure by Three Allied Intelligence Officers in World War II

Western Pilgrims: The Hill, Stockwell and Allied Families; Ancestors and Descendants of George J. Hill and Jessie Fidelia Stockwell, Who Were Married in Wright County, Iowa, in 1882

CPSIA information can be obtained
at www.ICGtesting.com
Printed in the USA
BVHW050007210619
551560BV00003B/81/P

9 780788 458767